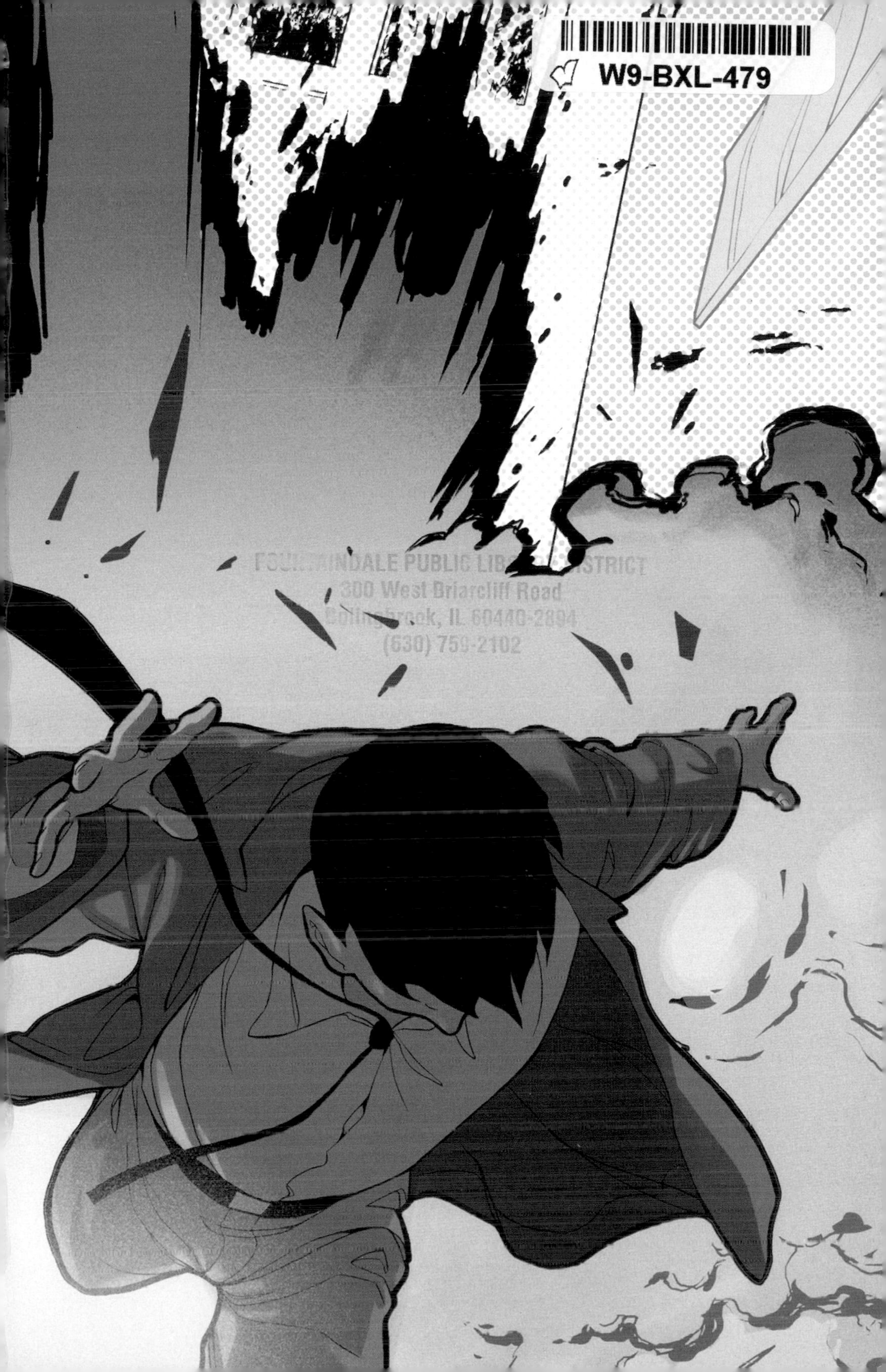

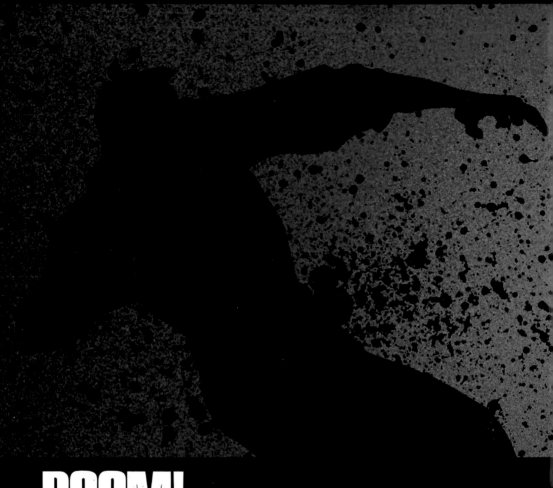

ROSS RICHIE
chief executive officer

MARK WAID
editor-in-chief

ADAM FORTIER
vice president,
publishing

CHIP MOSHER
marketing director

MATT GAGNON
managing editor

JENNY CHRISTOPHER
sales director

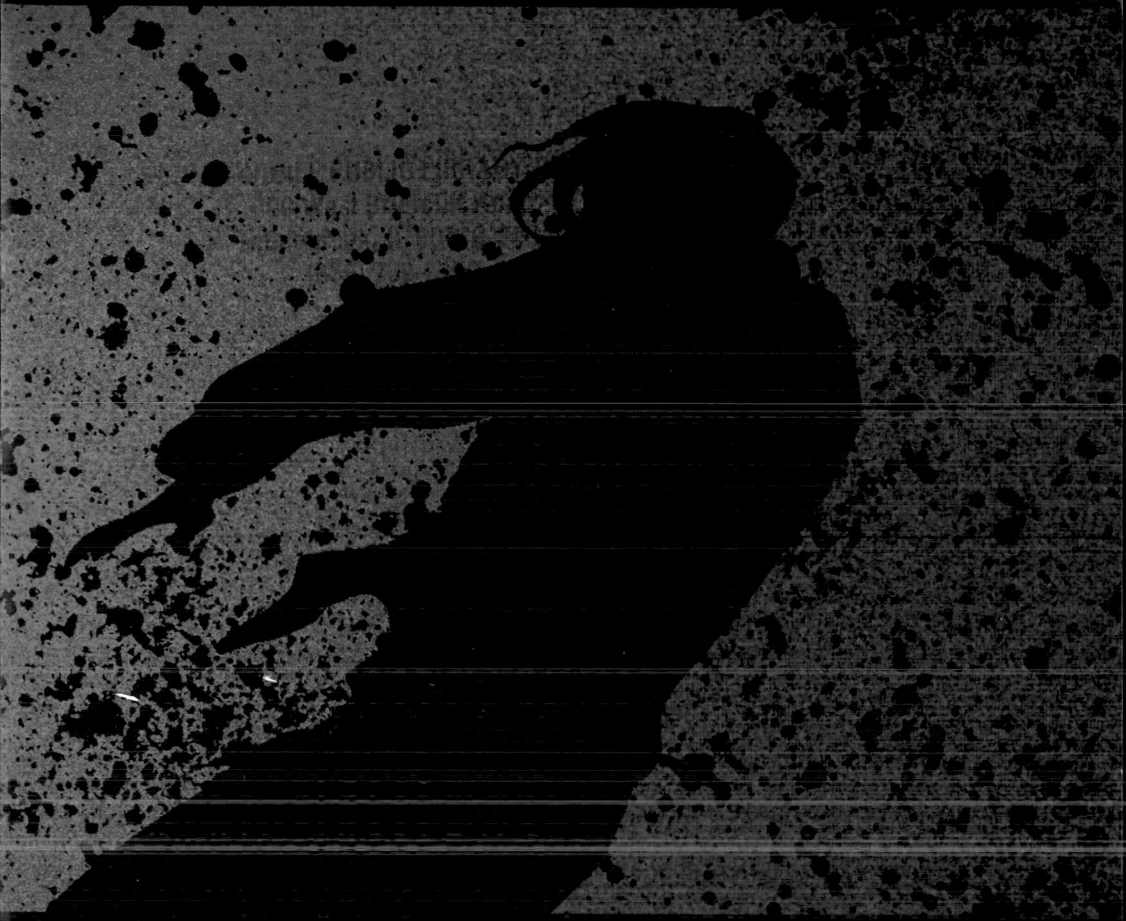

FIRST EDITION: NOVEMBER 2009

10 9 8 7 6 5 4 3 2 1

PRINTED IN KOREA

Office of publication: 6310 San Vicente Blvd Ste 404, Los Angeles, CA 90048-5457.

A catalog record for this book is available from the Library of Congress and on our website at WWW.BOOM-STUDIOS.COM on the Librarian Resource Page.

THE REMNANT

CREATED BY: STEPHEN BALDWIN
STORY BY: STEPHEN BALDWIN AND
ANDREW COSBY
SCRIPT: CALEB MONROE
ARTIST: JULIAN TOTINO TEDESCO

COLORIST: ANDRES LOZANO
LETTERER: ED DUKESHIRE
EDITOR: MATT GAGNON

COVER: PAUL AZACETA
COLORS / ANDREW DALHOUSE

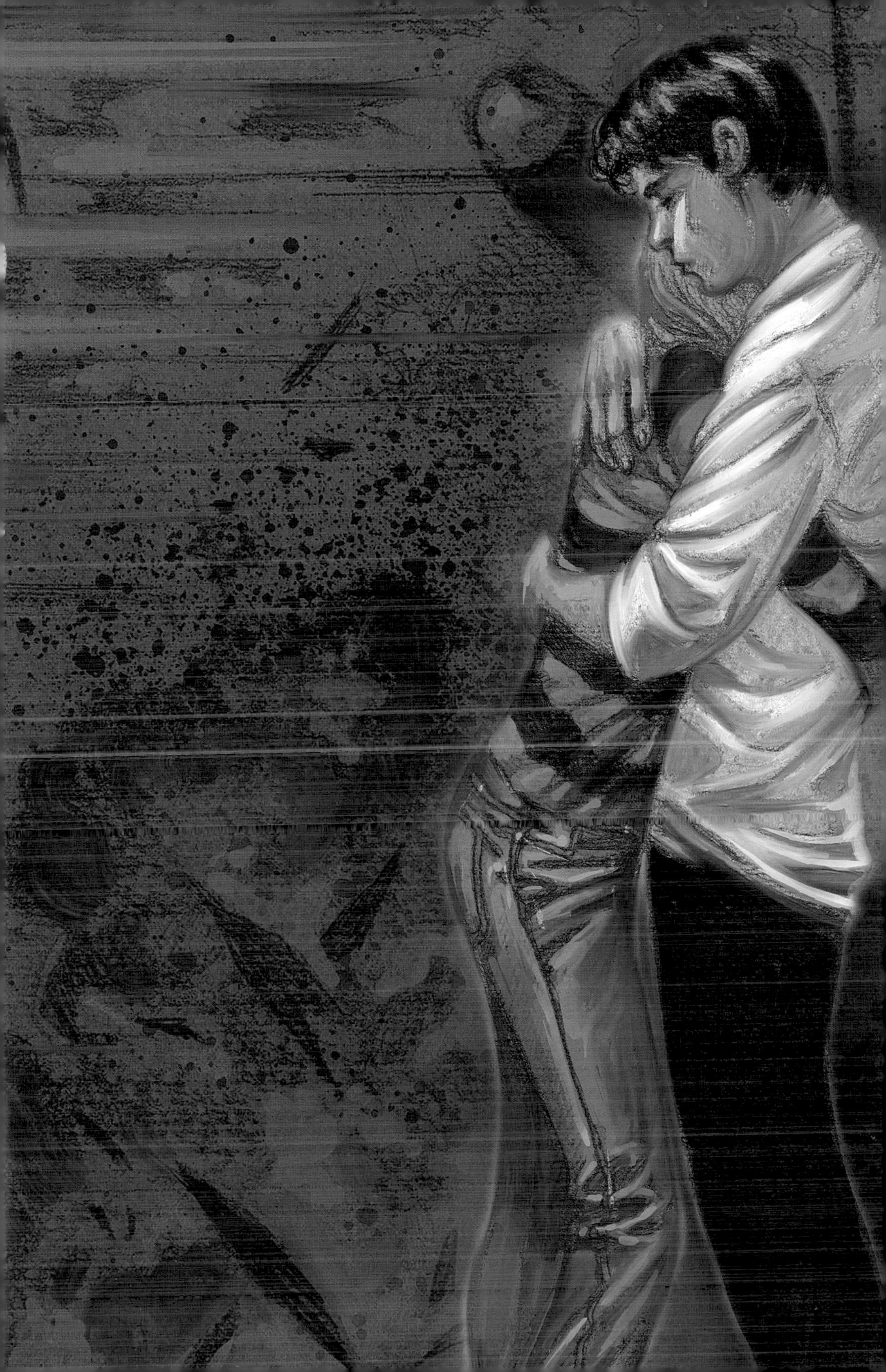

CHAPTER ONE

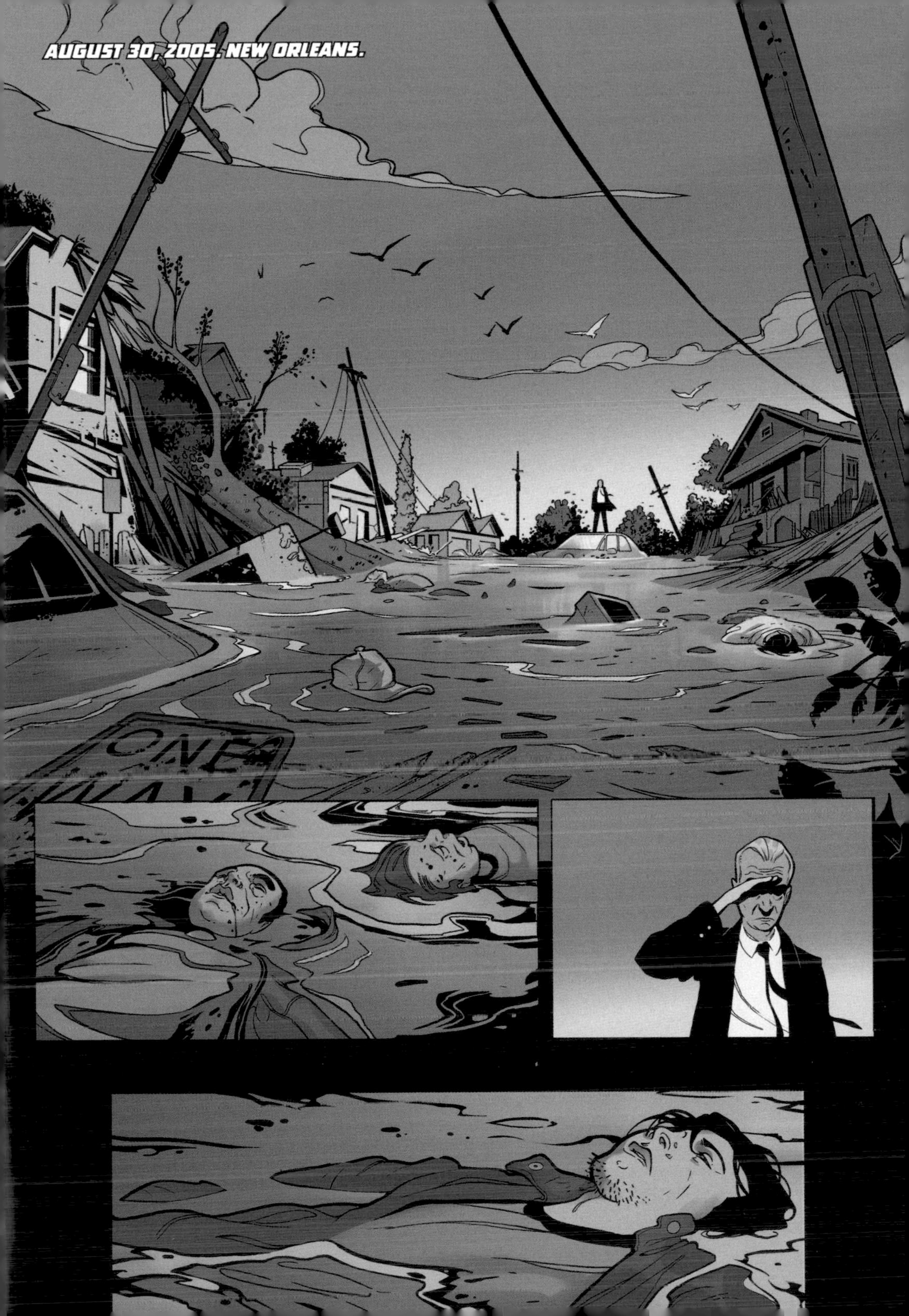
AUGUST 30, 2005. NEW ORLEANS.

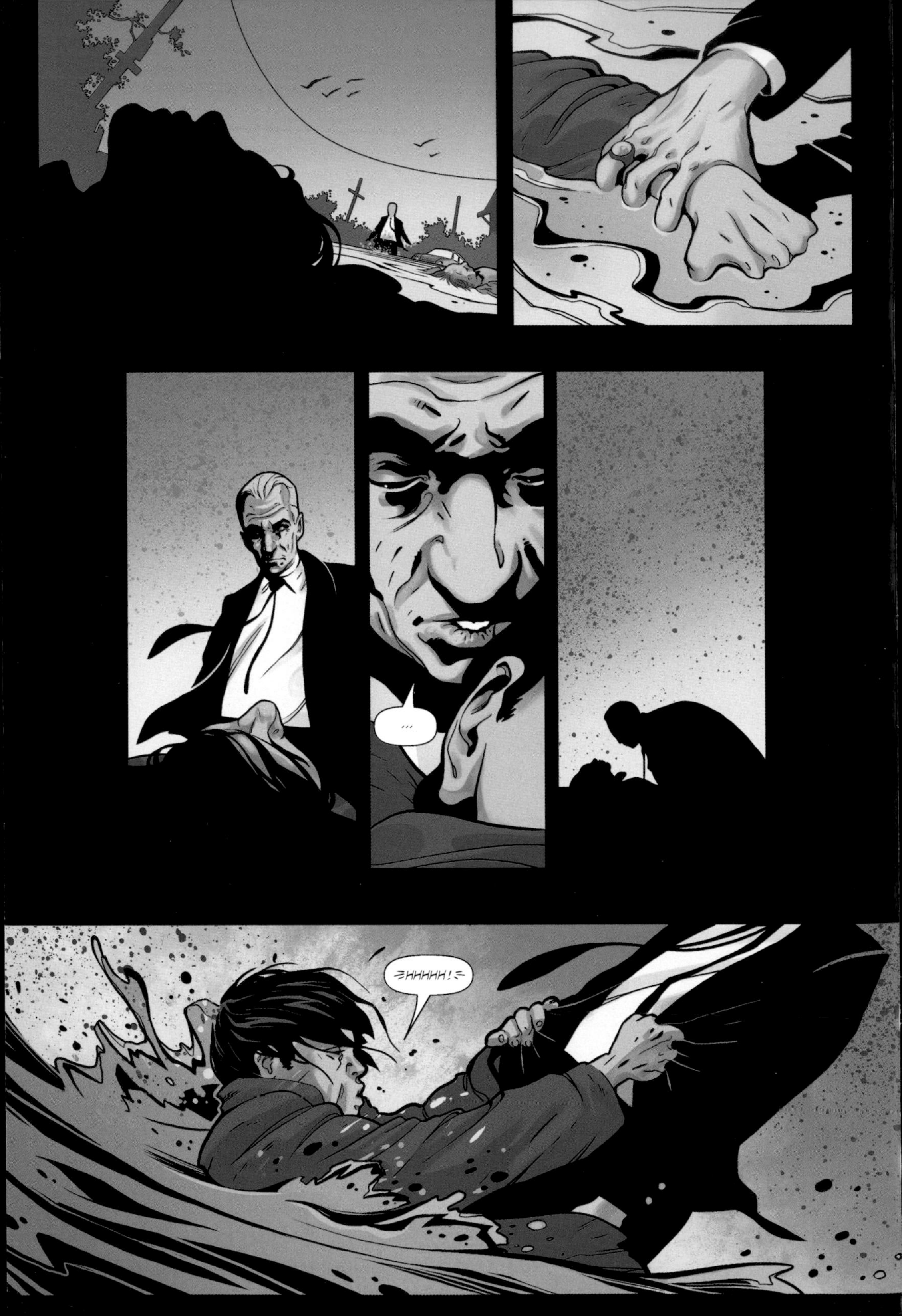
...
HHHHH!

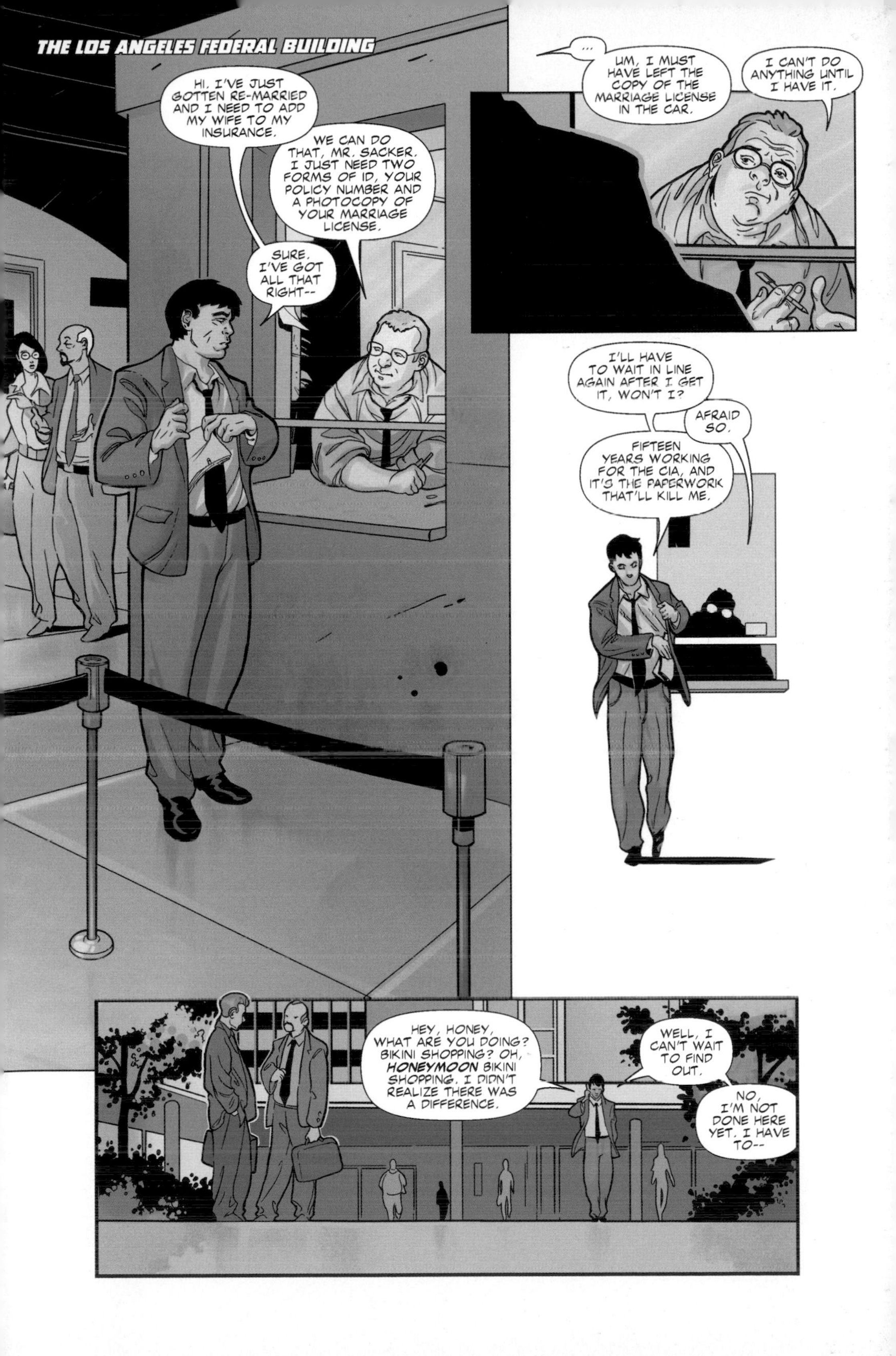
THE LOS ANGELES FEDERAL BUILDING
HI. I'VE JUST GOTTEN RE-MARRIED AND I NEED TO ADD MY WIFE TO MY INSURANCE.
WE CAN DO THAT, MR. SACKER. I JUST NEED TWO FORMS OF ID, YOUR POLICY NUMBER AND A PHOTOCOPY OF YOUR MARRIAGE LICENSE.
SURE. I'VE GOT ALL THAT RIGHT--
...
UM, I MUST HAVE LEFT THE COPY OF THE MARRIAGE LICENSE IN THE CAR.
I CAN'T DO ANYTHING UNTIL I HAVE IT.
I'LL HAVE TO WAIT IN LINE AGAIN AFTER I GET IT, WON'T I?
AFRAID SO.
FIFTEEN YEARS WORKING FOR THE CIA, AND IT'S THE PAPERWORK THAT'LL KILL ME.
HEY, HONEY, WHAT ARE YOU DOING? BIKINI SHOPPING? OH, HONEYMOON BIKINI SHOPPING. I DIDN'T REALIZE THERE WAS A DIFFERENCE.
WELL, I CAN'T WAIT TO FIND OUT.
NO, I'M NOT DONE HERE YET. I HAVE TO--

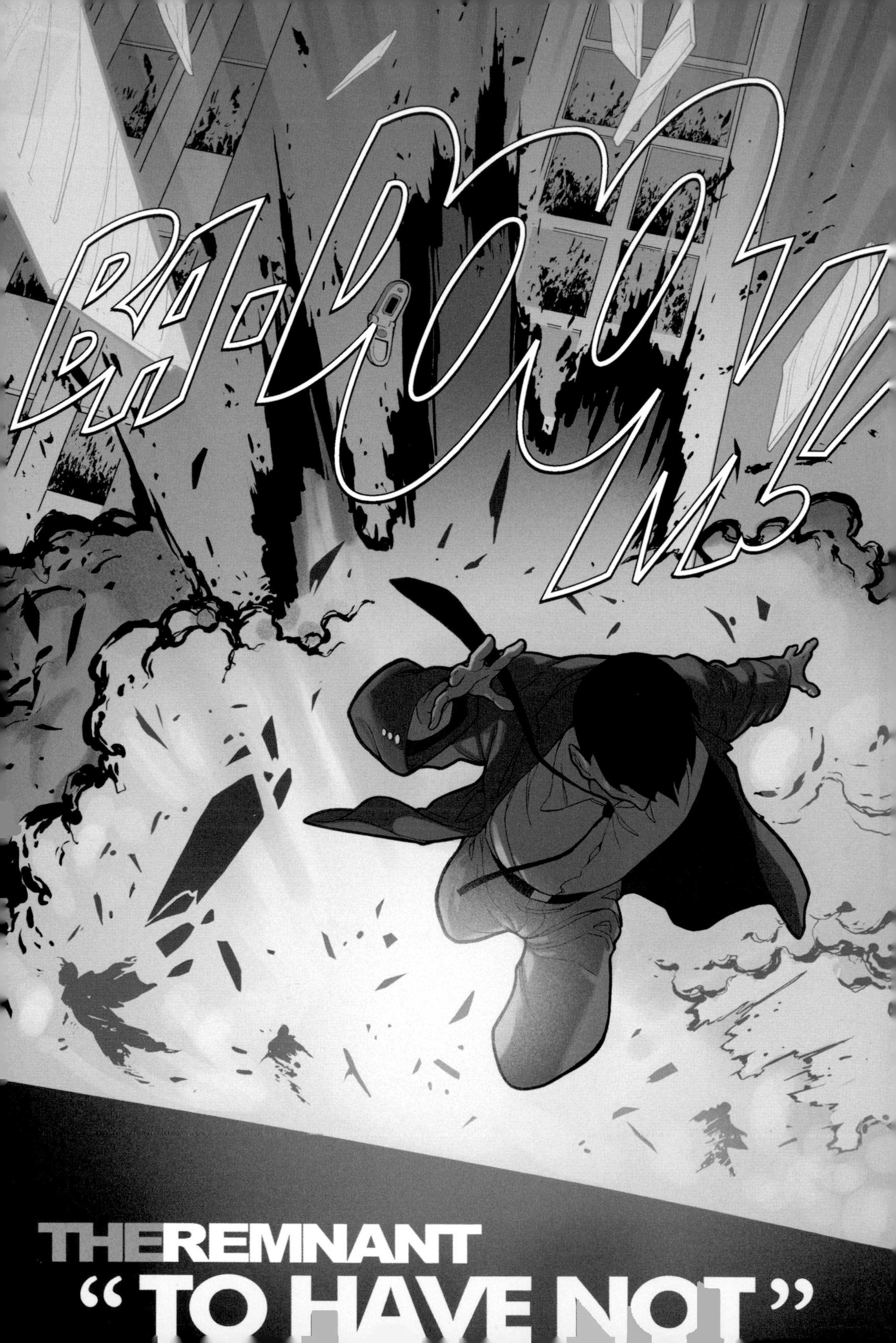
THE REMNANT
"TO HAVE NOT"

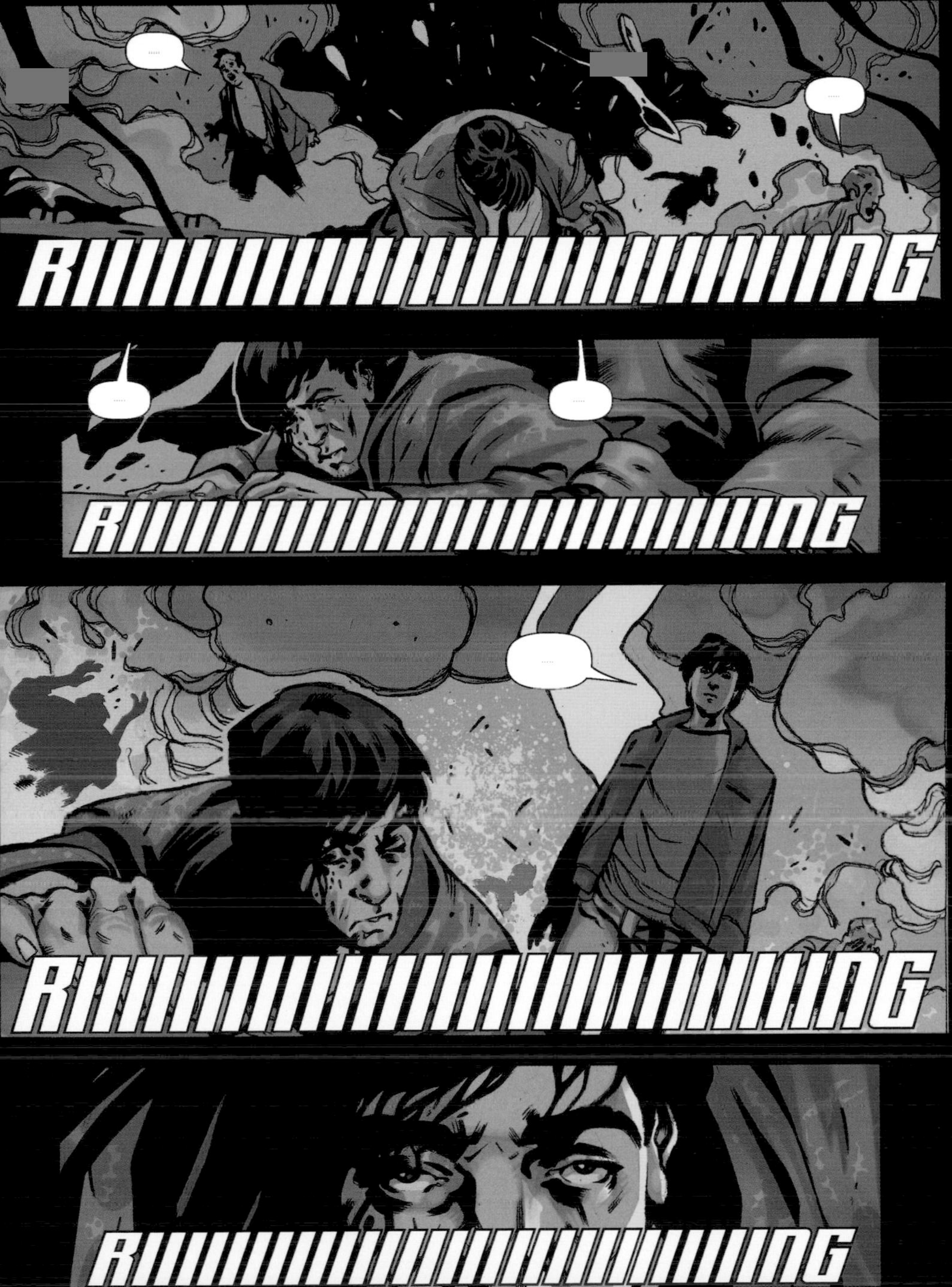
RIIIIIIIIIIIIIIIIIIIIIIIIIIIING
RIIIIIIIIIIIIIIIIIIIIIIIIING
RIIIIIIIIIIIIIIIIIIIIIIIIIIIING
RIIIIIIIIIIIIIIIIIIIIIIIIING

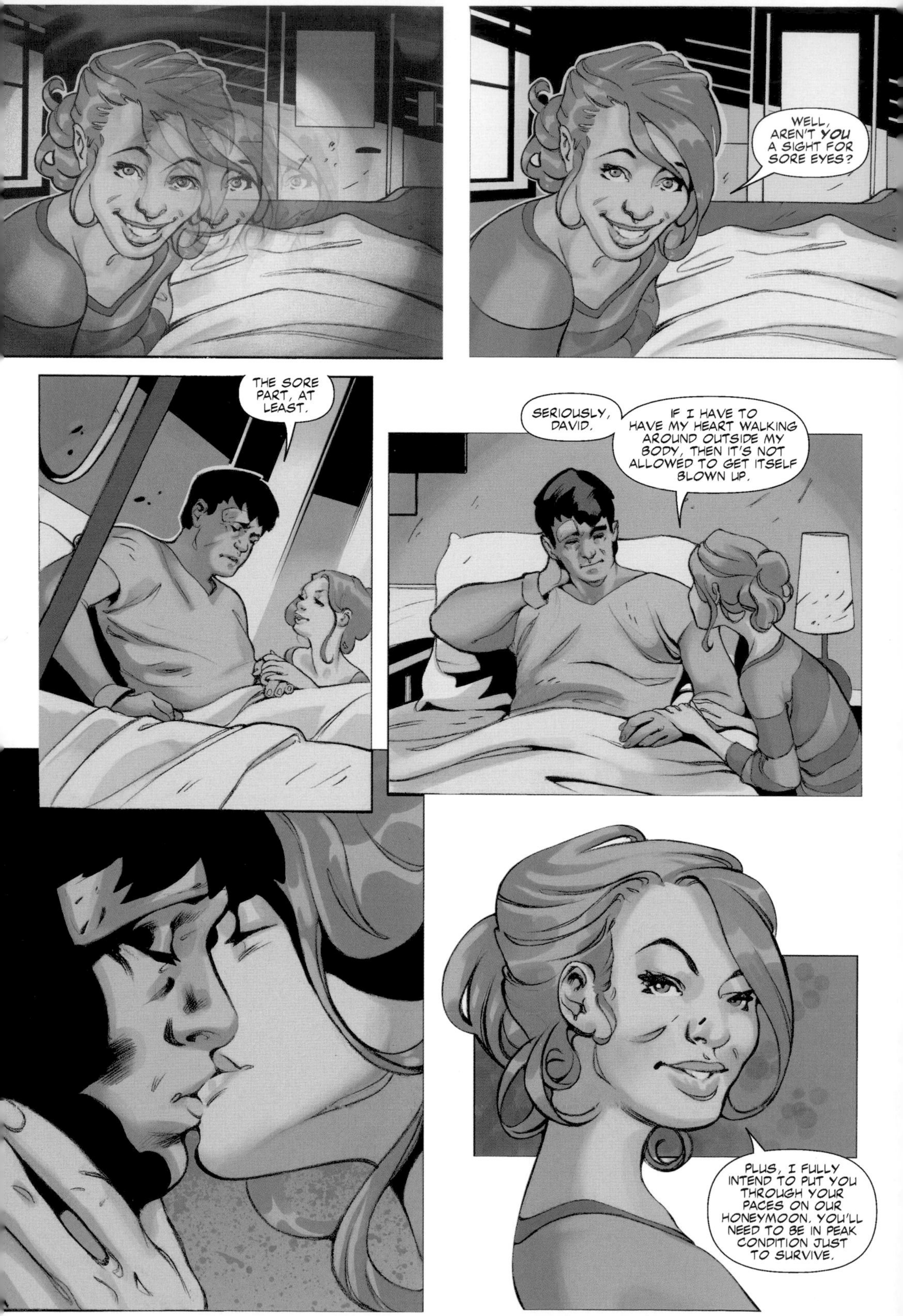
WELL, AREN'T YOU A SIGHT FOR SORE EYES?
THE SORE PART, AT LEAST.
SERIOUSLY, DAVID.
IF I HAVE TO HAVE MY HEART WALKING AROUND OUTSIDE MY BODY, THEN IT'S NOT ALLOWED TO GET ITSELF BLOWN UP.
PLUS, I FULLY INTEND TO PUT YOU THROUGH YOUR PACES ON OUR HONEYMOON. YOU'LL NEED TO BE IN PEAK CONDITION JUST TO SURVIVE.

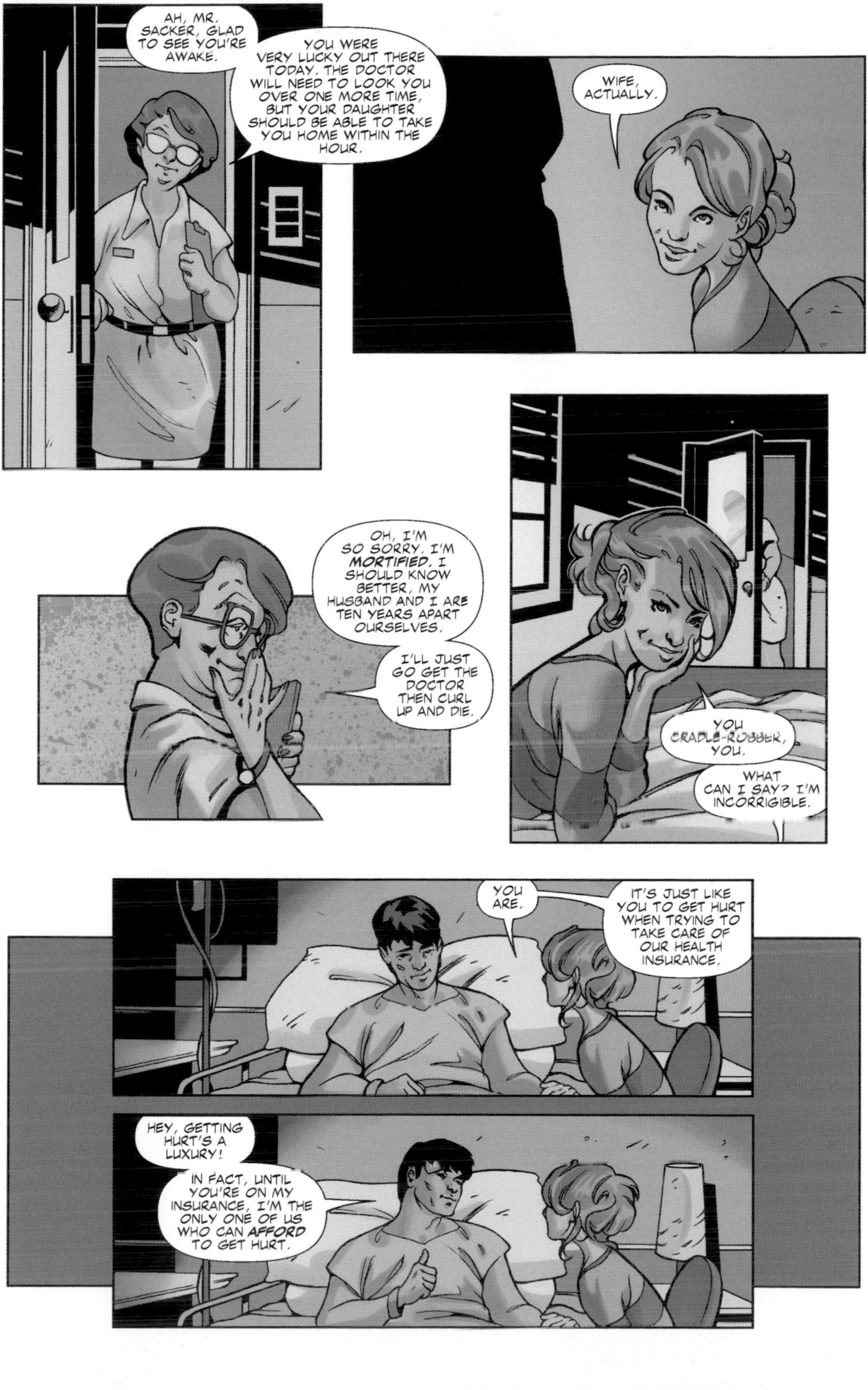
AH, MR. SACKER, GLAD TO SEE YOU'RE AWAKE.
YOU WERE VERY LUCKY OUT THERE TODAY. THE DOCTOR WILL NEED TO LOOK YOU OVER ONE MORE TIME, BUT YOUR DAUGHTER SHOULD BE ABLE TO TAKE YOU HOME WITHIN THE HOUR.
WIFE, ACTUALLY.
OH, I'M SO SORRY. I'M MORTIFIED. I SHOULD KNOW BETTER, MY HUSBAND AND I ARE TEN YEARS APART OURSELVES.
I'LL JUST GO GET THE DOCTOR THEN CURL UP AND DIE.
YOU CRADLE-ROBBER, YOU.
WHAT CAN I SAY? I'M INCORRIGIBLE.
YOU ARE.
IT'S JUST LIKE YOU TO GET HURT WHEN TRYING TO TAKE CARE OF OUR HEALTH INSURANCE.
HEY, GETTING HURT'S A LUXURY!
IN FACT, UNTIL YOU'RE ON MY INSURANCE, I'M THE ONLY ONE OF US WHO CAN AFFORD TO GET HURT.

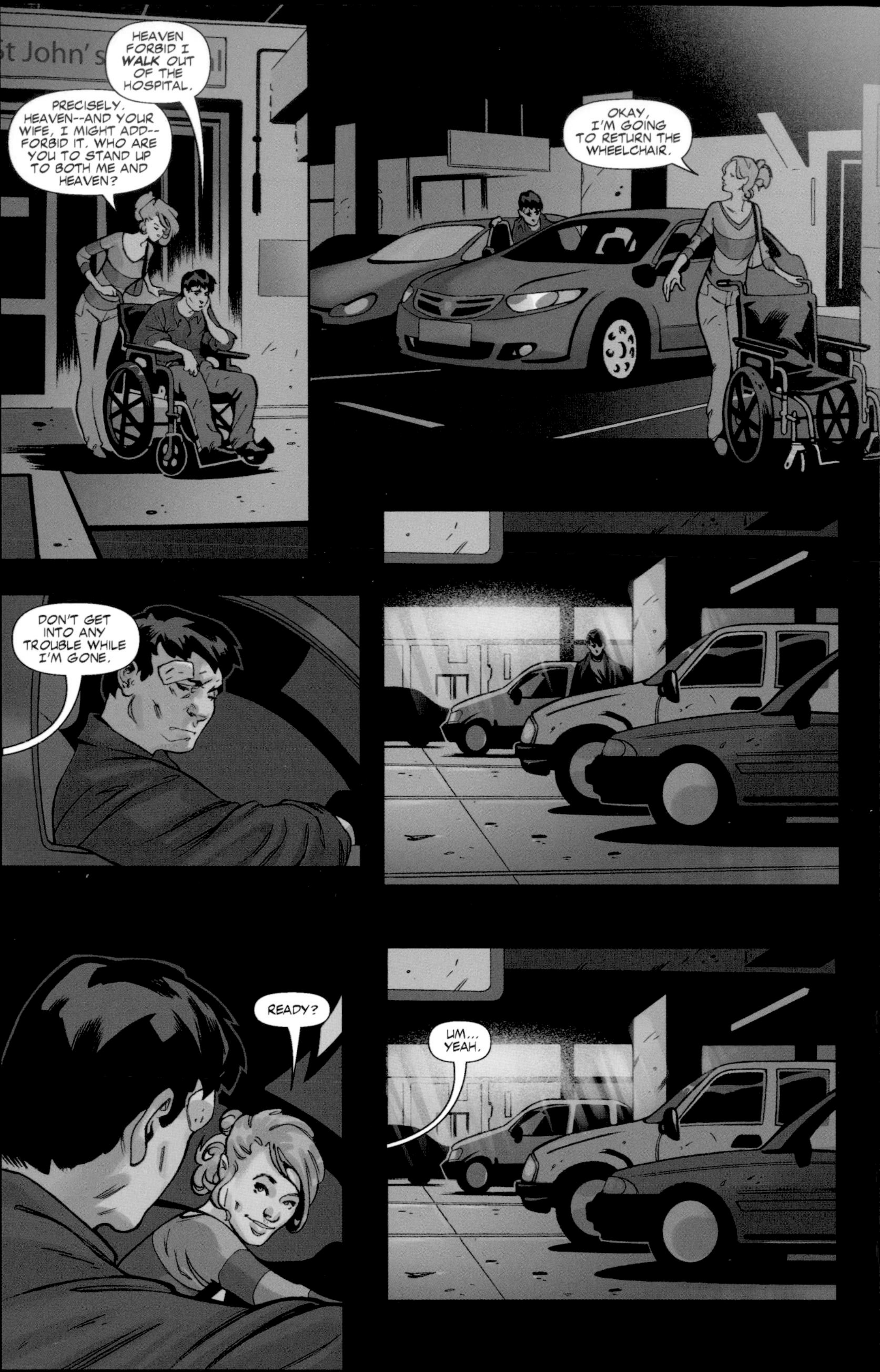
St John's
HEAVEN FORBID I WALK OUT OF THE HOSPITAL.
PRECISELY. HEAVEN--AND YOUR WIFE, I MIGHT ADD--FORBID IT. WHO ARE YOU TO STAND UP TO BOTH ME AND HEAVEN?
OKAY, I'M GOING TO RETURN THE WHEELCHAIR.
DON'T GET INTO ANY TROUBLE WHILE I'M GONE.
READY?
UM... YEAH.

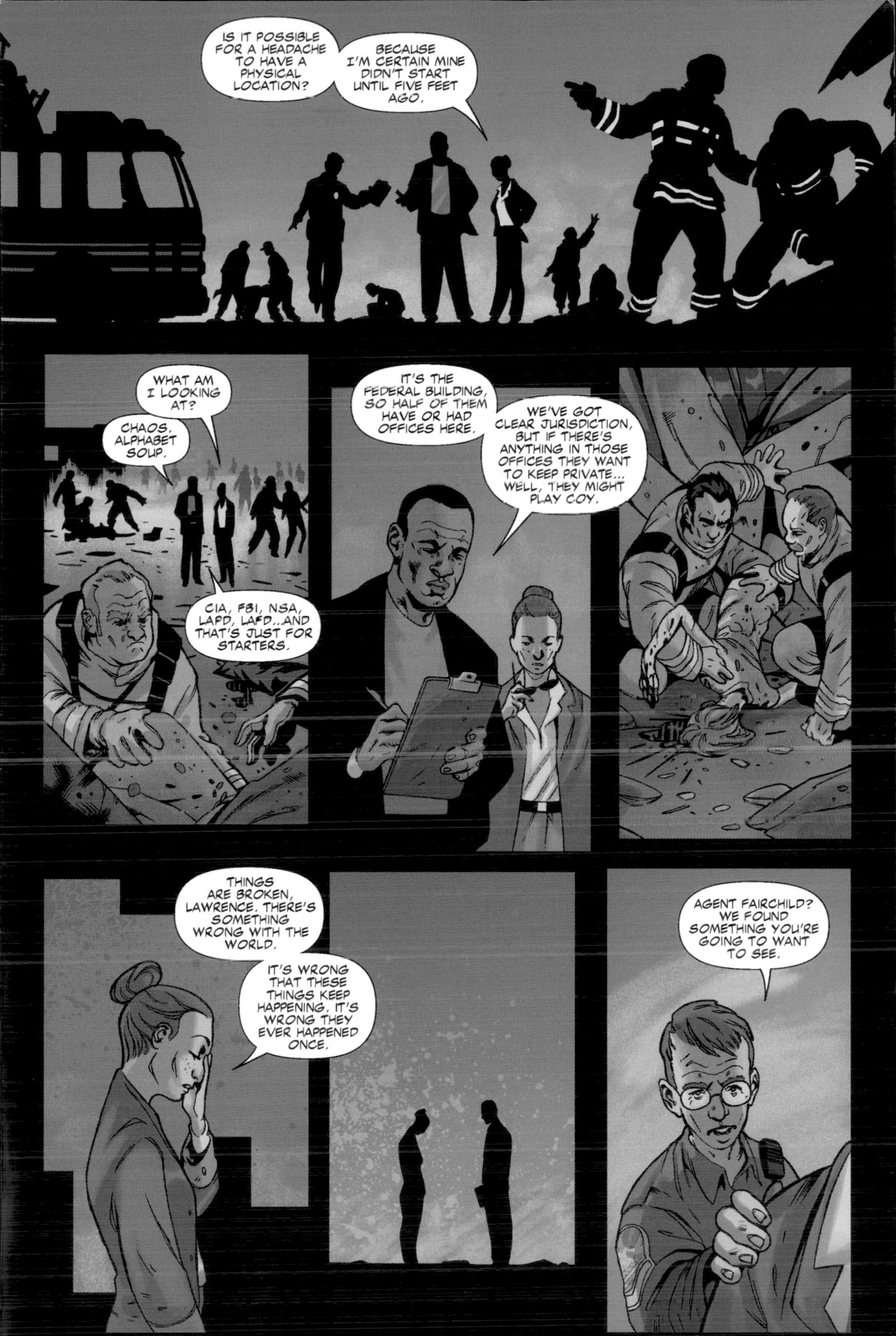
IS IT POSSIBLE FOR A HEADACHE TO HAVE A PHYSICAL LOCATION?
BECAUSE I'M CERTAIN MINE DIDN'T START UNTIL FIVE FEET AGO.
WHAT AM I LOOKING AT?
CHAOS. ALPHABET SOUP.
CIA, FBI, NSA, LAPD, LAFD...AND THAT'S JUST FOR STARTERS.
IT'S THE FEDERAL BUILDING, SO HALF OF THEM HAVE OR HAD OFFICES HERE.
WE'VE GOT CLEAR JURISDICTION, BUT IF THERE'S ANYTHING IN THOSE OFFICES THEY WANT TO KEEP PRIVATE... WELL, THEY MIGHT PLAY COY.
THINGS ARE BROKEN, LAWRENCE. THERE'S SOMETHING WRONG WITH THE WORLD.
IT'S WRONG THAT THESE THINGS KEEP HAPPENING. IT'S WRONG THEY EVER HAPPENED ONCE.
AGENT FAIRCHILD? WE FOUND SOMETHING YOU'RE GOING TO WANT TO SEE.

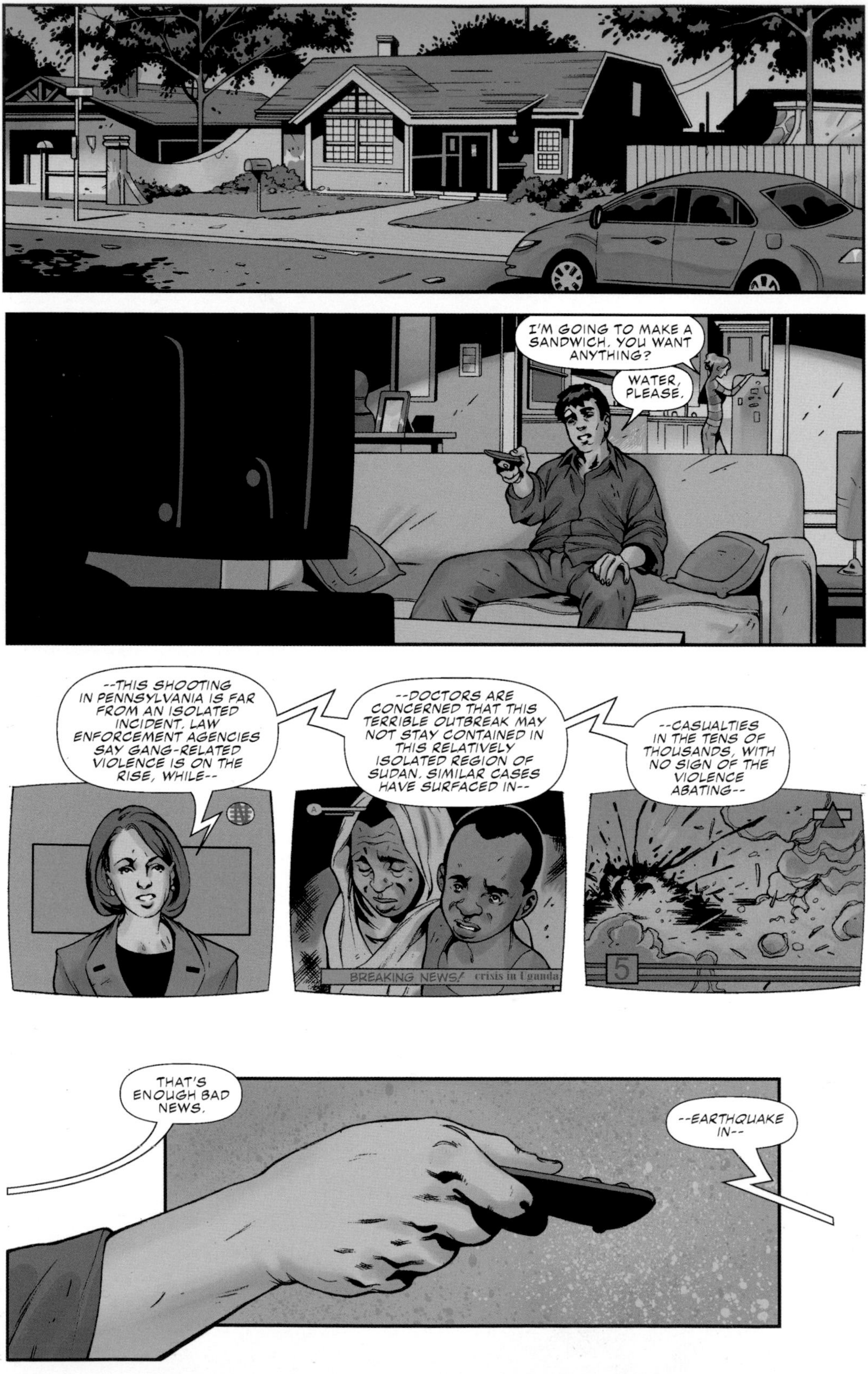
I'M GOING TO MAKE A SANDWICH. YOU WANT ANYTHING?
WATER, PLEASE.
--THIS SHOOTING IN PENNSYLVANIA IS FAR FROM AN ISOLATED INCIDENT. LAW ENFORCEMENT AGENCIES SAY GANG-RELATED VIOLENCE IS ON THE RISE, WHILE--
--DOCTORS ARE CONCERNED THAT THIS TERRIBLE OUTBREAK MAY NOT STAY CONTAINED IN THIS RELATIVELY ISOLATED REGION OF SUDAN. SIMILAR CASES HAVE SURFACED IN--
BREAKING NEWS! crisis in Uganda
--CASUALTIES IN THE TENS OF THOUSANDS, WITH NO SIGN OF THE VIOLENCE ABATING--
5
THAT'S ENOUGH BAD NEWS.
--EARTHQUAKE IN--

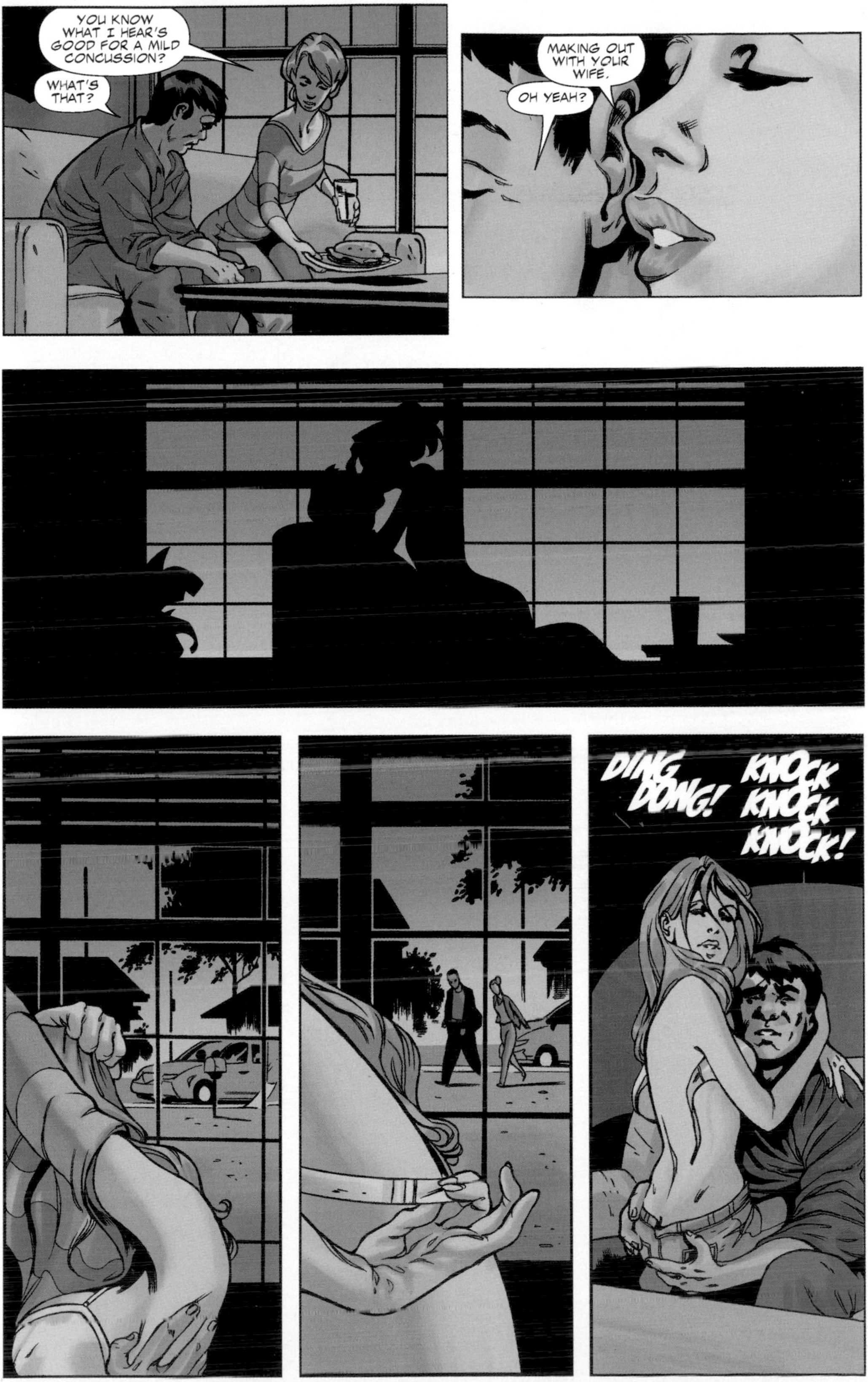
YOU KNOW WHAT I HEAR'S GOOD FOR A MILD CONCUSSION?
WHAT'S THAT?
MAKING OUT WITH YOUR WIFE.
OH YEAH?
DING DONG!
KNOCK KNOCK KNOCK!

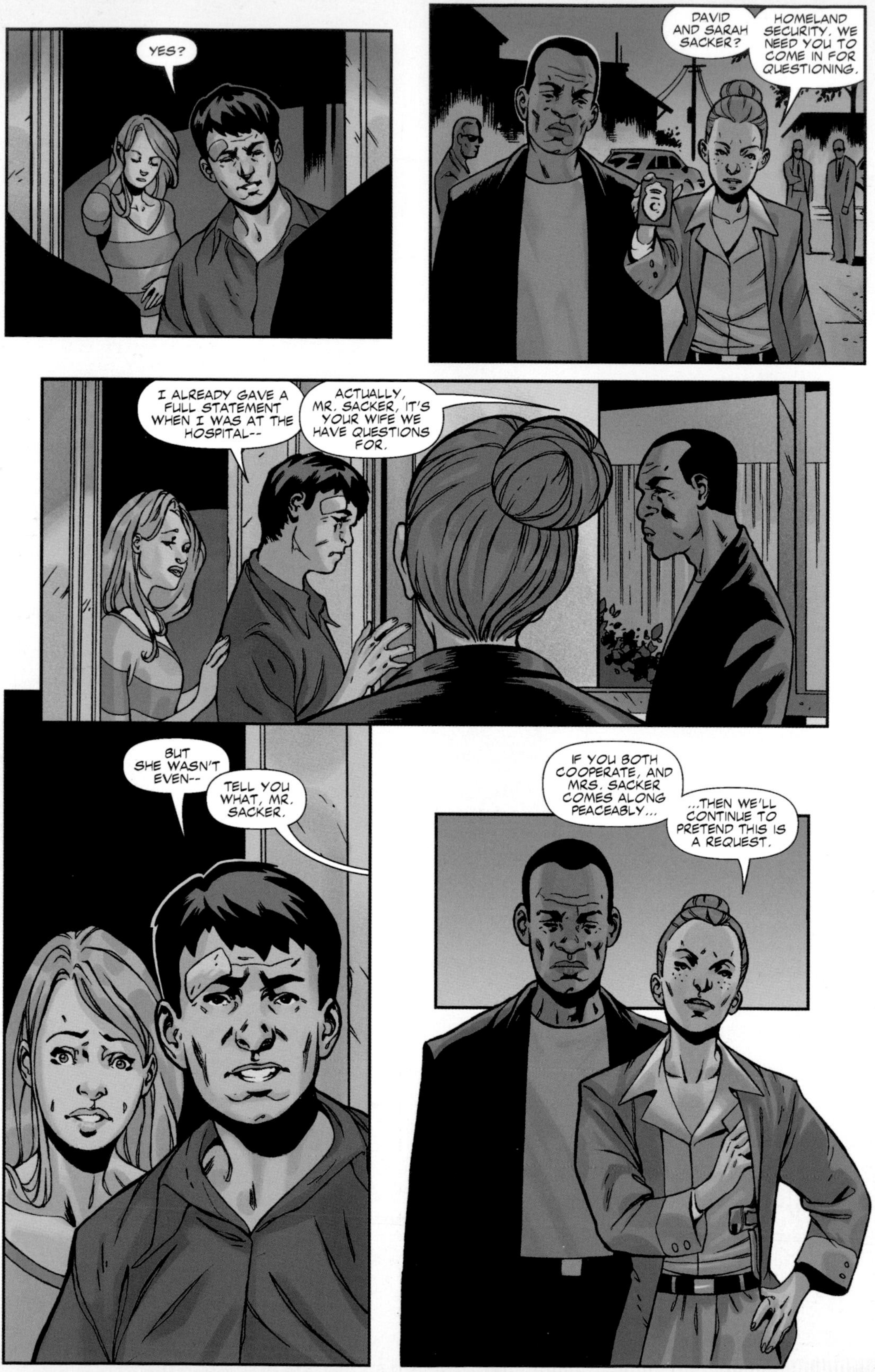
YES?
DAVID AND SARAH SACKER?
HOMELAND SECURITY. WE NEED YOU TO COME IN FOR QUESTIONING.
I ALREADY GAVE A FULL STATEMENT WHEN I WAS AT THE HOSPITAL--
ACTUALLY, MR. SACKER, IT'S YOUR WIFE WE HAVE QUESTIONS FOR.
BUT SHE WASN'T EVEN--
TELL YOU WHAT, MR. SACKER.
IF YOU BOTH COOPERATE, AND MRS. SACKER COMES ALONG PEACEABLY...
...THEN WE'LL CONTINUE TO PRETEND THIS IS A REQUEST.

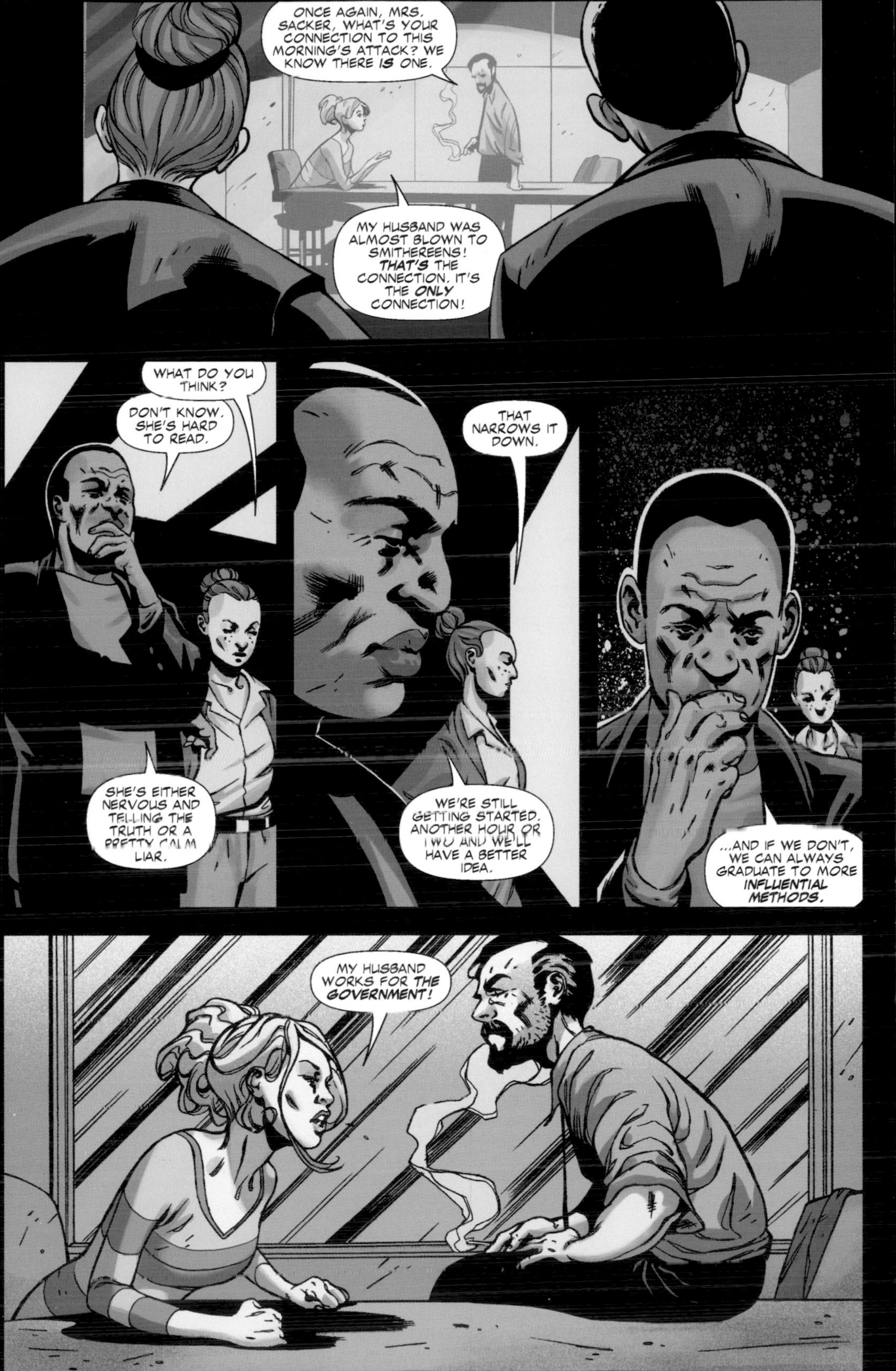
ONCE AGAIN, MRS. SACKER, WHAT'S YOUR CONNECTION TO THIS MORNING'S ATTACK? WE KNOW THERE IS ONE.
MY HUSBAND WAS ALMOST BLOWN TO SMITHEREENS! THAT'S THE CONNECTION. IT'S THE ONLY CONNECTION!
WHAT DO YOU THINK?
DON'T KNOW. SHE'S HARD TO READ.
SHE'S EITHER NERVOUS AND TELLING THE TRUTH OR A PRETTY CALM LIAR.
THAT NARROWS IT DOWN.
WE'RE STILL GETTING STARTED. ANOTHER HOUR OR TWO AND WE'LL HAVE A BETTER IDEA.
...AND IF WE DON'T, WE CAN ALWAYS GRADUATE TO MORE INFLUENTIAL METHODS.
MY HUSBAND WORKS FOR THE GOVERNMENT!

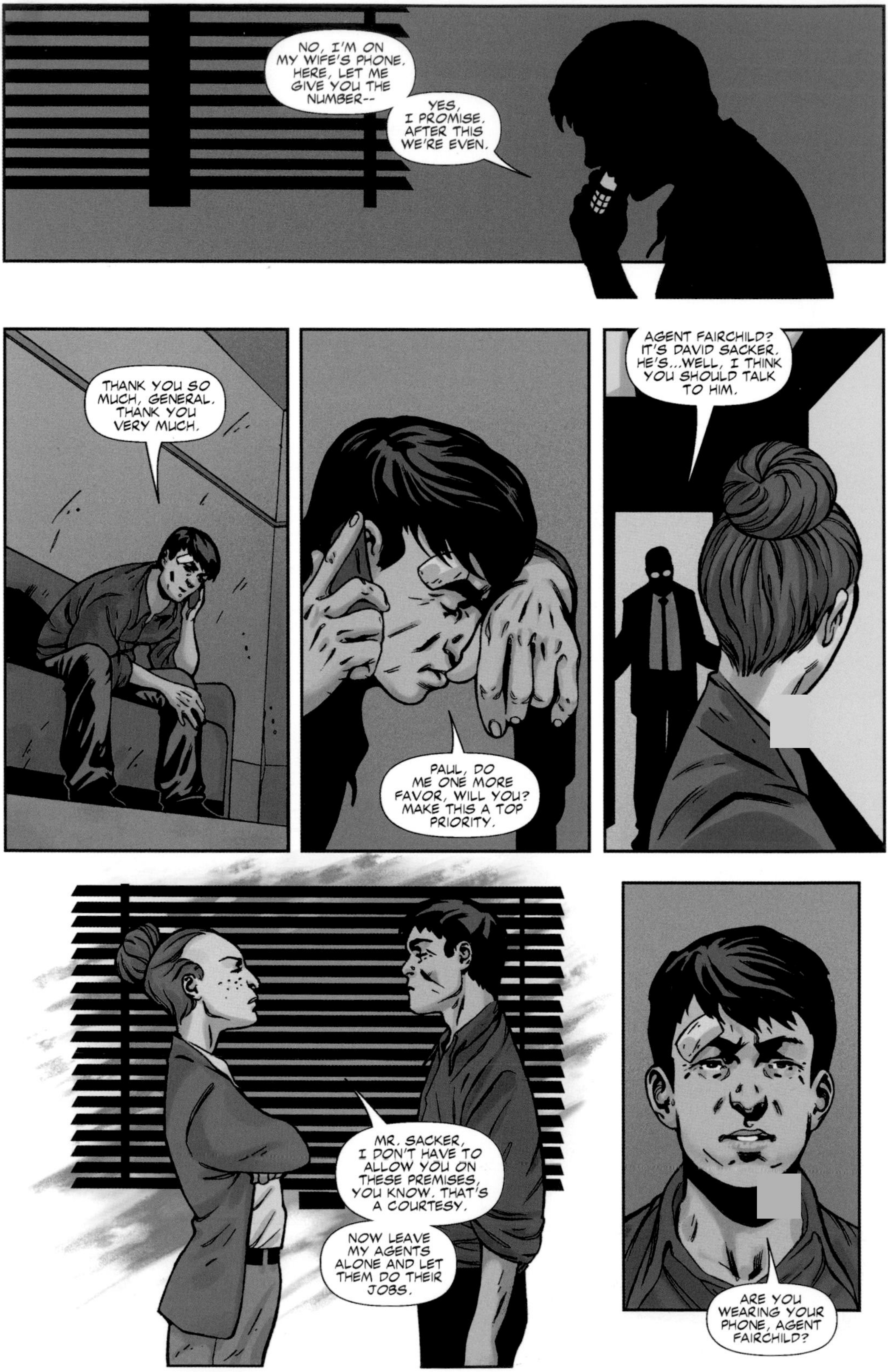
NO, I'M ON MY WIFE'S PHONE. HERE, LET ME GIVE YOU THE NUMBER--
YES, I PROMISE. AFTER THIS WE'RE EVEN.
THANK YOU SO MUCH, GENERAL. THANK YOU VERY MUCH.
PAUL, DO ME ONE MORE FAVOR, WILL YOU? MAKE THIS A TOP PRIORITY.
AGENT FAIRCHILD? IT'S DAVID SACKER. HE'S...WELL, I THINK YOU SHOULD TALK TO HIM.
MR. SACKER, I DON'T HAVE TO ALLOW YOU ON THESE PREMISES, YOU KNOW. THAT'S A COURTESY.
NOW LEAVE MY AGENTS ALONE AND LET THEM DO THEIR JOBS.
ARE YOU WEARING YOUR PHONE, AGENT FAIRCHILD?

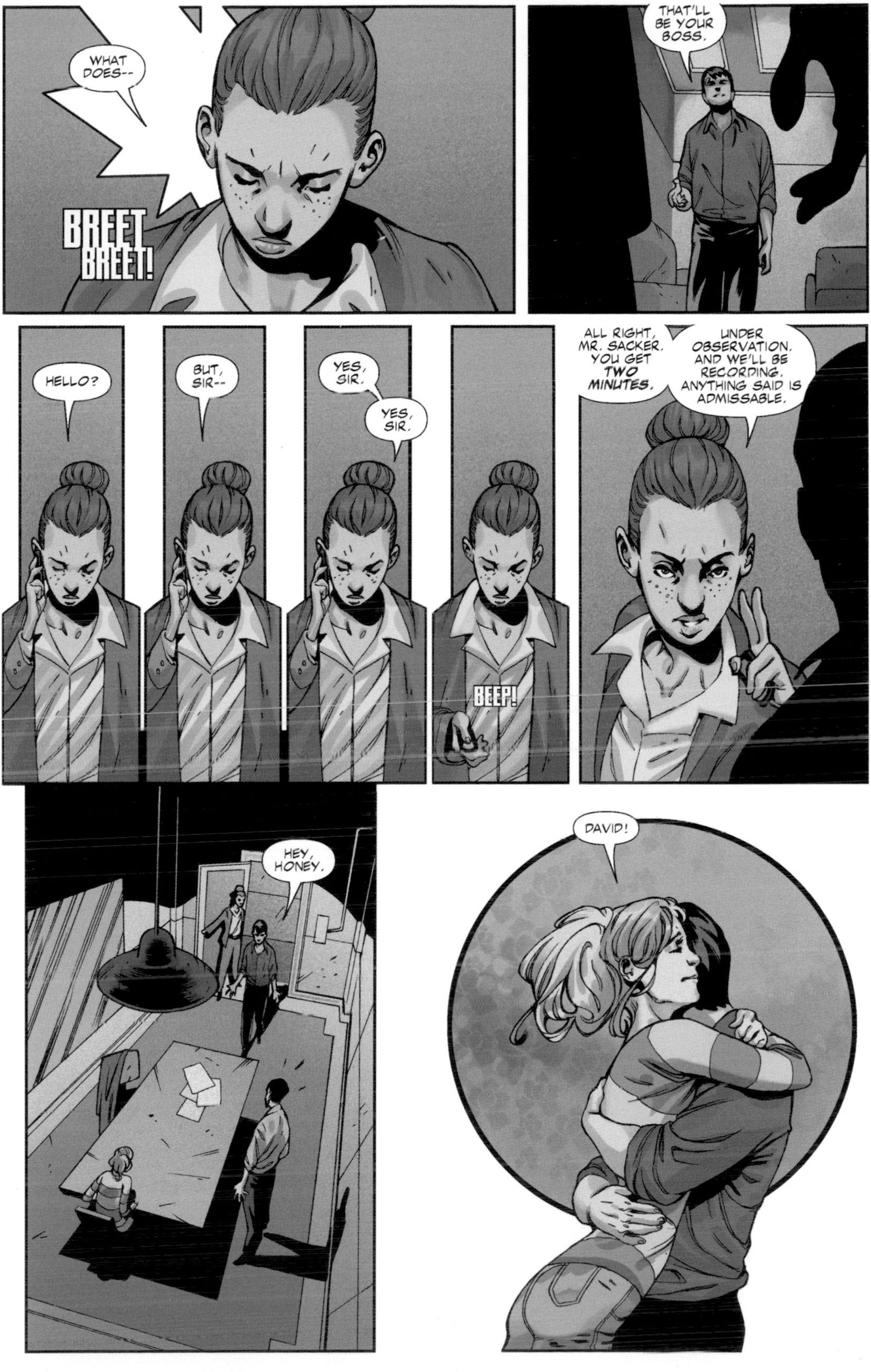

WHAT DOES--
BREET BREET!
THAT'LL BE YOUR BOSS.
HELLO?
BUT, SIR--
YES, SIR.
YES, SIR.
BEEP!
ALL RIGHT, MR. SACKER. YOU GET TWO MINUTES.
UNDER OBSERVATION. AND WE'LL BE RECORDING. ANYTHING SAID IS ADMISSABLE.
HEY, HONEY.
DAVID!

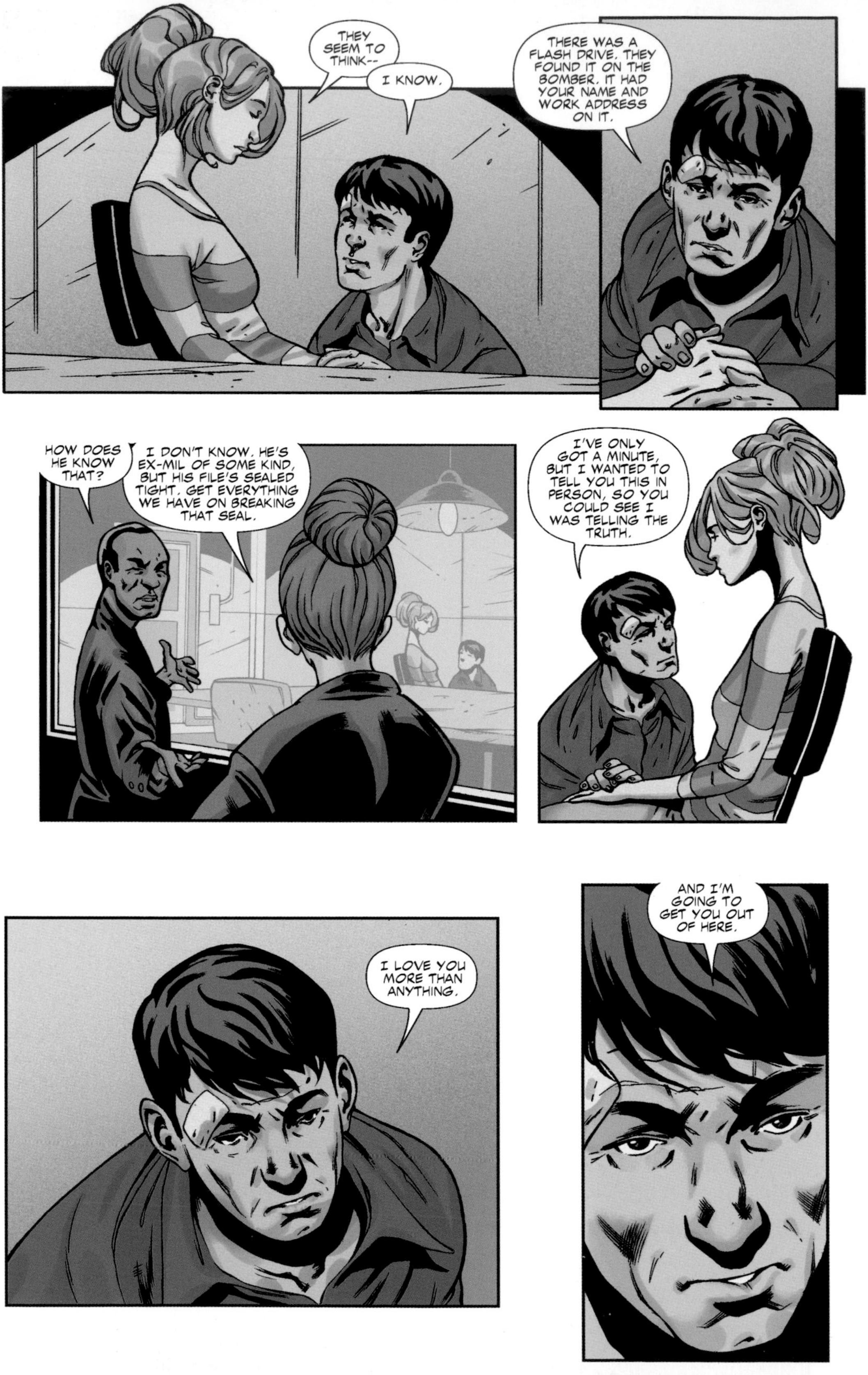
THEY SEEM TO THINK--
I KNOW.
THERE WAS A FLASH DRIVE. THEY FOUND IT ON THE BOMBER. IT HAD YOUR NAME AND WORK ADDRESS ON IT.
HOW DOES HE KNOW THAT?
I DON'T KNOW. HE'S EX-MIL OF SOME KIND, BUT HIS FILE'S SEALED TIGHT. GET EVERYTHING WE HAVE ON BREAKING THAT SEAL.
I'VE ONLY GOT A MINUTE, BUT I WANTED TO TELL YOU THIS IN PERSON, SO YOU COULD SEE I WAS TELLING THE TRUTH.
I LOVE YOU MORE THAN ANYTHING.
AND I'M GOING TO GET YOU OUT OF HERE.

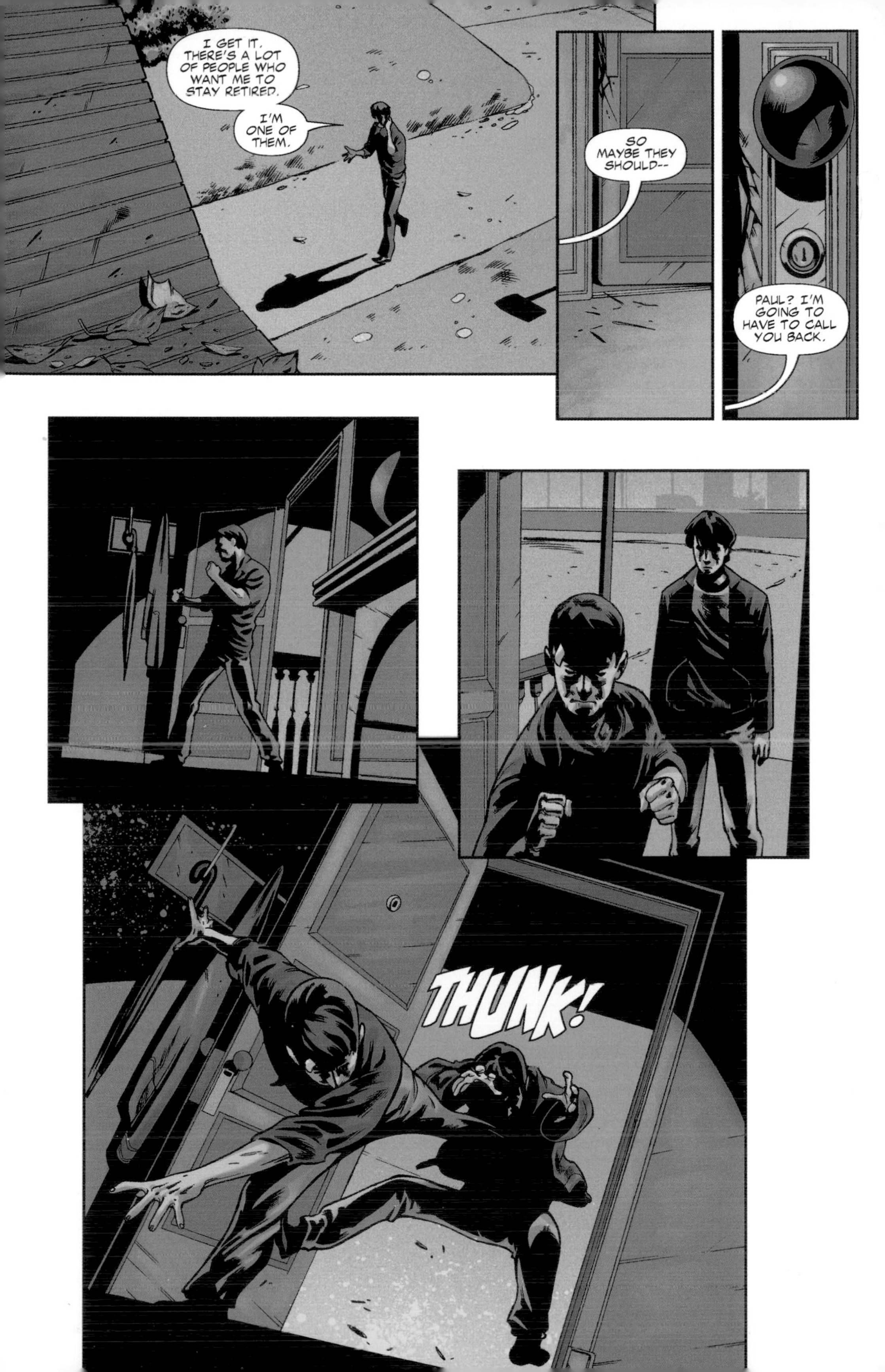
I GET IT. THERE'S A LOT OF PEOPLE WHO WANT ME TO STAY RETIRED.
I'M ONE OF THEM.
SO MAYBE THEY SHOULD--
PAUL? I'M GOING TO HAVE TO CALL YOU BACK.
THUNK!

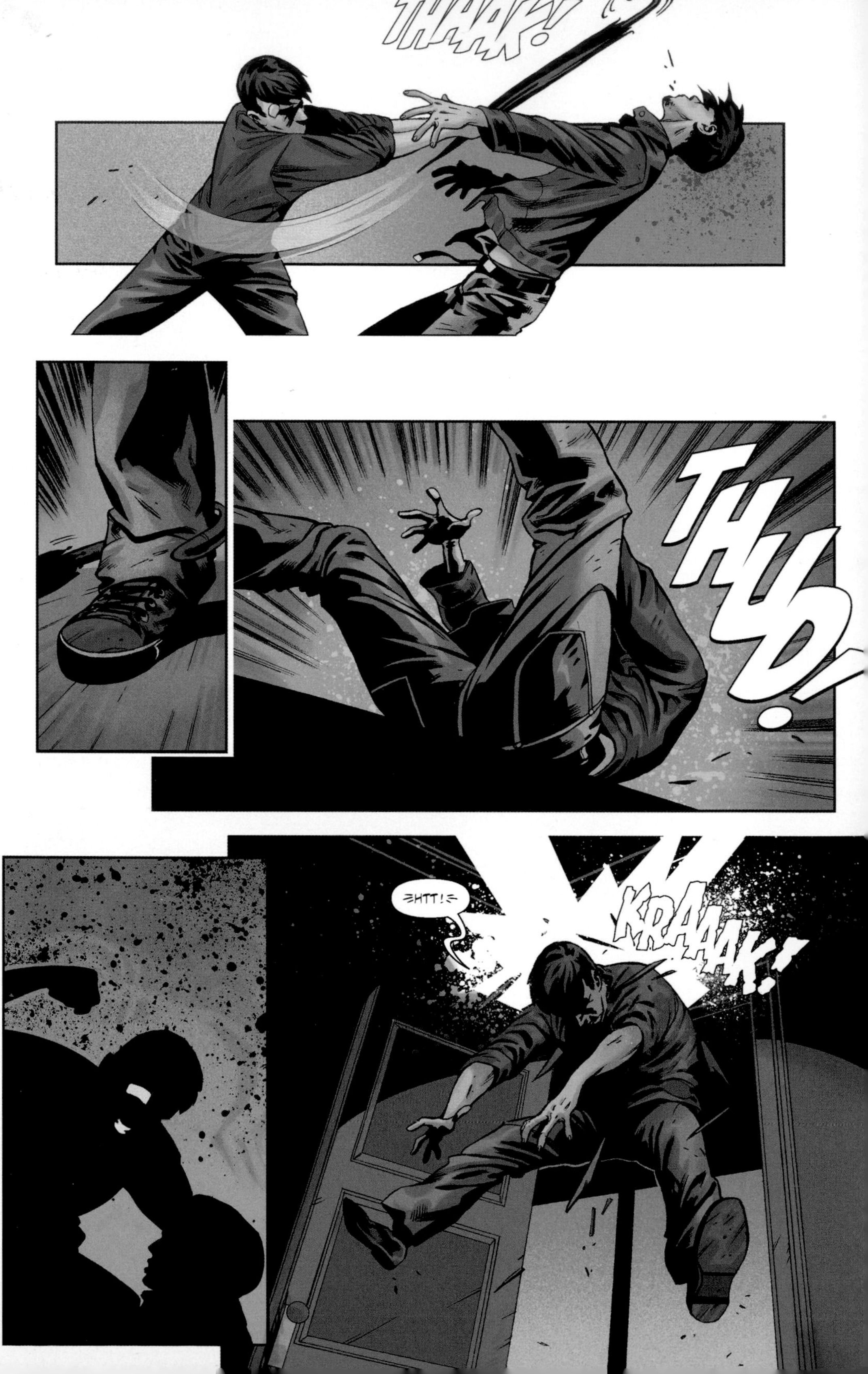
THAAK!
THUD!
HTT!
KRAAAK!

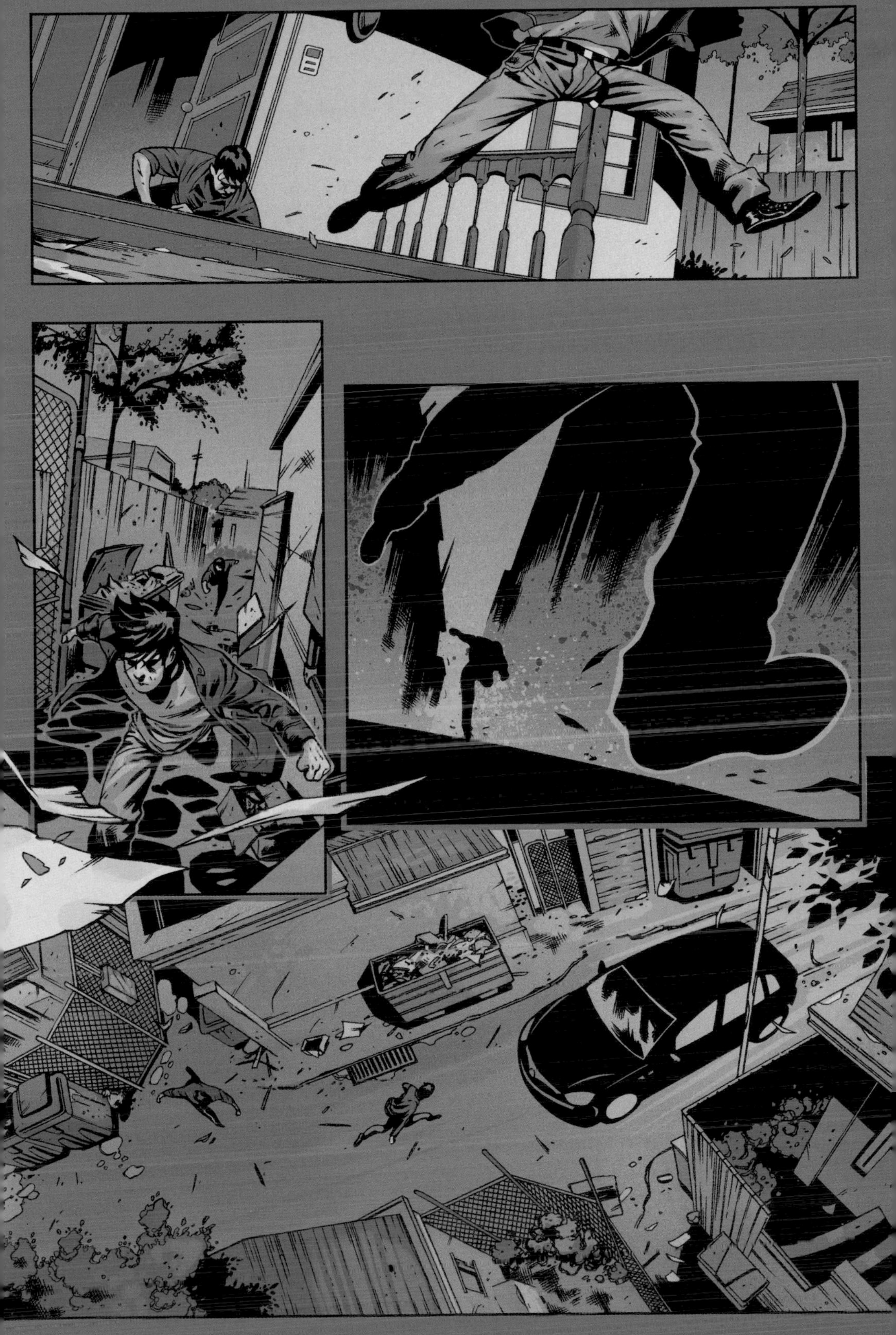

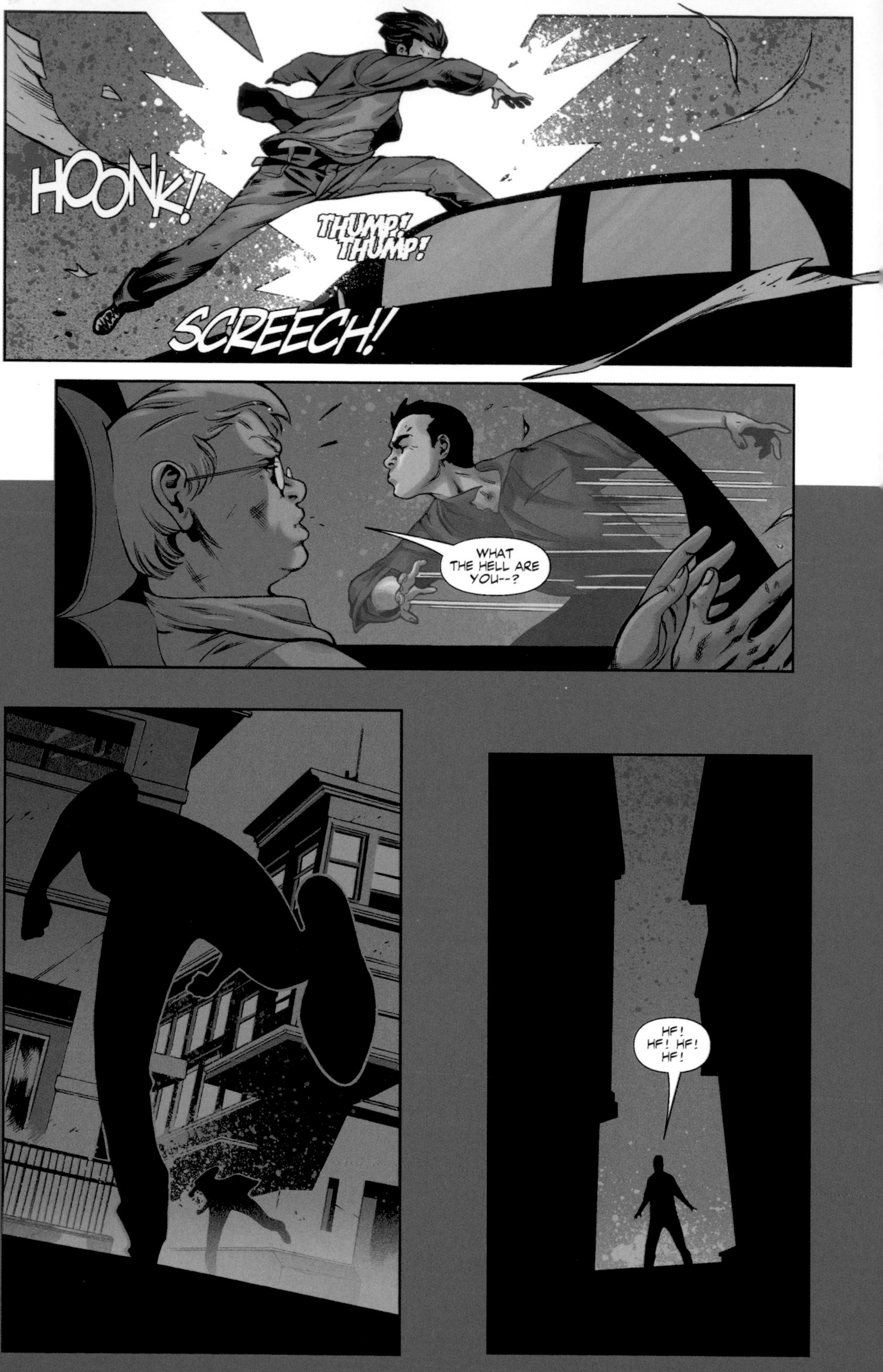
HOONK!
THUMP! THUMP!
SCREECH!
WHAT THE HELL ARE YOU--?
HF! HF! HF! HF!

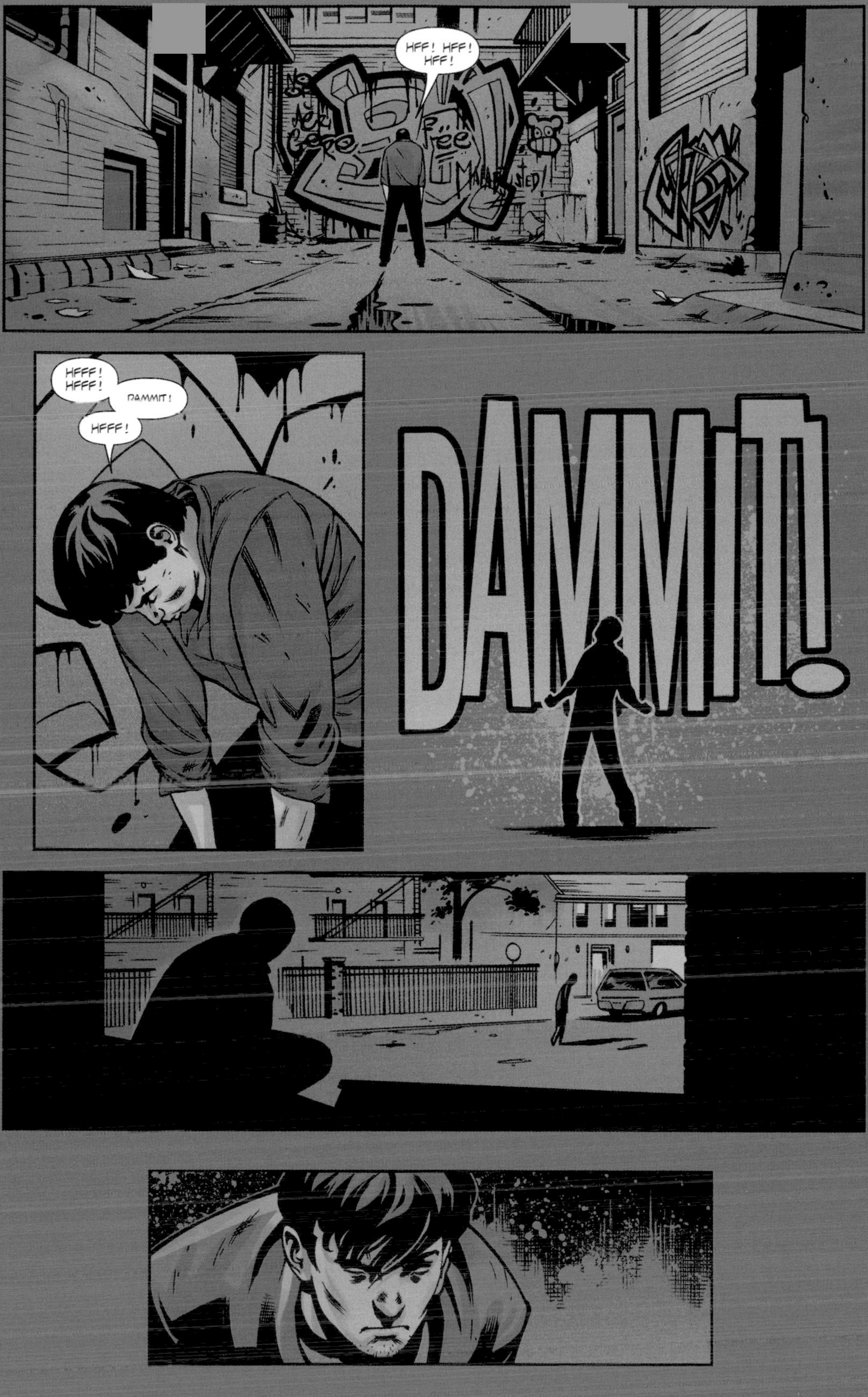
HFF! HFF!
HFF!
HFFF!
HFFF!
DAMMIT!
HFFF!
DAMMIT!

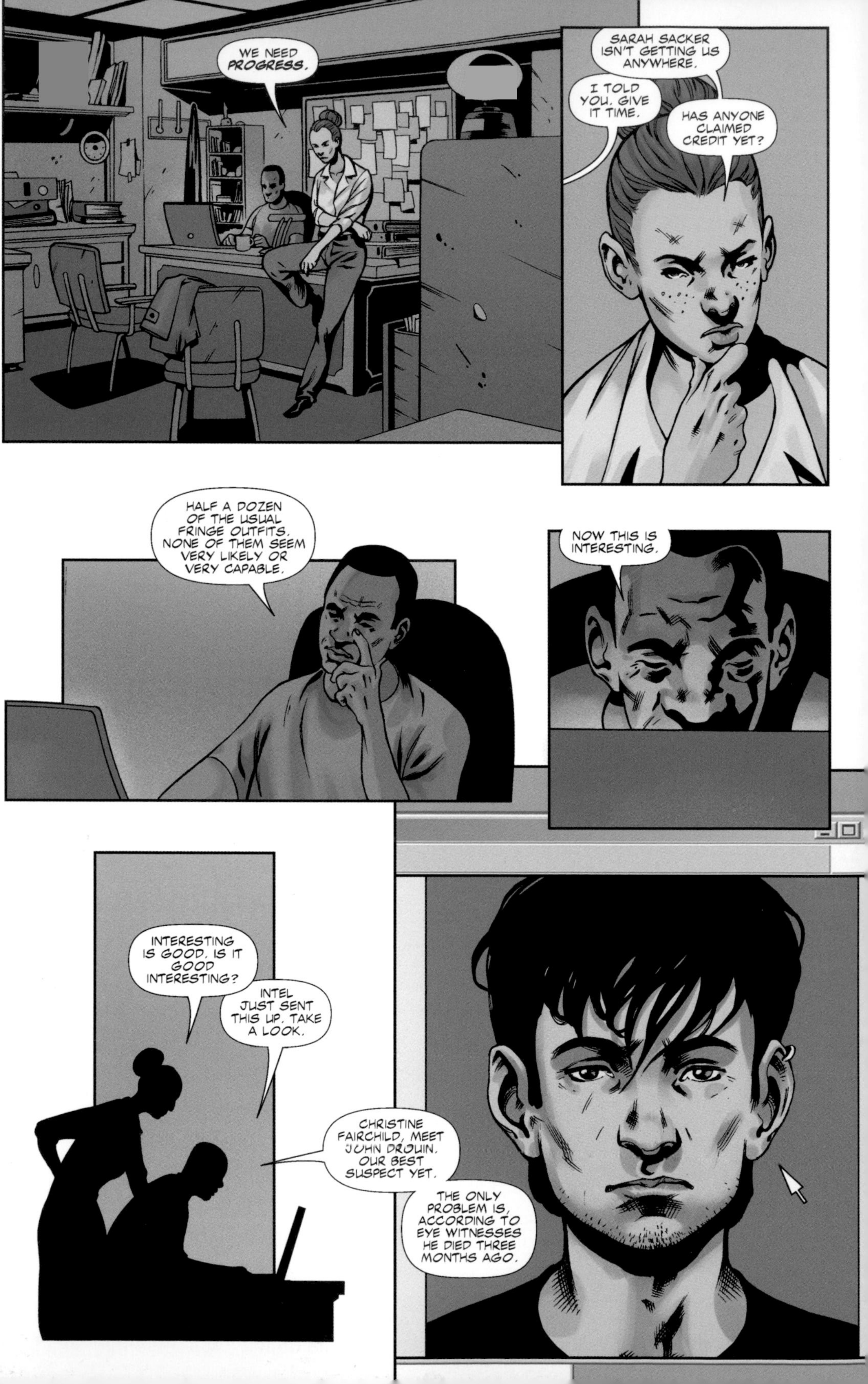
WE NEED PROGRESS.
SARAH SACKER ISN'T GETTING US ANYWHERE.
I TOLD YOU. GIVE IT TIME.
HAS ANYONE CLAIMED CREDIT YET?
HALF A DOZEN OF THE USUAL FRINGE OUTFITS. NONE OF THEM SEEM VERY LIKELY OR VERY CAPABLE.
NOW THIS IS INTERESTING.
INTERESTING IS GOOD. IS IT GOOD INTERESTING?
INTEL JUST SENT THIS UP. TAKE A LOOK.
CHRISTINE FAIRCHILD, MEET JOHN DROUIN. OUR BEST SUSPECT YET.
THE ONLY PROBLEM IS, ACCORDING TO EYE WITNESSES HE DIED THREE MONTHS AGO.

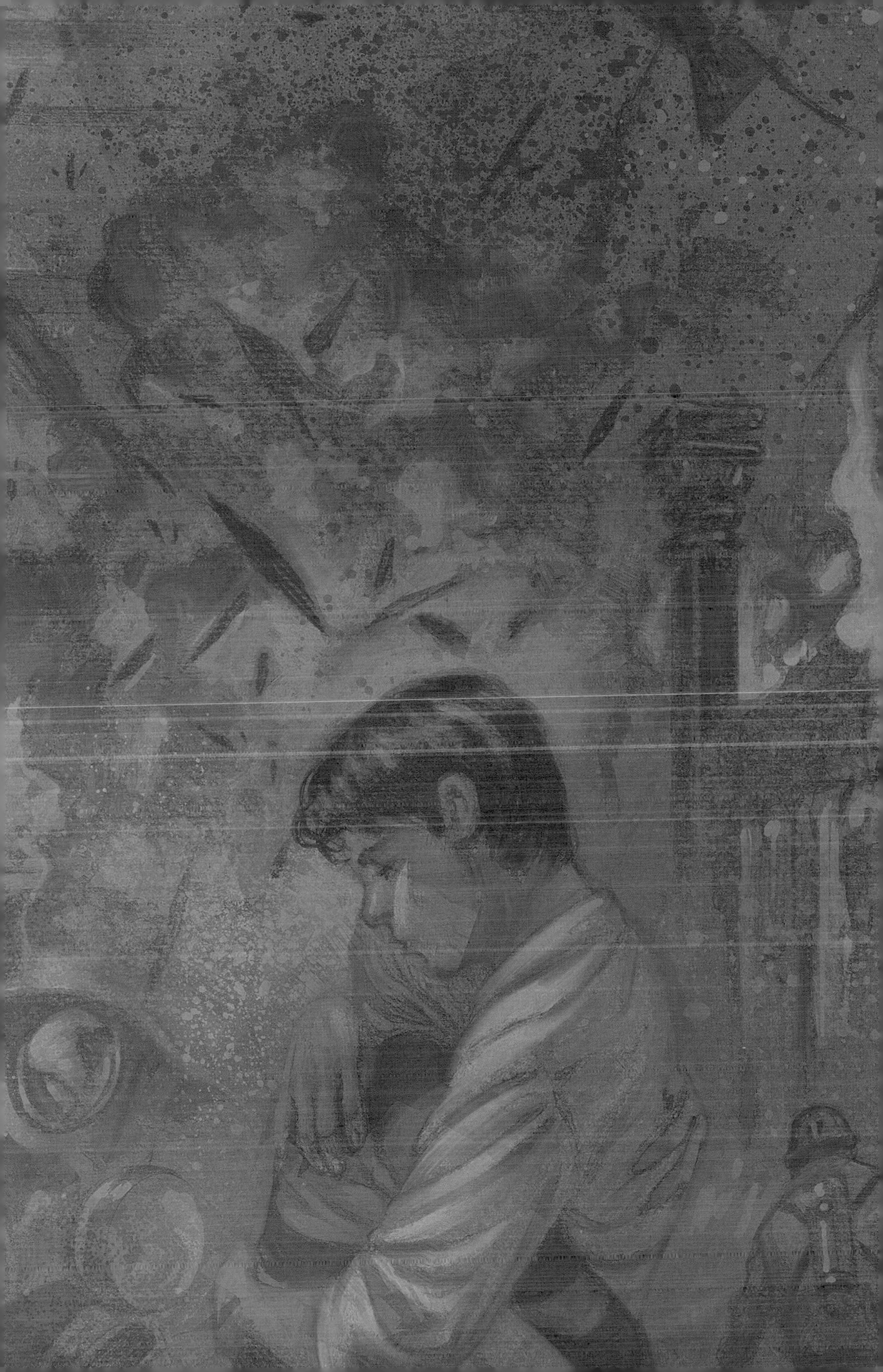

CHAPTER TWO

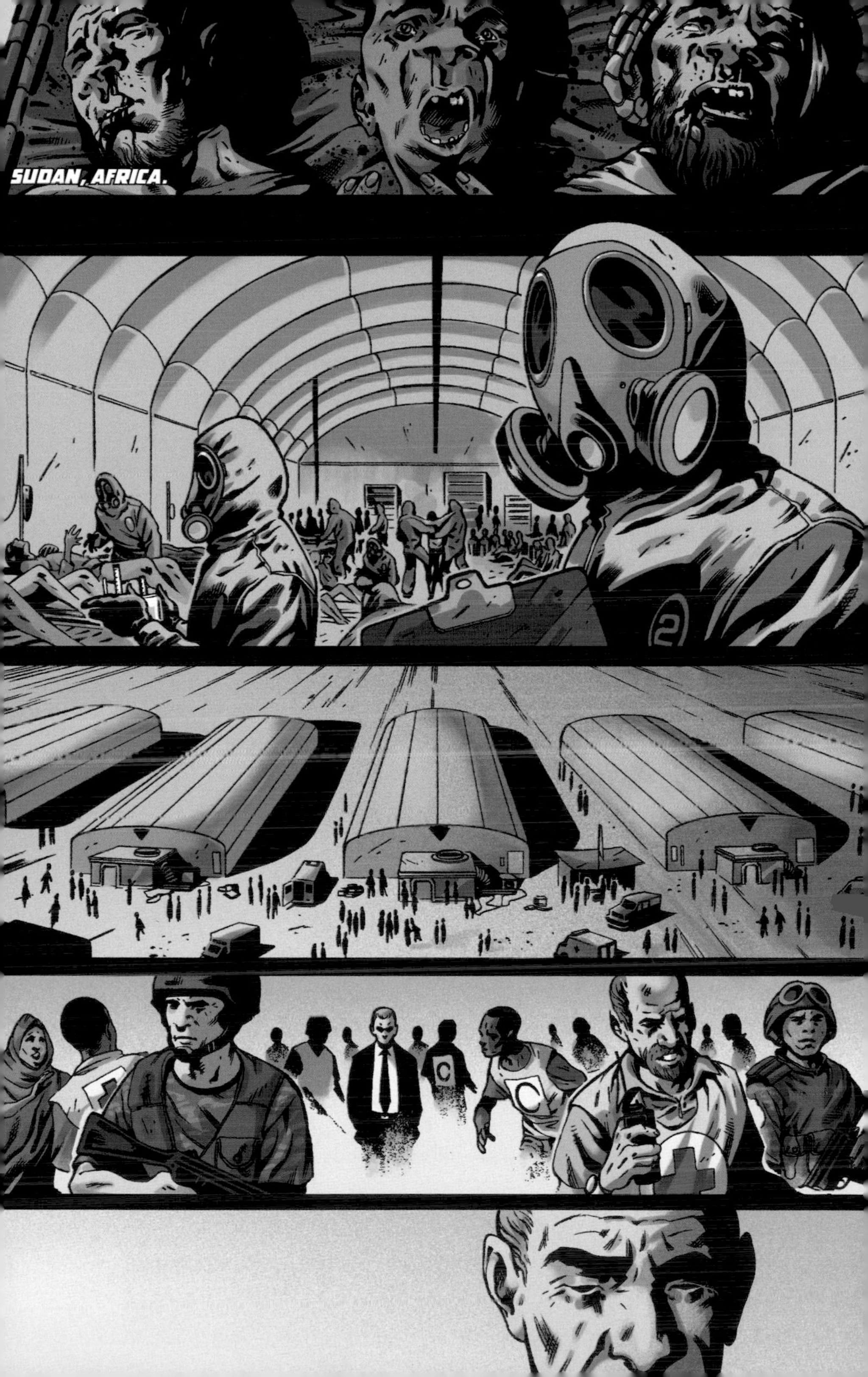
SUDAN, AFRICA.

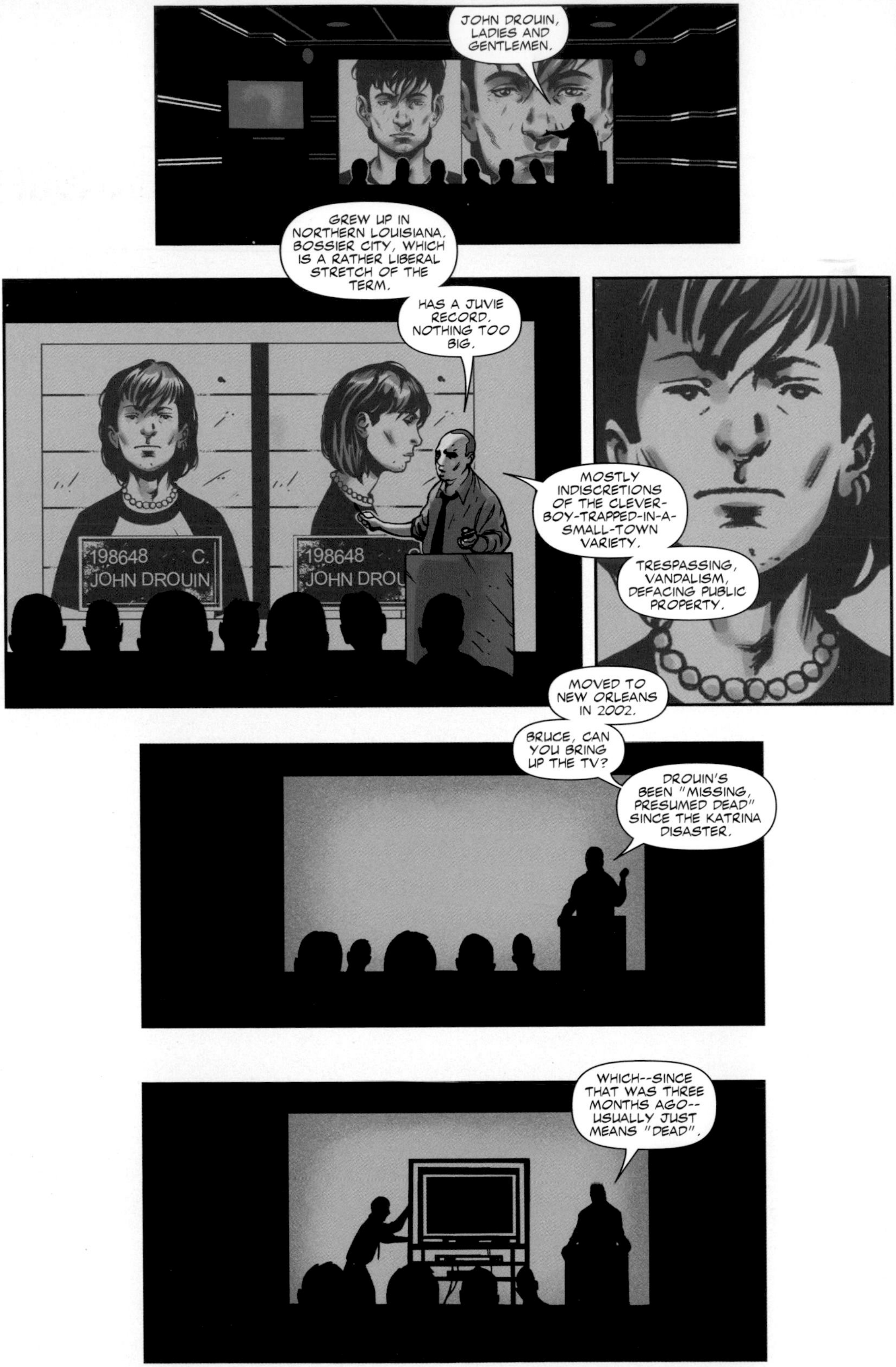
JOHN DROUIN, LADIES AND GENTLEMEN.
GREW UP IN NORTHERN LOUISIANA. BOSSIER CITY, WHICH IS A RATHER LIBERAL STRETCH OF THE TERM.
HAS A JUVIE RECORD. NOTHING TOO BIG.
198648 C. JOHN DROUIN
198648 C JOHN DROU
MOSTLY INDISCRETIONS OF THE CLEVER-BOY-TRAPPED-IN-A-SMALL-TOWN VARIETY.
TRESPASSING, VANDALISM, DEFACING PUBLIC PROPERTY.
MOVED TO NEW ORLEANS IN 2002.
BRUCE, CAN YOU BRING UP THE TV?
DROUIN'S BEEN "MISSING, PRESUMED DEAD" SINCE THE KATRINA DISASTER.
WHICH--SINCE THAT WAS THREE MONTHS AGO--USUALLY JUST MEANS "DEAD".

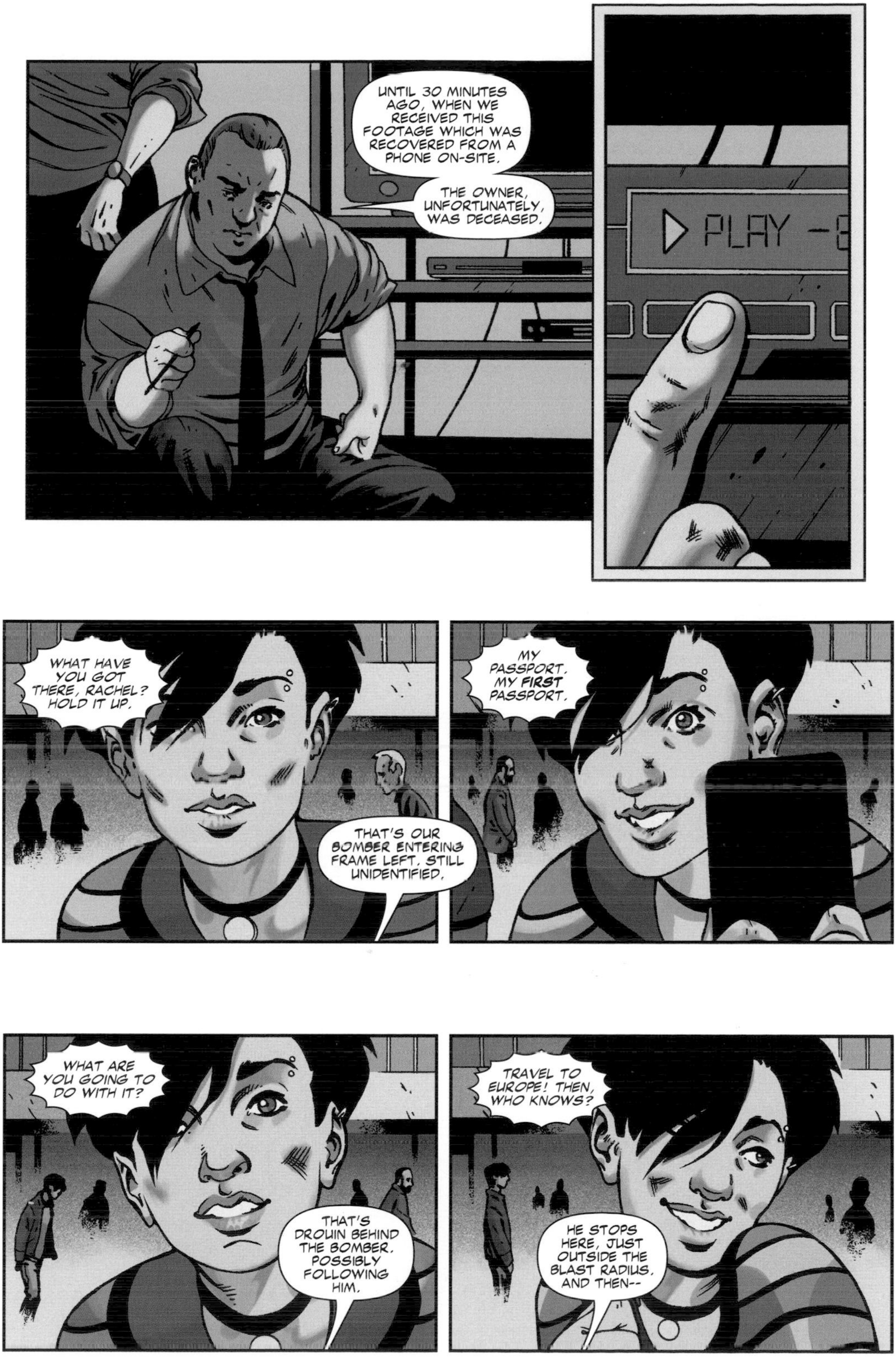
UNTIL 30 MINUTES AGO, WHEN WE RECEIVED THIS FOOTAGE WHICH WAS RECOVERED FROM A PHONE ON-SITE.
THE OWNER, UNFORTUNATELY, WAS DECEASED.
PLAY
WHAT HAVE YOU GOT THERE, RACHEL? HOLD IT UP.
THAT'S OUR BOMBER ENTERING FRAME LEFT. STILL UNIDENTIFIED.
MY PASSPORT. MY FIRST PASSPORT.
WHAT ARE YOU GOING TO DO WITH IT?
THAT'S DROUIN BEHIND THE BOMBER. POSSIBLY FOLLOWING HIM.
TRAVEL TO EUROPE! THEN, WHO KNOWS?
HE STOPS HERE, JUST OUTSIDE THE BLAST RADIUS, AND THEN--

--BOOM.

BA-DOO--*

THIS IS WHERE WE LOSE SOUND.

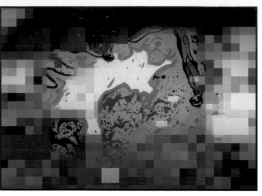

THERE, DROUIN DOESN'T SEEM TO HAVE MOVED.

THAT'S DAVID SACKER ON THE GROUND, THEY SEEM TO LOOK AT EACH OTHER--

--THEN SACKER APPARENTLY PASSES OUT.

DO WE HAVE SACKER'S FILE YET?

NO, IT'S TIGHTER THAN A DRUM, AND BURIED DEEP.

GET ME THAT FILE. YESTERDAY.

HE'S IMPORTANT IN ALL THIS, I KNOW IT.

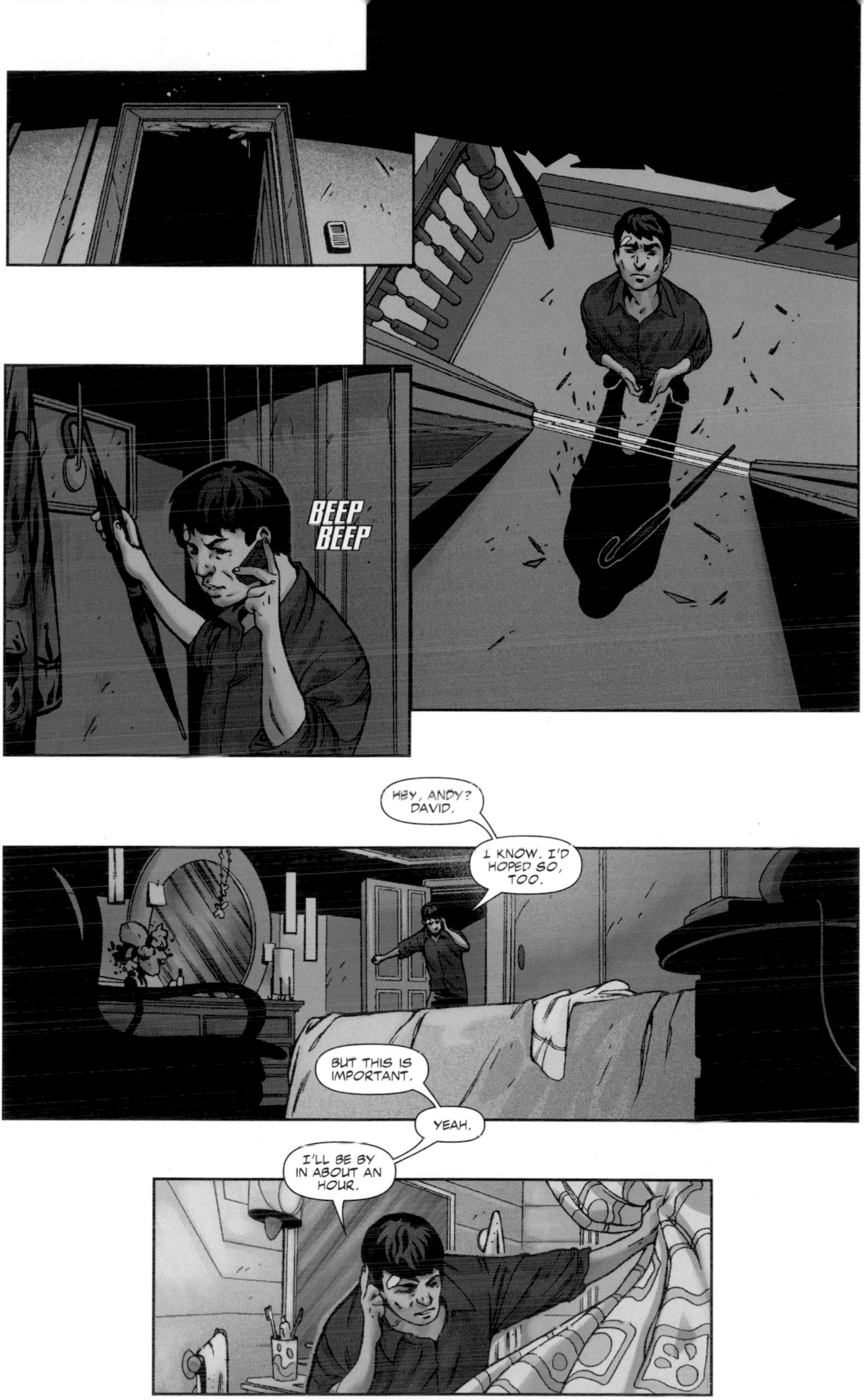
BEEP
BEEP
HEY, ANDY? DAVID.
I KNOW. I'D HOPED SO, TOO.
BUT THIS IS IMPORTANT.
YEAH.
I'LL BE BY IN ABOUT AN HOUR.

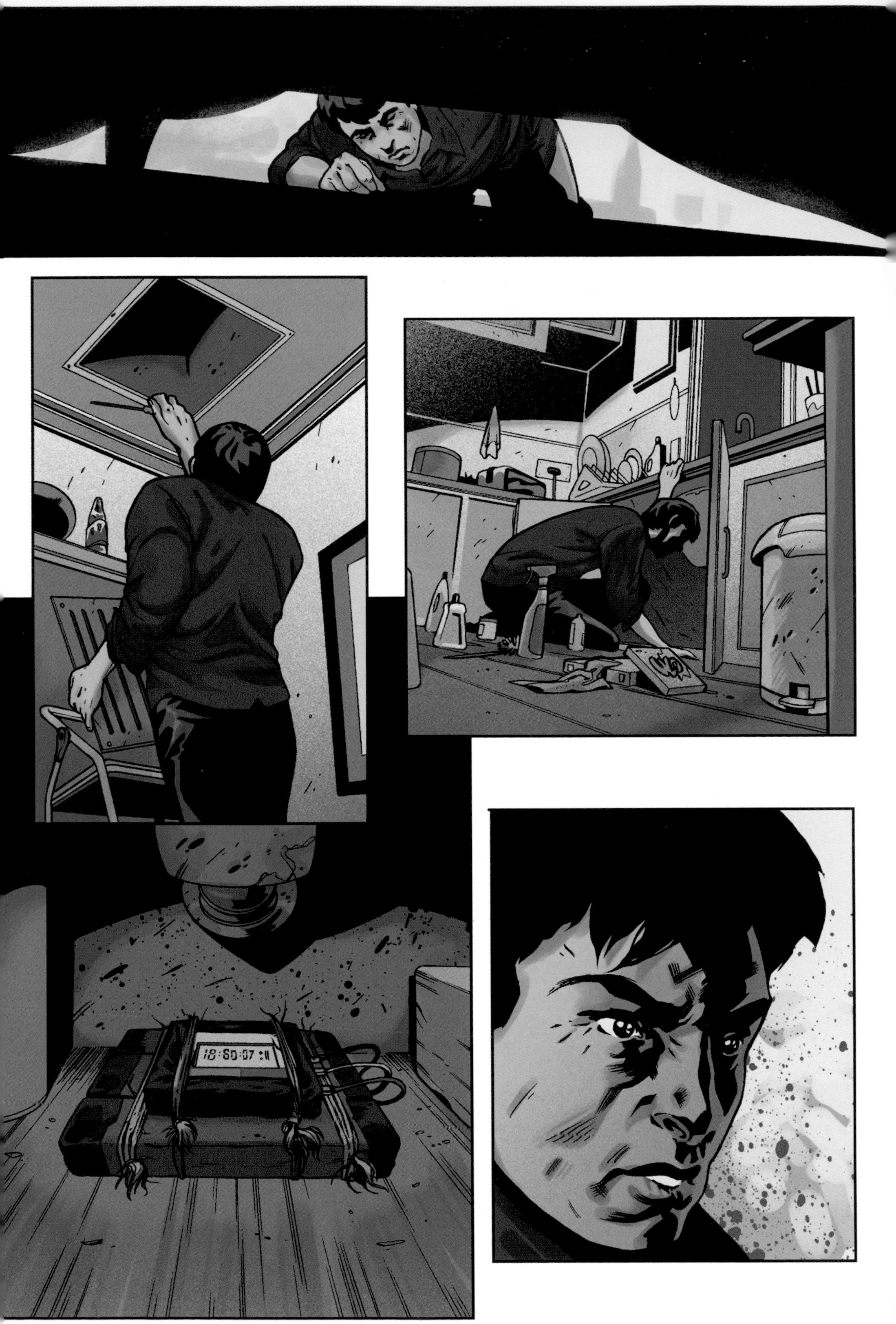

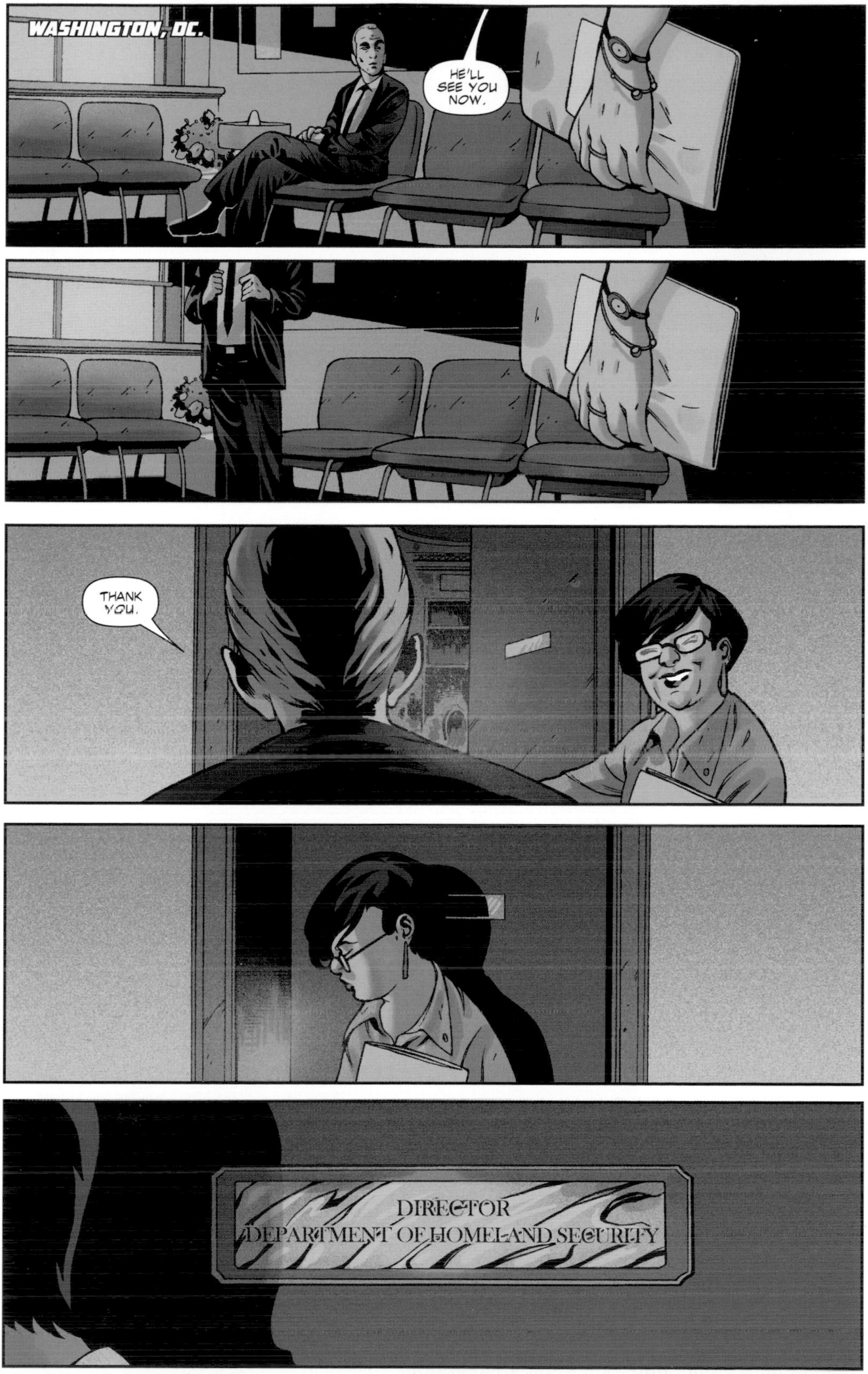
WASHINGTON, DC.
HE'LL SEE YOU NOW.
THANK YOU.
DIRECTOR
DEPARTMENT OF HOMELAND SECURITY

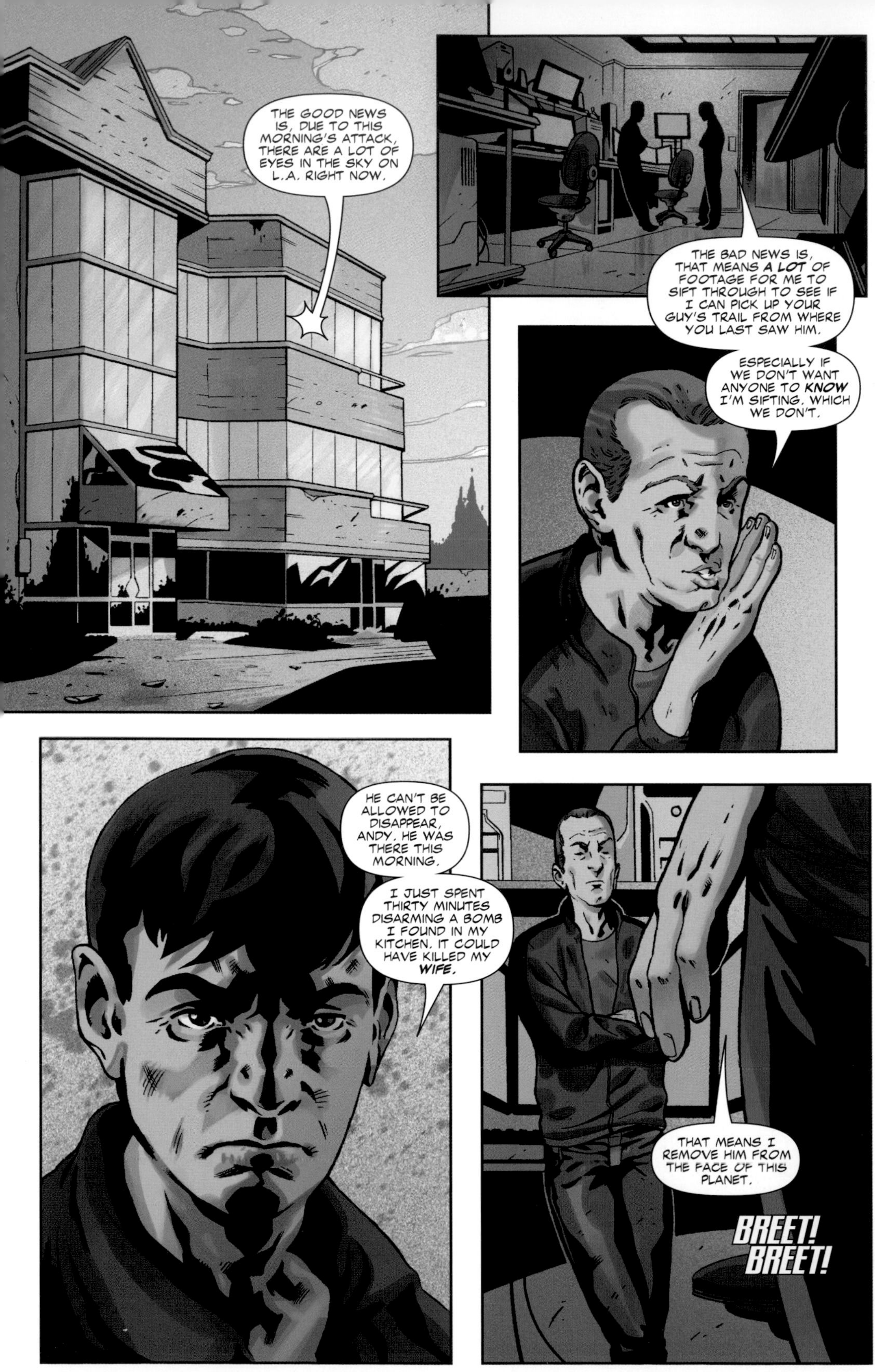
THE GOOD NEWS IS, DUE TO THIS MORNING'S ATTACK, THERE ARE A LOT OF EYES IN THE SKY ON L.A. RIGHT NOW.
THE BAD NEWS IS, THAT MEANS **A LOT** OF FOOTAGE FOR ME TO SIFT THROUGH TO SEE IF I CAN PICK UP YOUR GUY'S TRAIL FROM WHERE YOU LAST SAW HIM.
ESPECIALLY IF WE DON'T WANT ANYONE TO **KNOW** I'M SIFTING, WHICH WE DON'T.
HE CAN'T BE ALLOWED TO DISAPPEAR, ANDY. HE WAS THERE THIS MORNING.
I JUST SPENT THIRTY MINUTES DISARMING A BOMB I FOUND IN MY KITCHEN. IT COULD HAVE KILLED MY **WIFE.**
THAT MEANS I REMOVE HIM FROM THE FACE OF THIS PLANET.
BREET! BREET!

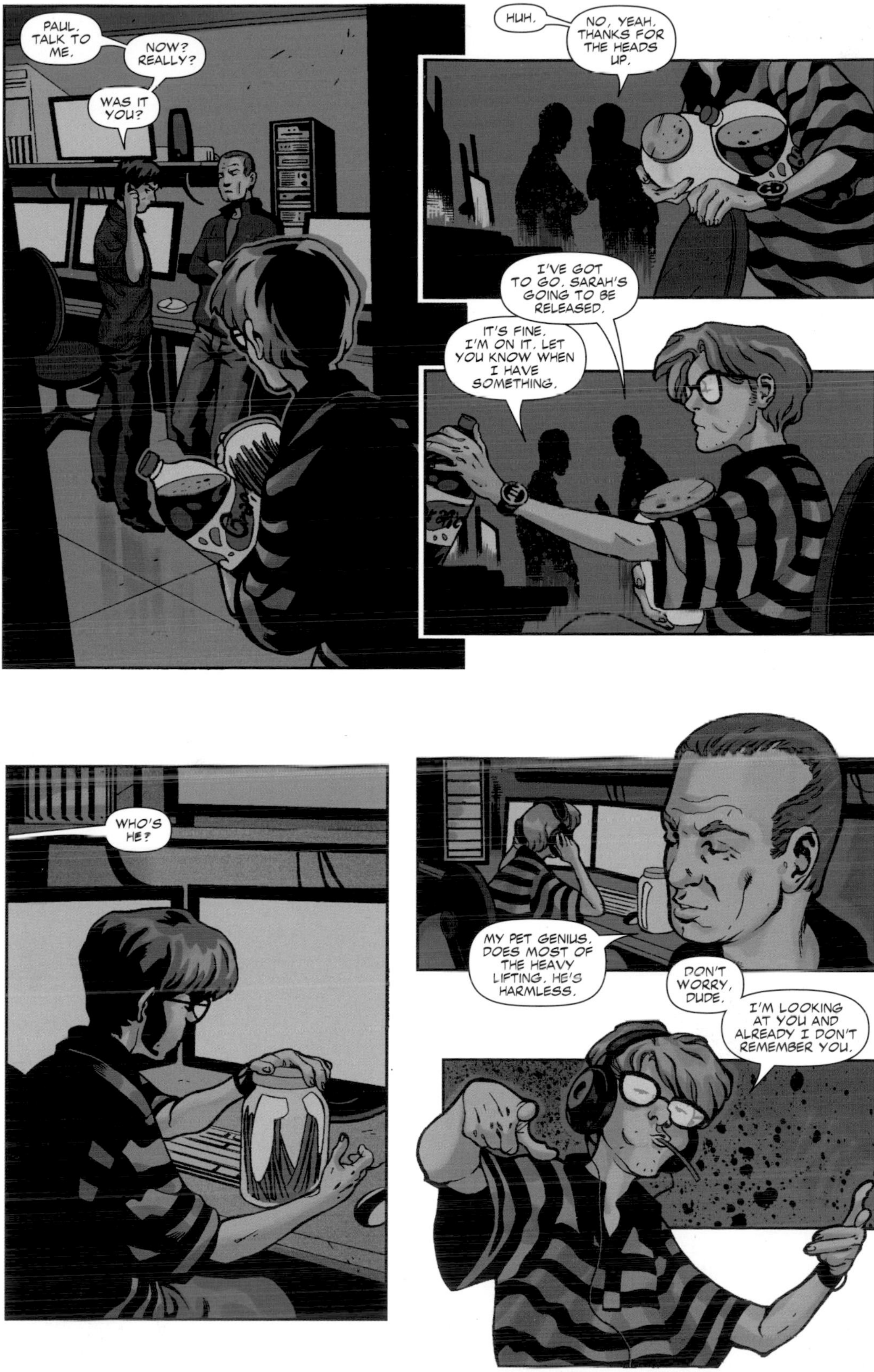
PAUL. TALK TO ME.
NOW? REALLY?
WAS IT YOU?
HUH.
NO, YEAH. THANKS FOR THE HEADS UP.
I'VE GOT TO GO. SARAH'S GOING TO BE RELEASED.
IT'S FINE. I'M ON IT. LET YOU KNOW WHEN I HAVE SOMETHING.
WHO'S HE?
MY PET GENIUS. DOES MOST OF THE HEAVY LIFTING. HE'S HARMLESS.
DON'T WORRY, DUDE.
I'M LOOKING AT YOU AND ALREADY I DON'T REMEMBER YOU.

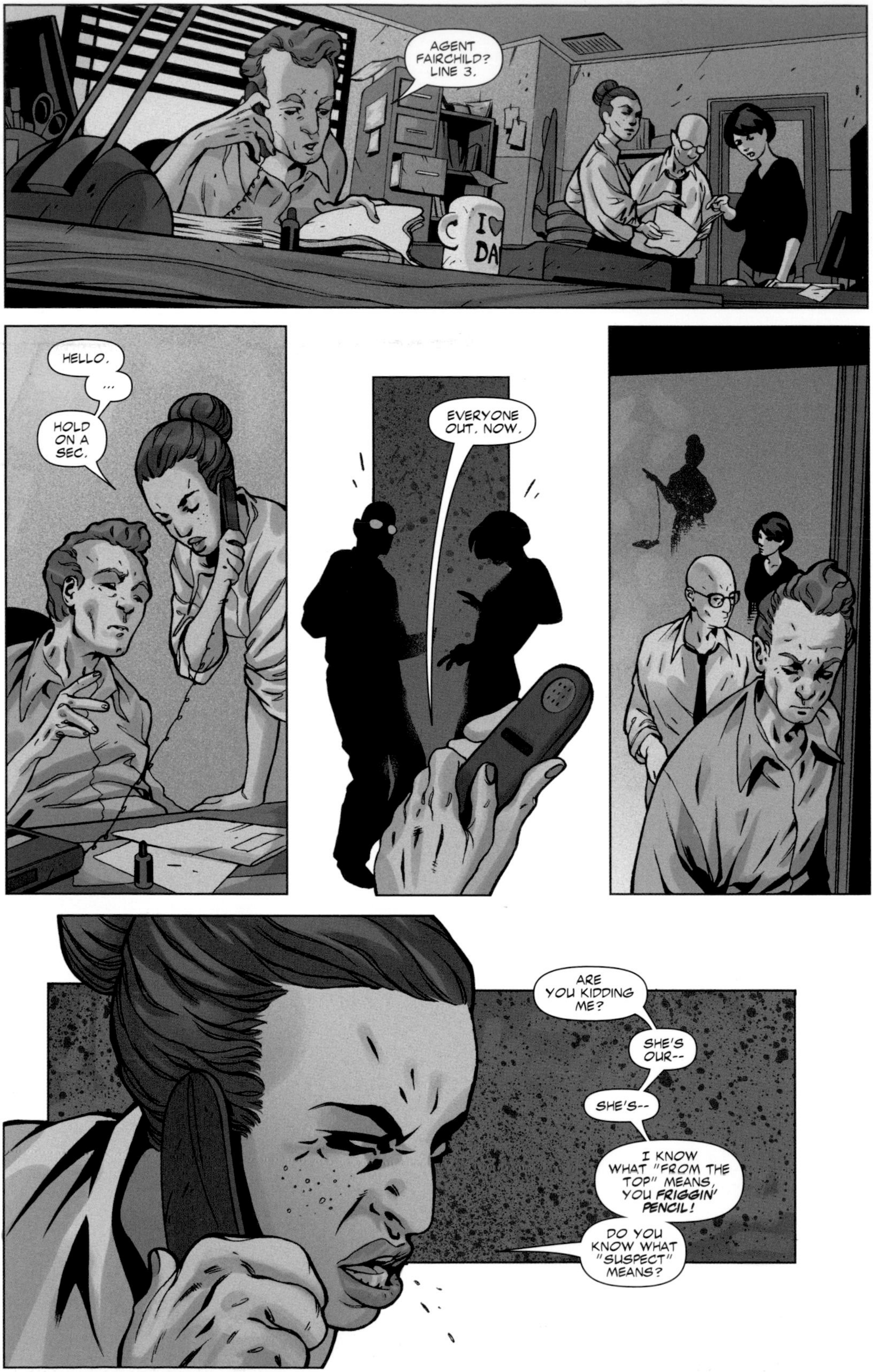
AGENT FAIRCHILD? LINE 3.
HELLO.
...
HOLD ON A SEC.
EVERYONE OUT. NOW.
ARE YOU KIDDING ME?
SHE'S OUR--
SHE'S--
I KNOW WHAT "FROM THE TOP" MEANS, YOU **FRIGGIN' PENCIL!**
DO YOU KNOW WHAT "SUSPECT" MEANS?

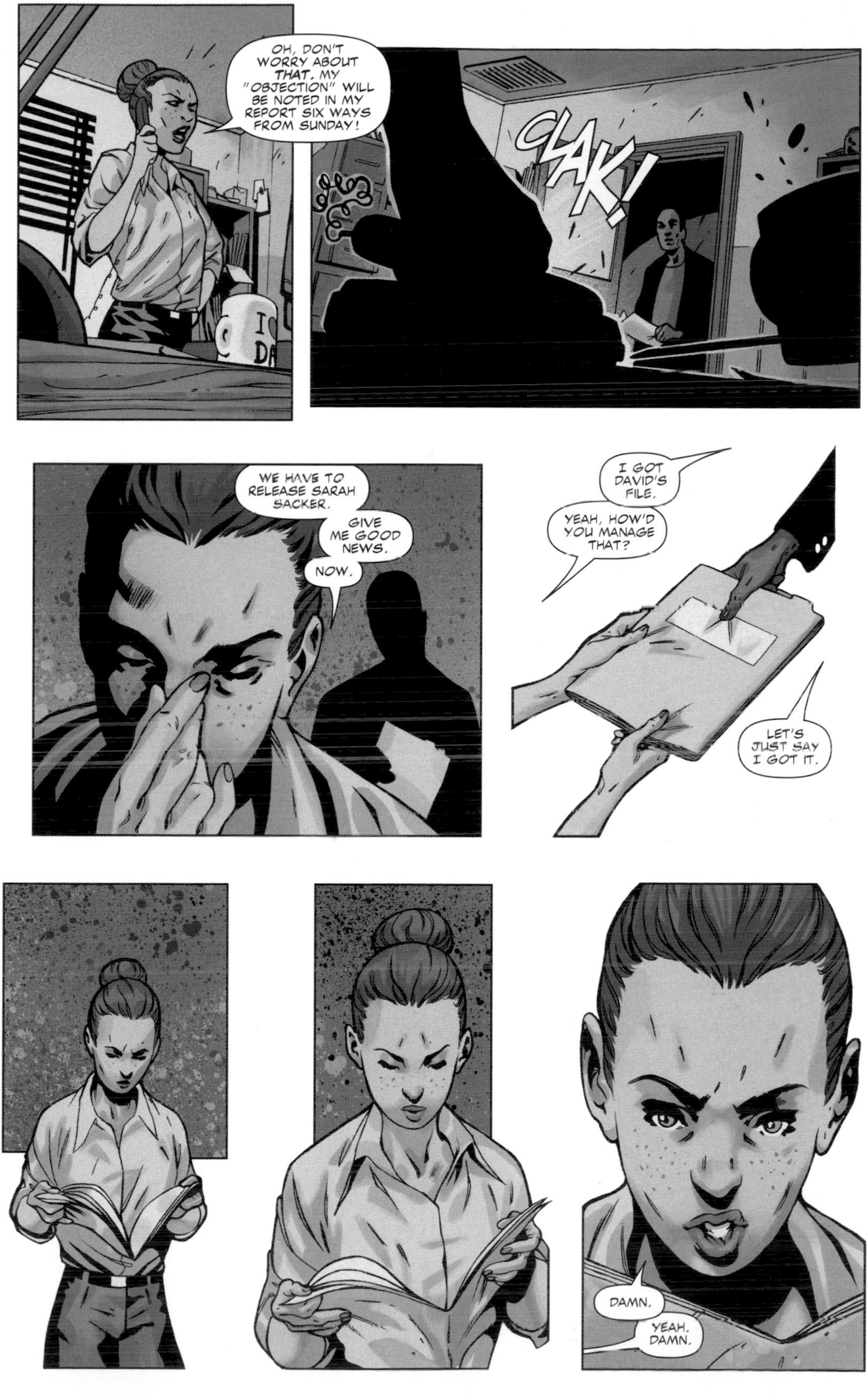
OH, DON'T WORRY ABOUT THAT. MY "OBJECTION" WILL BE NOTED IN MY REPORT SIX WAYS FROM SUNDAY!
CLAK!
WE HAVE TO RELEASE SARAH SACKER.
GIVE ME GOOD NEWS.
NOW.
I GOT DAVID'S FILE.
YEAH, HOW'D YOU MANAGE THAT?
LET'S JUST SAY I GOT IT.
DAMN.
YEAH. DAMN.

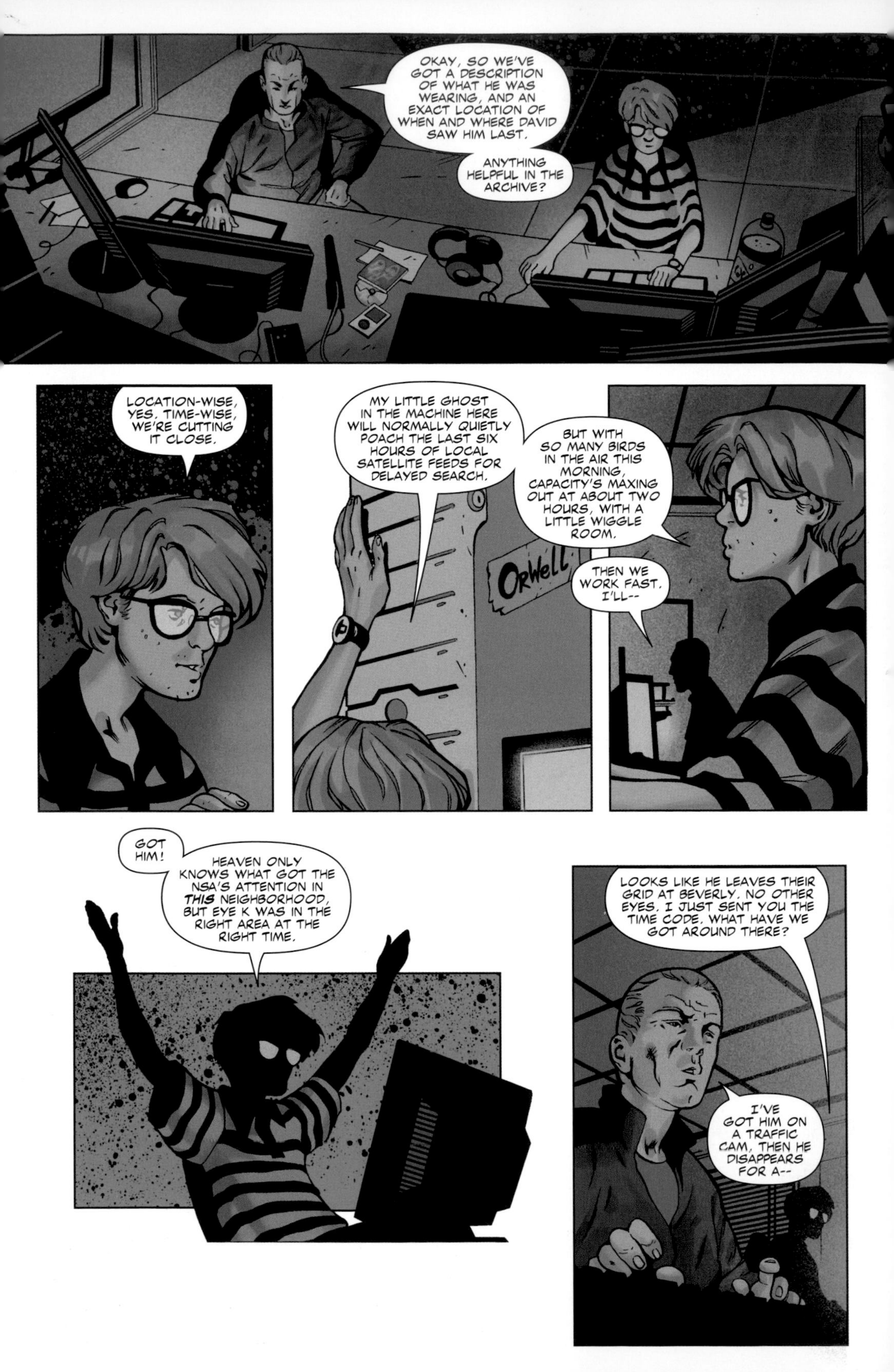
OKAY, SO WE'VE GOT A DESCRIPTION OF WHAT HE WAS WEARING, AND AN EXACT LOCATION OF WHEN AND WHERE DAVID SAW HIM LAST.
ANYTHING HELPFUL IN THE ARCHIVE?
LOCATION-WISE, YES. TIME-WISE, WE'RE CUTTING IT CLOSE.
MY LITTLE GHOST IN THE MACHINE HERE WILL NORMALLY QUIETLY POACH THE LAST SIX HOURS OF LOCAL SATELLITE FEEDS FOR DELAYED SEARCH.
ORWELL
BUT WITH SO MANY BIRDS IN THE AIR THIS MORNING, CAPACITY'S MAXING OUT AT ABOUT TWO HOURS, WITH A LITTLE WIGGLE ROOM.
THEN WE WORK FAST. I'LL--
GOT HIM!
HEAVEN ONLY KNOWS WHAT GOT THE NSA'S ATTENTION IN THIS NEIGHBORHOOD, BUT EYE K WAS IN THE RIGHT AREA AT THE RIGHT TIME.
LOOKS LIKE HE LEAVES THEIR GRID AT BEVERLY. NO OTHER EYES. I JUST SENT YOU THE TIME CODE. WHAT HAVE WE GOT AROUND THERE?
I'VE GOT HIM ON A TRAFFIC CAM, THEN HE DISAPPEARS FOR A--

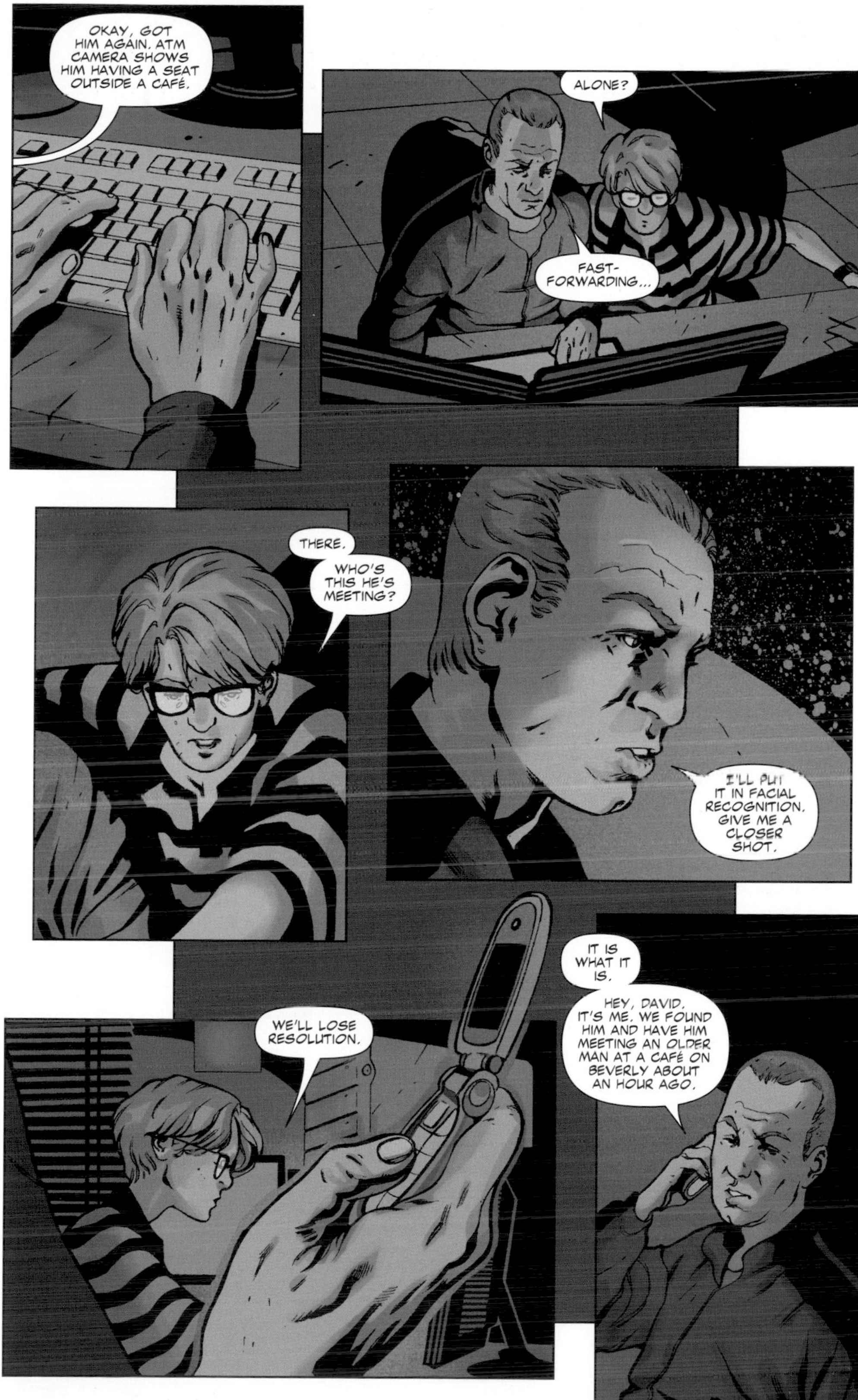
OKAY, GOT HIM AGAIN. ATM CAMERA SHOWS HIM HAVING A SEAT OUTSIDE A CAFÉ.
ALONE?
FAST-FORWARDING...
THERE.
WHO'S THIS HE'S MEETING?
I'LL PUT IT IN FACIAL RECOGNITION. GIVE ME A CLOSER SHOT.
WE'LL LOSE RESOLUTION.
IT IS WHAT IT IS.
HEY, DAVID. IT'S ME. WE FOUND HIM AND HAVE HIM MEETING AN OLDER MAN AT A CAFÉ ON BEVERLY ABOUT AN HOUR AGO.

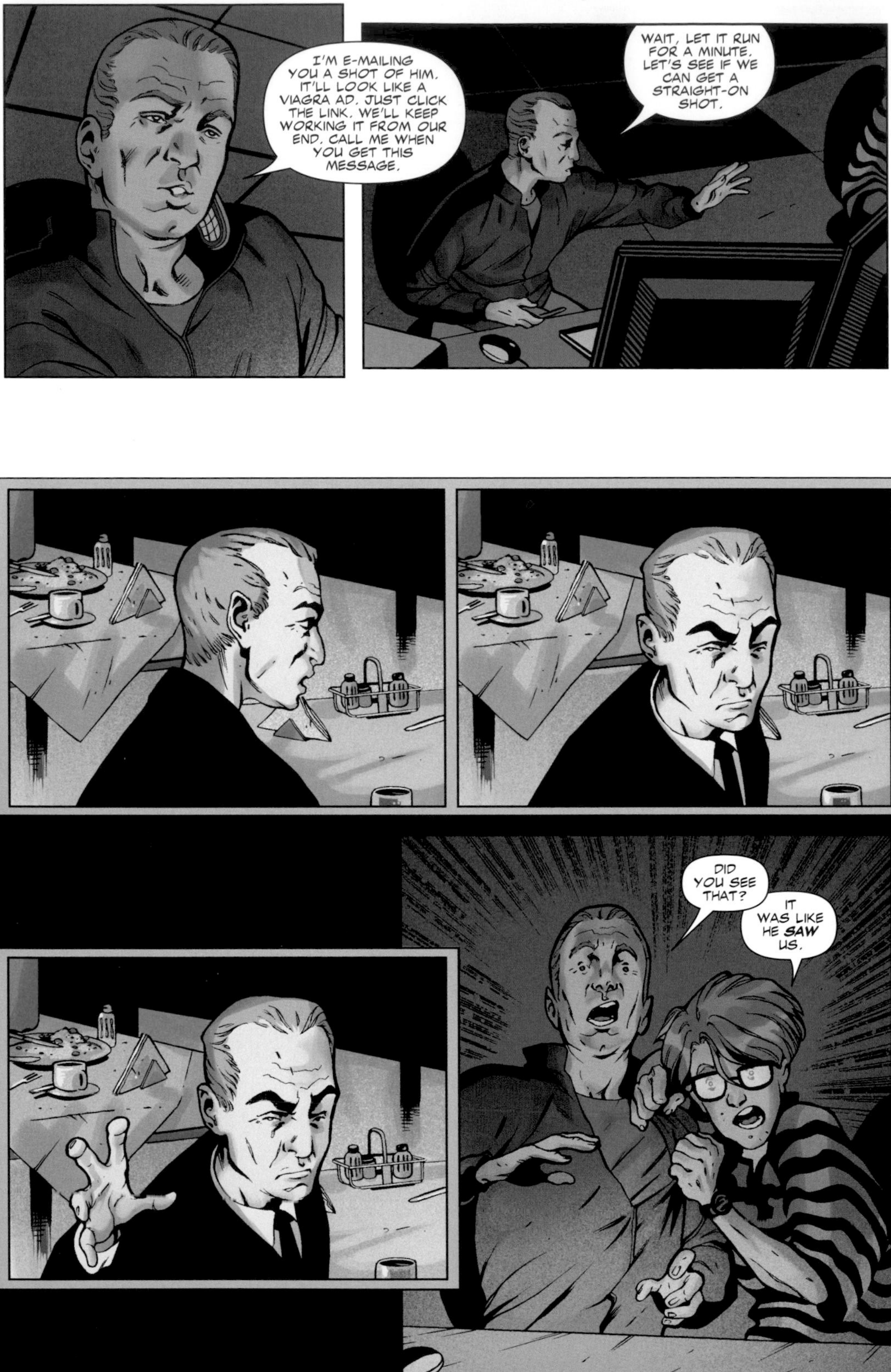
I'M E-MAILING YOU A SHOT OF HIM. IT'LL LOOK LIKE A VIAGRA AD. JUST CLICK THE LINK. WE'LL KEEP WORKING IT FROM OUR END. CALL ME WHEN YOU GET THIS MESSAGE.
WAIT, LET IT RUN FOR A MINUTE. LET'S SEE IF WE CAN GET A STRAIGHT-ON SHOT.
DID YOU SEE THAT?
IT WAS LIKE HE **SAW** US.

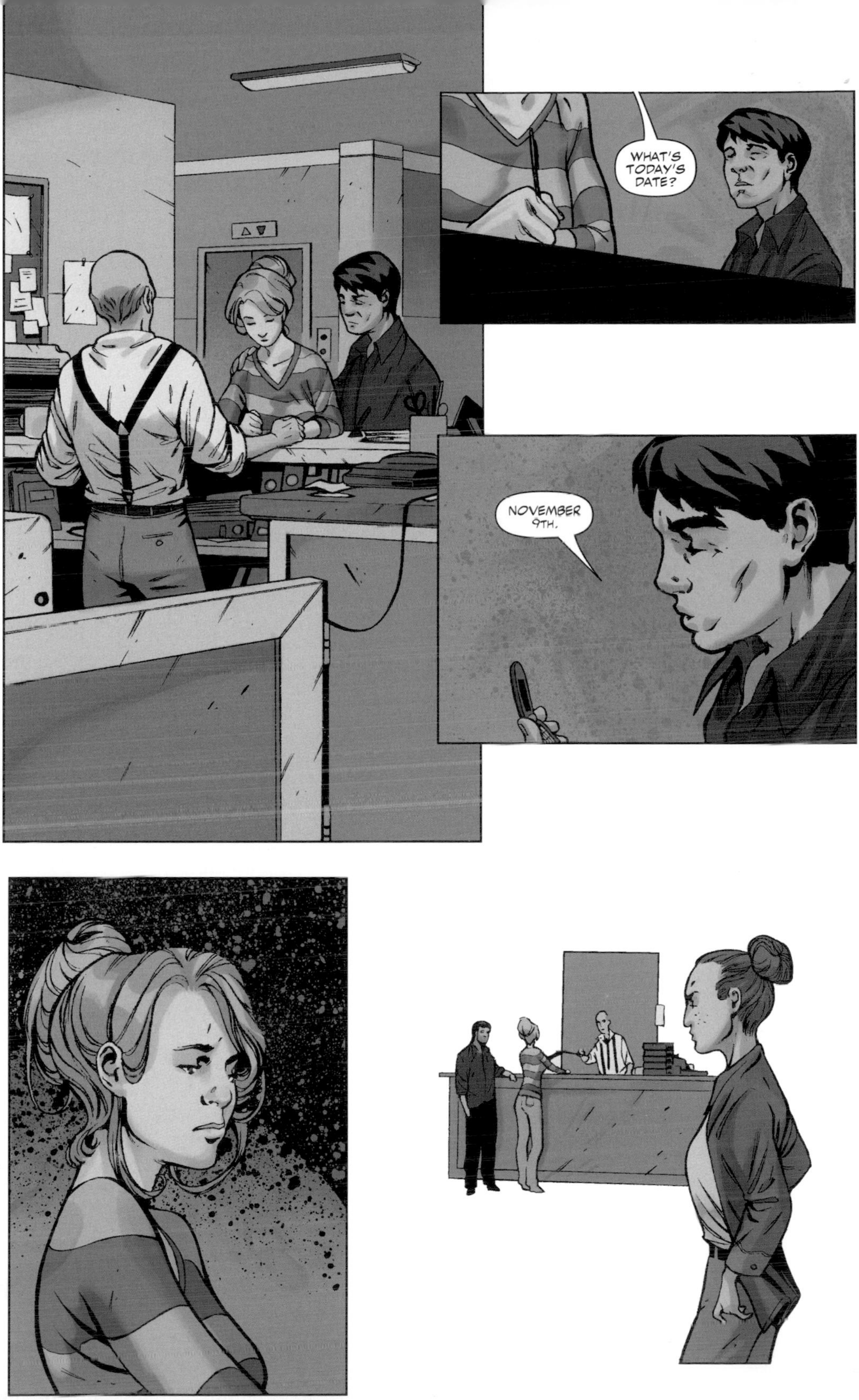
WHAT'S TODAY'S DATE?
NOVEMBER 9TH.

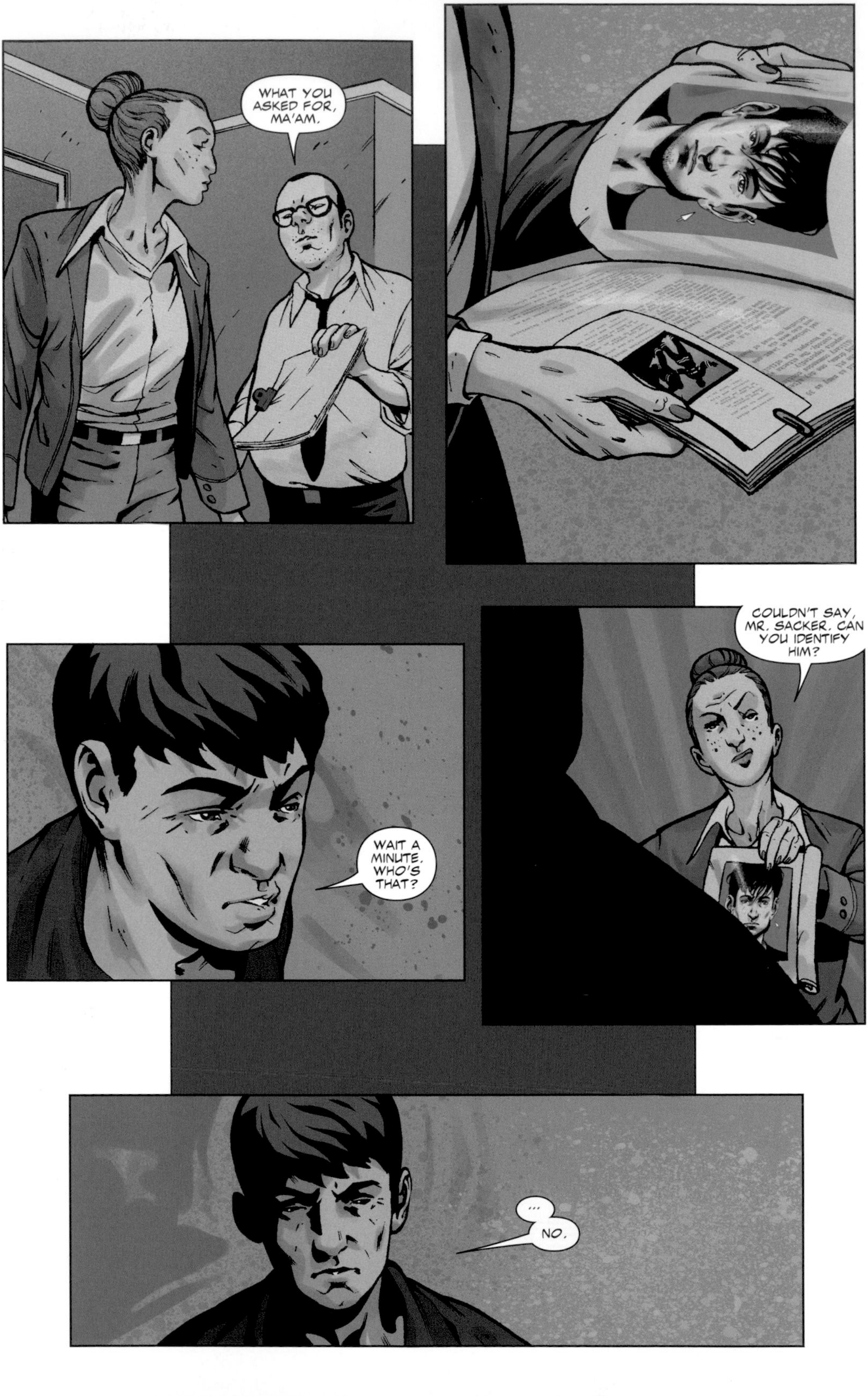
WHAT YOU ASKED FOR, MA'AM.
WAIT A MINUTE. WHO'S THAT?
COULDN'T SAY, MR. SACKER. CAN YOU IDENTIFY HIM?
...
NO.

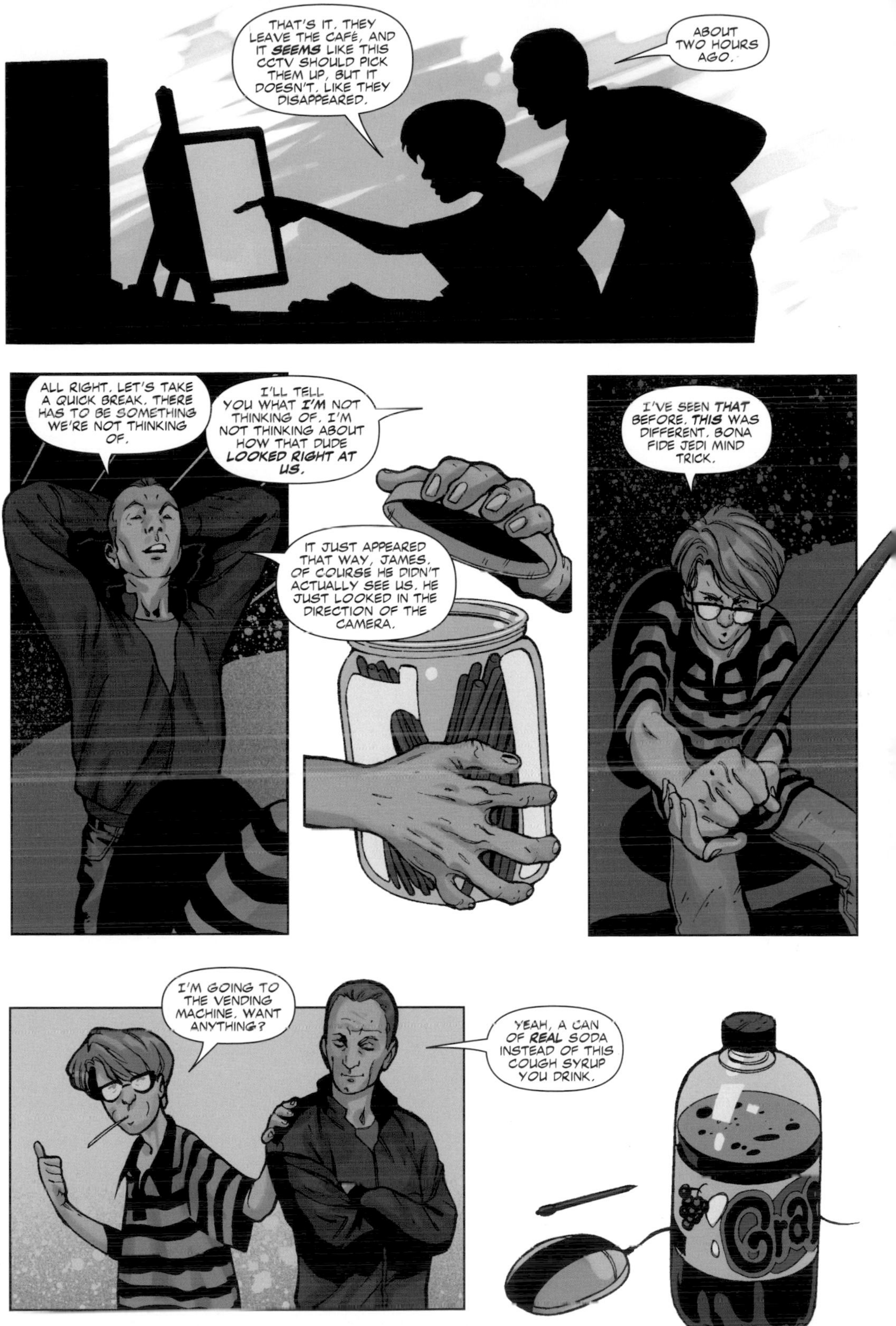
THAT'S IT. THEY LEAVE THE CAFÉ, AND IT SEEMS LIKE THIS CCTV SHOULD PICK THEM UP, BUT IT DOESN'T. LIKE THEY DISAPPEARED.
ABOUT TWO HOURS AGO.
ALL RIGHT. LET'S TAKE A QUICK BREAK. THERE HAS TO BE SOMETHING WE'RE NOT THINKING OF.
I'LL TELL YOU WHAT I'M NOT THINKING OF. I'M NOT THINKING ABOUT HOW THAT DUDE LOOKED RIGHT AT US.
IT JUST APPEARED THAT WAY, JAMES. OF COURSE HE DIDN'T ACTUALLY SEE US. HE JUST LOOKED IN THE DIRECTION OF THE CAMERA.
I'VE SEEN THAT BEFORE. THIS WAS DIFFERENT. BONA FIDE JEDI MIND TRICK.
I'M GOING TO THE VENDING MACHINE. WANT ANYTHING?
YEAH, A CAN OF REAL SODA INSTEAD OF THIS COUGH SYRUP YOU DRINK.

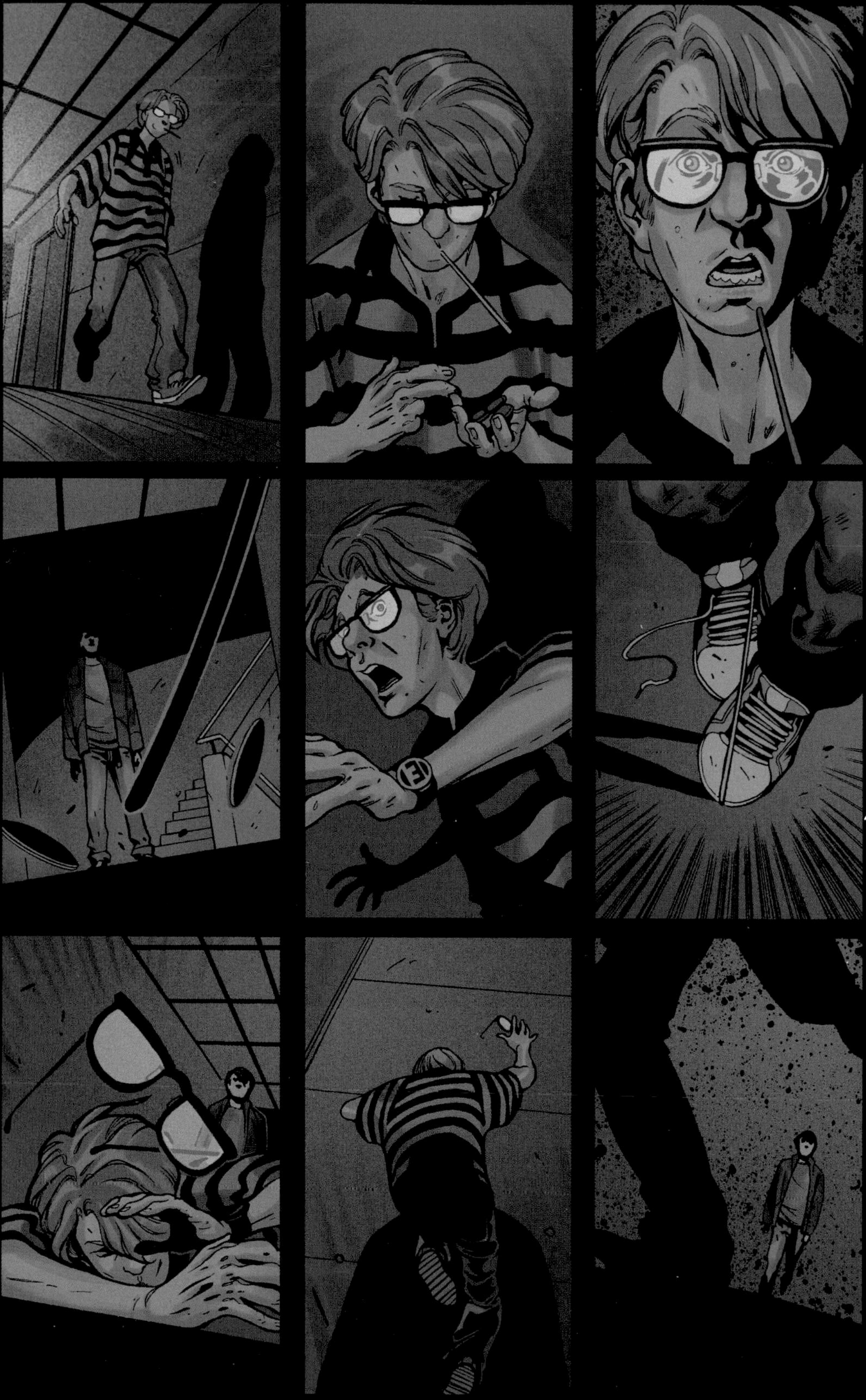

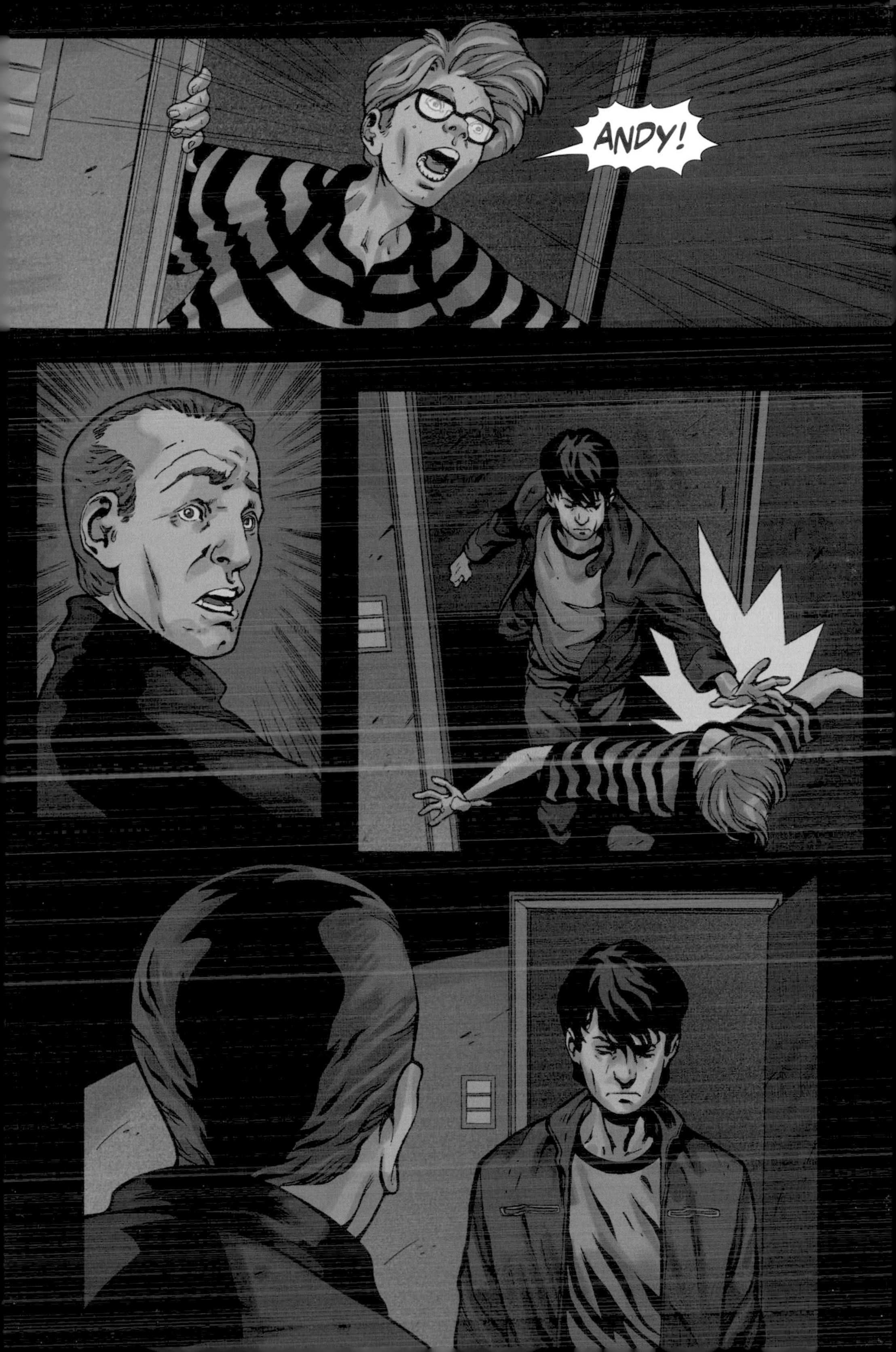
ANDY!

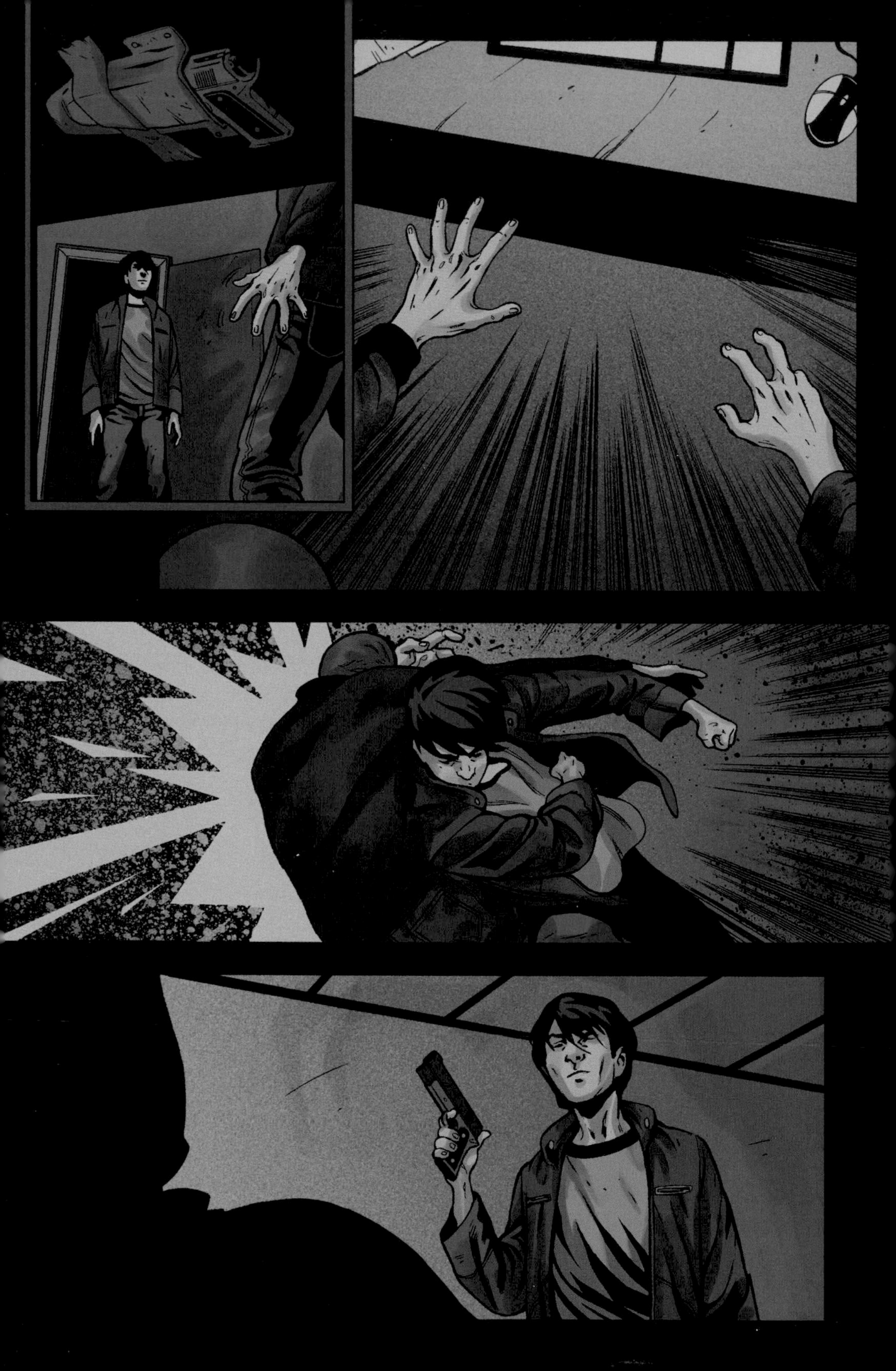

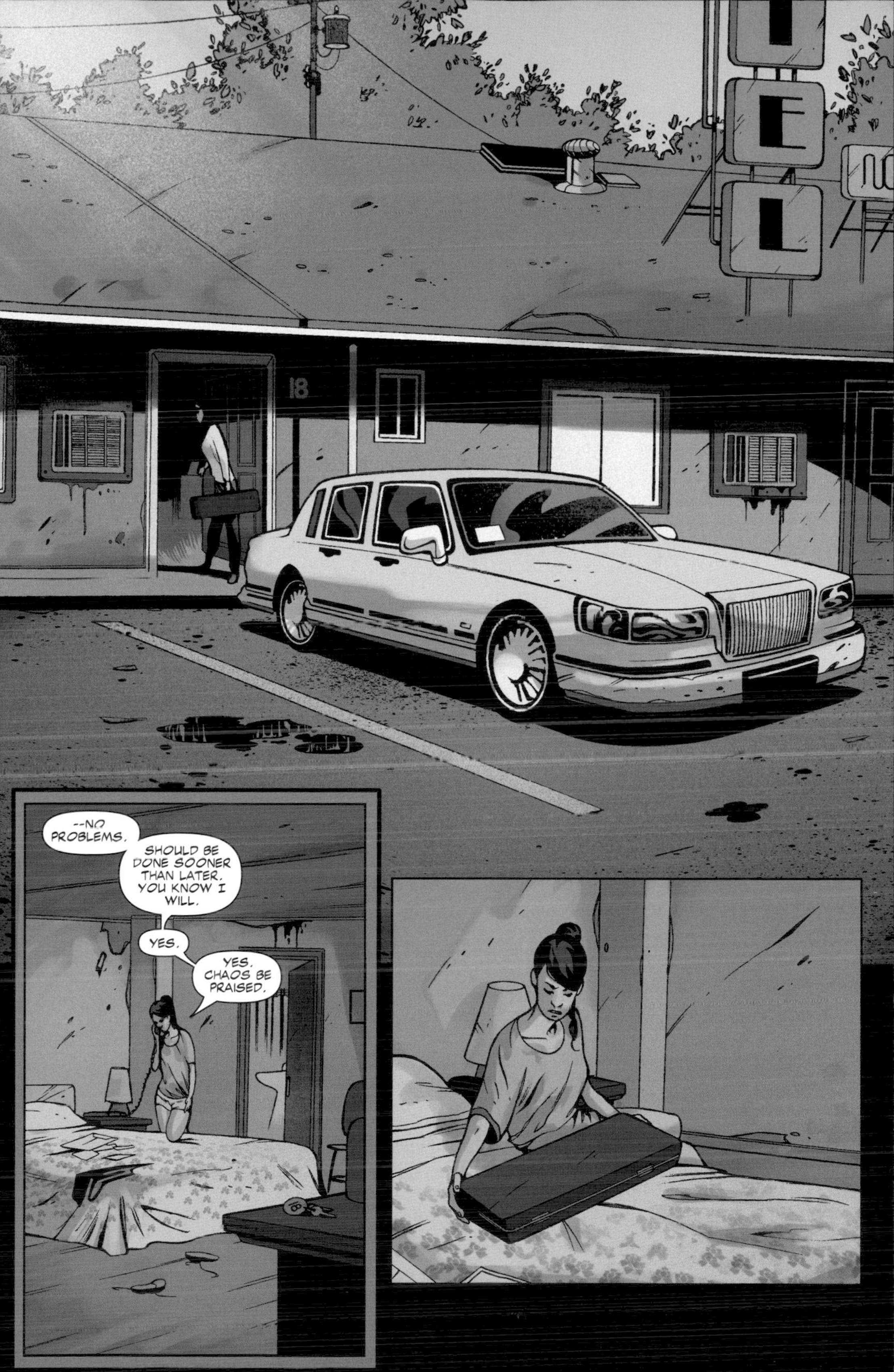
18
--NO PROBLEMS.
SHOULD BE DONE SOONER THAN LATER. YOU KNOW I WILL.
YES.
YES. CHAOS BE PRAISED.

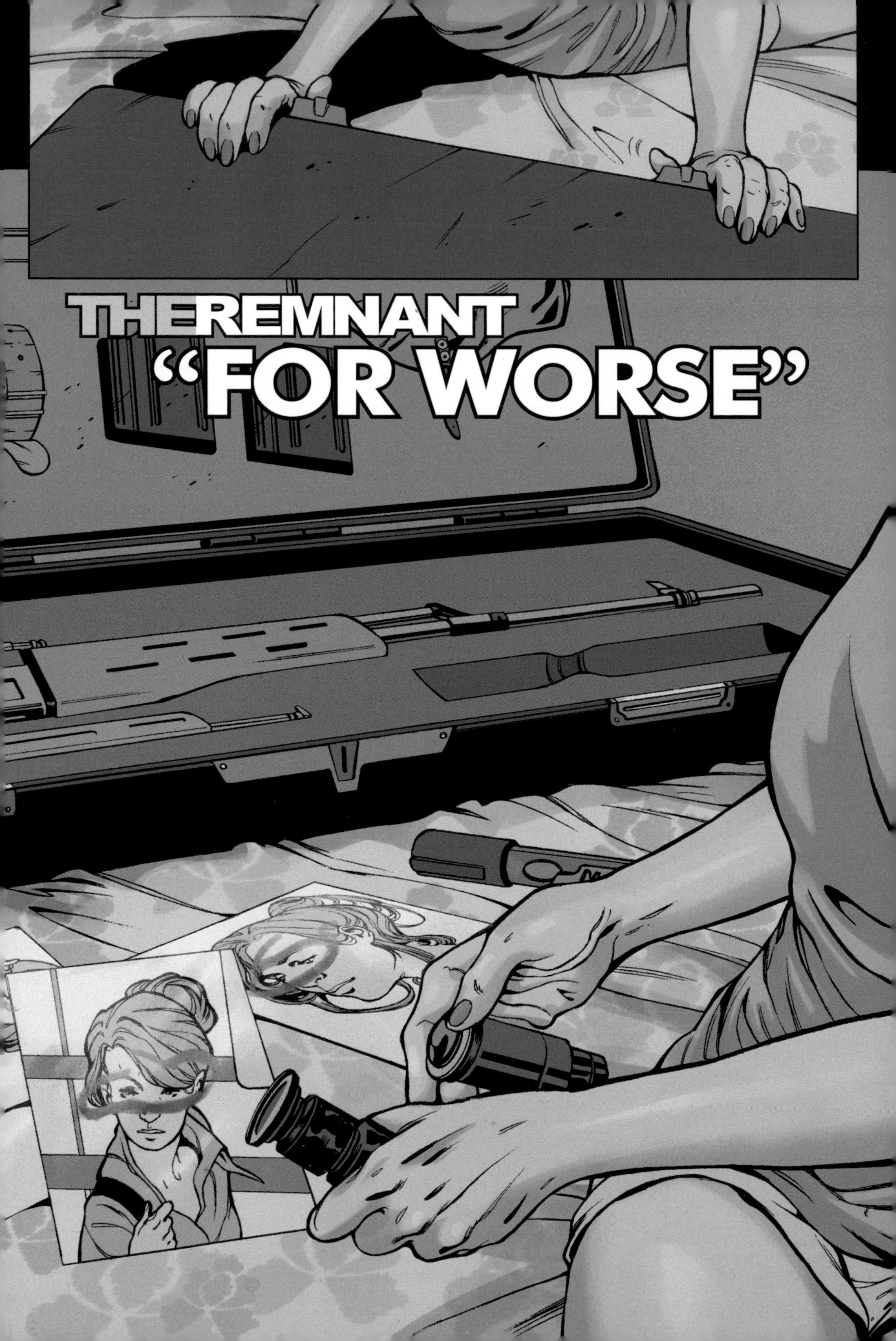
THE REMNANT
"FOR WORSE"

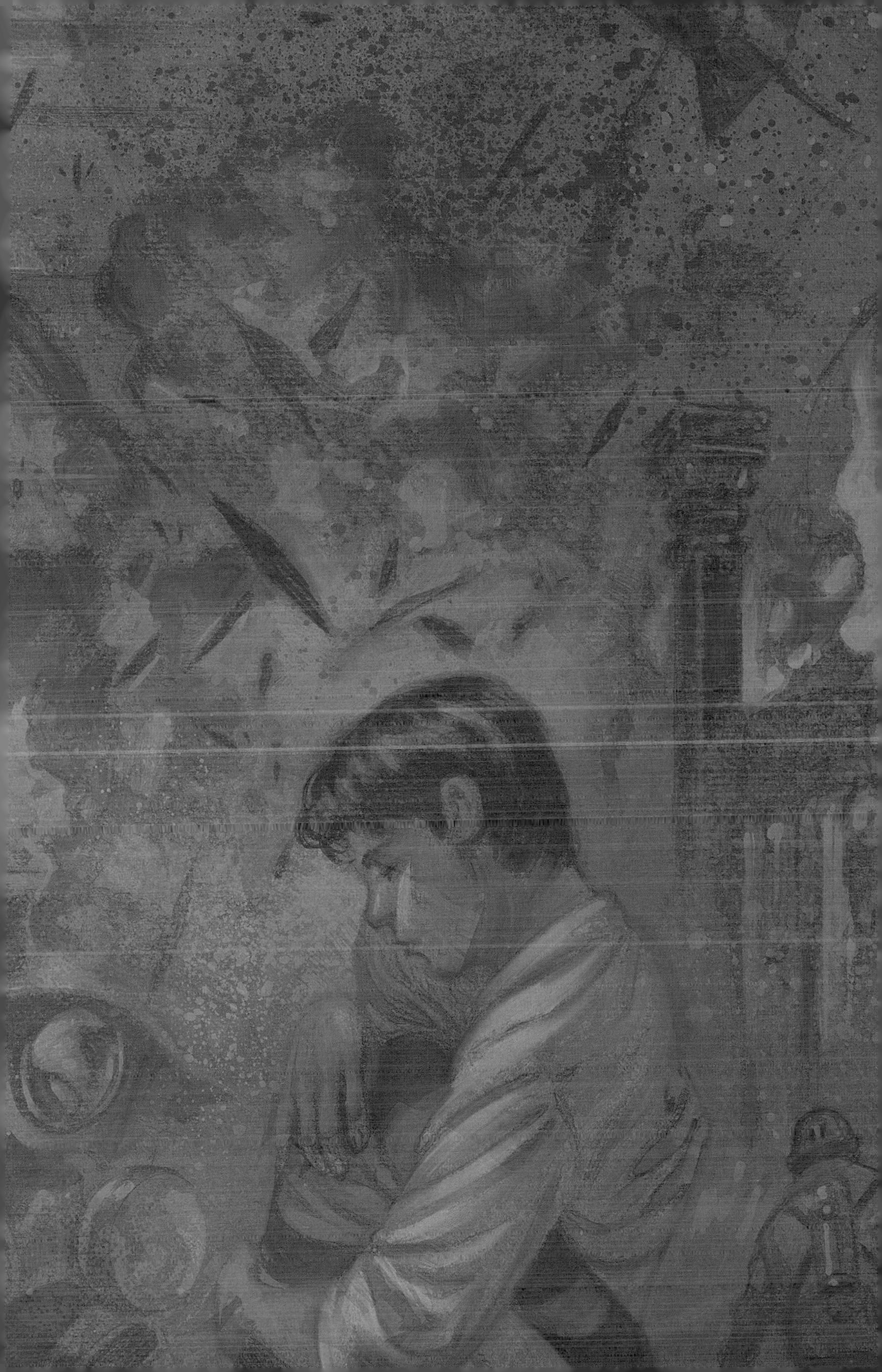

CHAPTER THREE

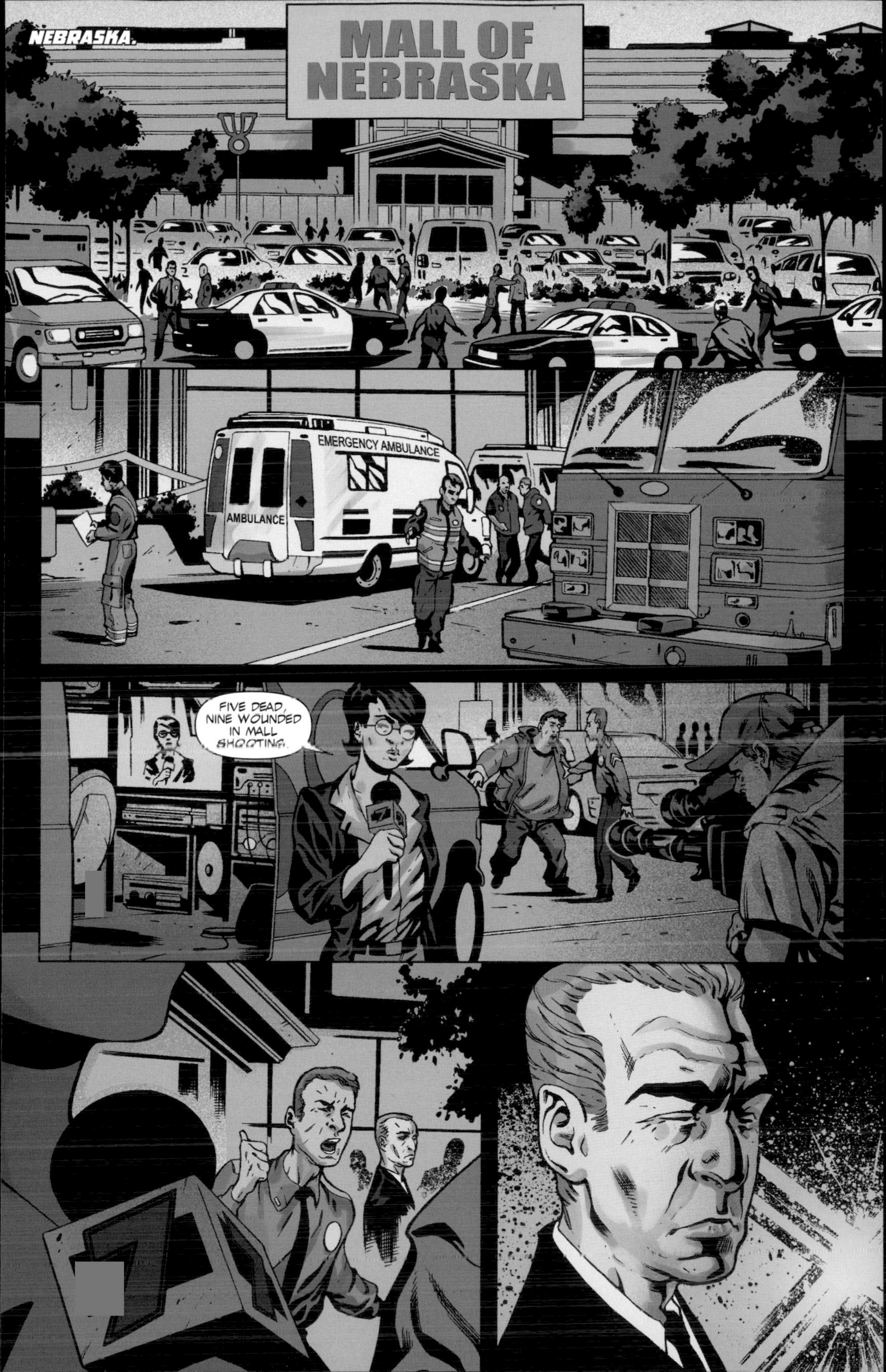
NEBRASKA.
MALL OF NEBRASKA
EMERGENCY AMBULANCE
AMBULANCE
FIVE DEAD, NINE WOUNDED IN MALL SHOOTING.

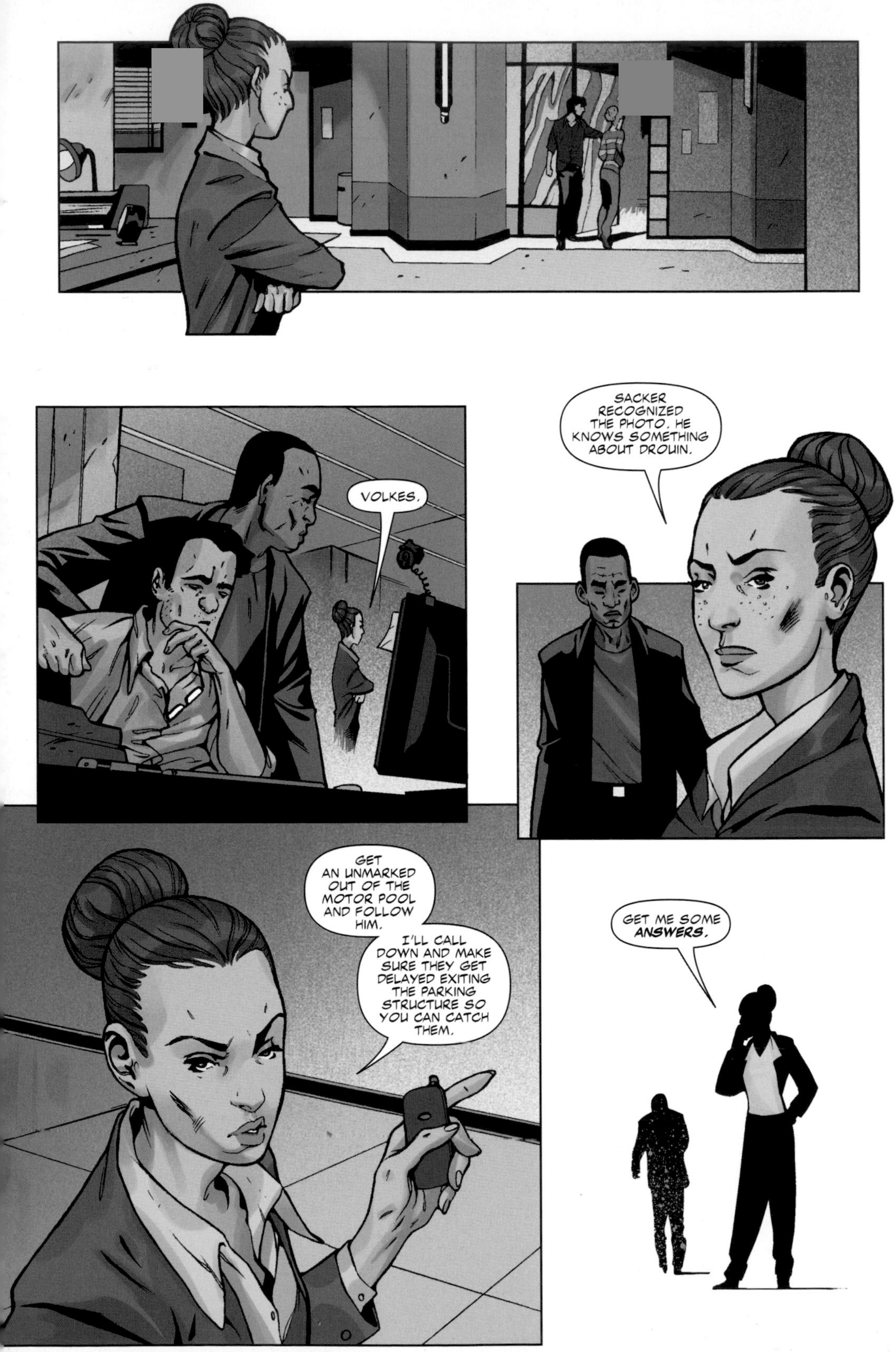
VOLKES.
SACKER RECOGNIZED THE PHOTO. HE KNOWS SOMETHING ABOUT DROUIN.
GET AN UNMARKED OUT OF THE MOTOR POOL AND FOLLOW HIM.
I'LL CALL DOWN AND MAKE SURE THEY GET DELAYED EXITING THE PARKING STRUCTURE SO YOU CAN CATCH THEM.
GET ME SOME **ANSWERS.**

THE REMNANT
"TILL DEATH"

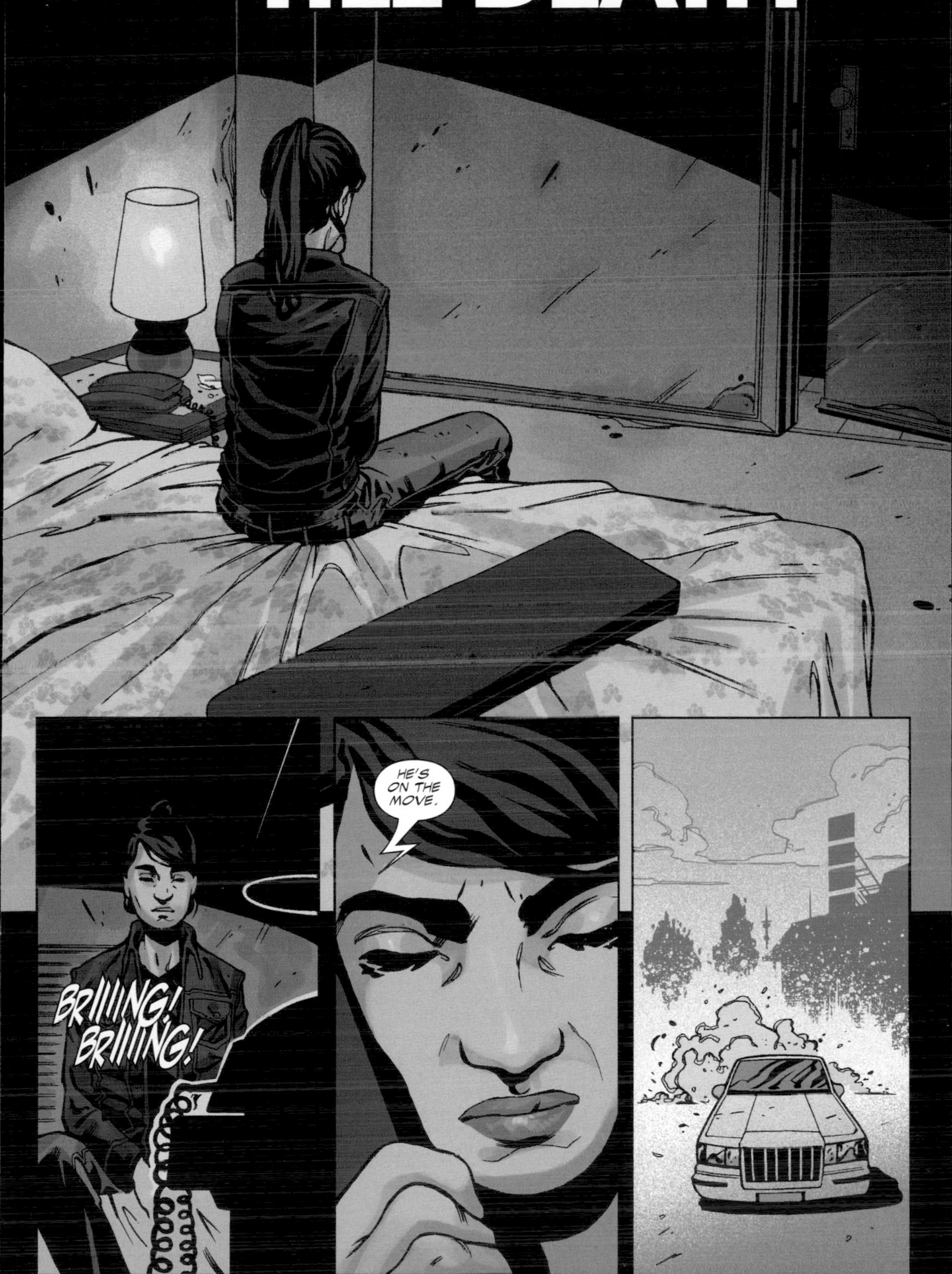
BRIIING! BRIIING!
HE'S ON THE MOVE.

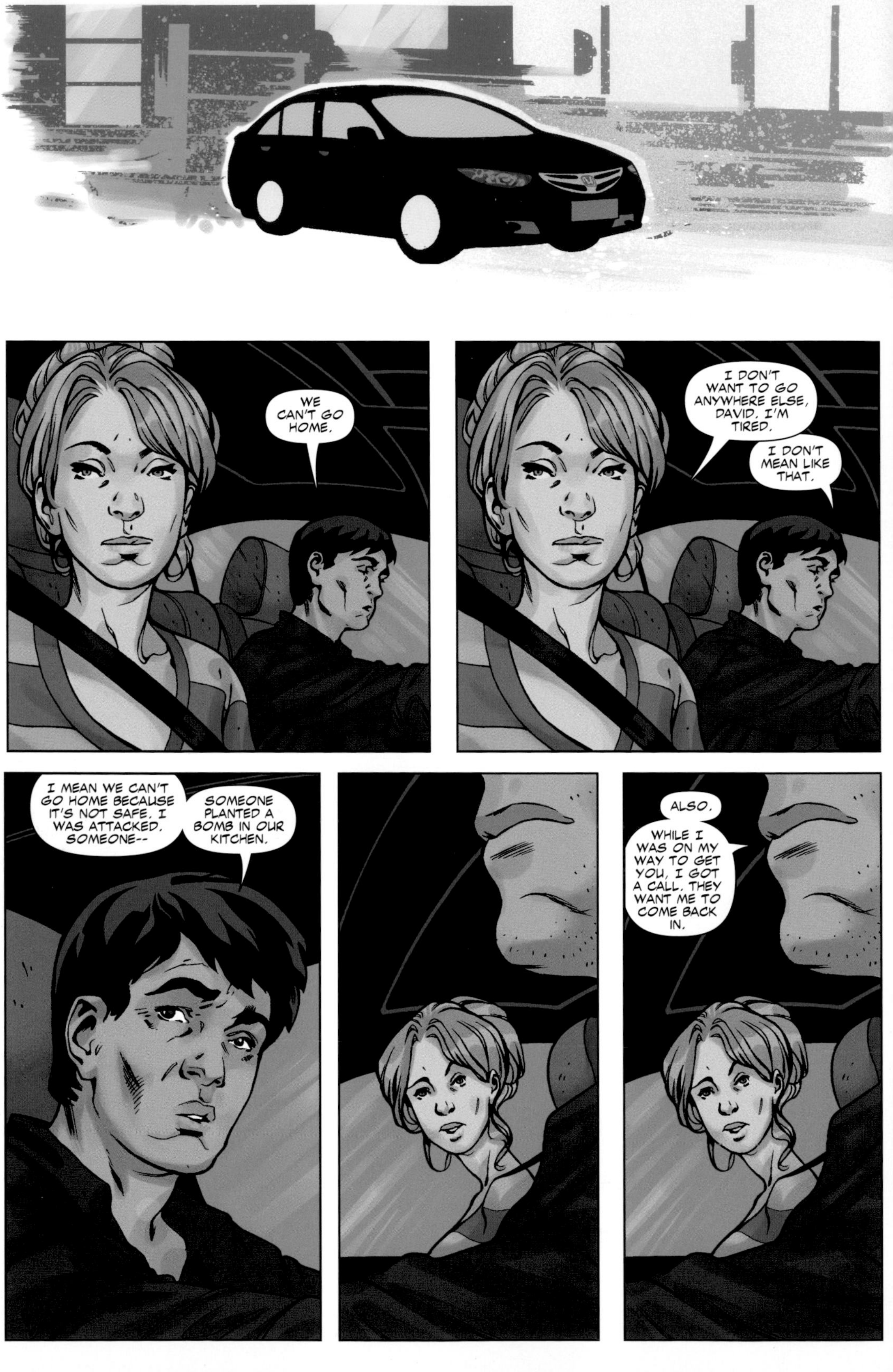
WE CAN'T GO HOME.
I DON'T WANT TO GO ANYWHERE ELSE, DAVID. I'M TIRED.
I DON'T MEAN LIKE THAT.
I MEAN WE CAN'T GO HOME BECAUSE IT'S NOT SAFE. I WAS ATTACKED. SOMEONE--
SOMEONE PLANTED A BOMB IN OUR KITCHEN.
ALSO.
WHILE I WAS ON MY WAY TO GET YOU, I GOT A CALL. THEY WANT ME TO COME BACK IN.

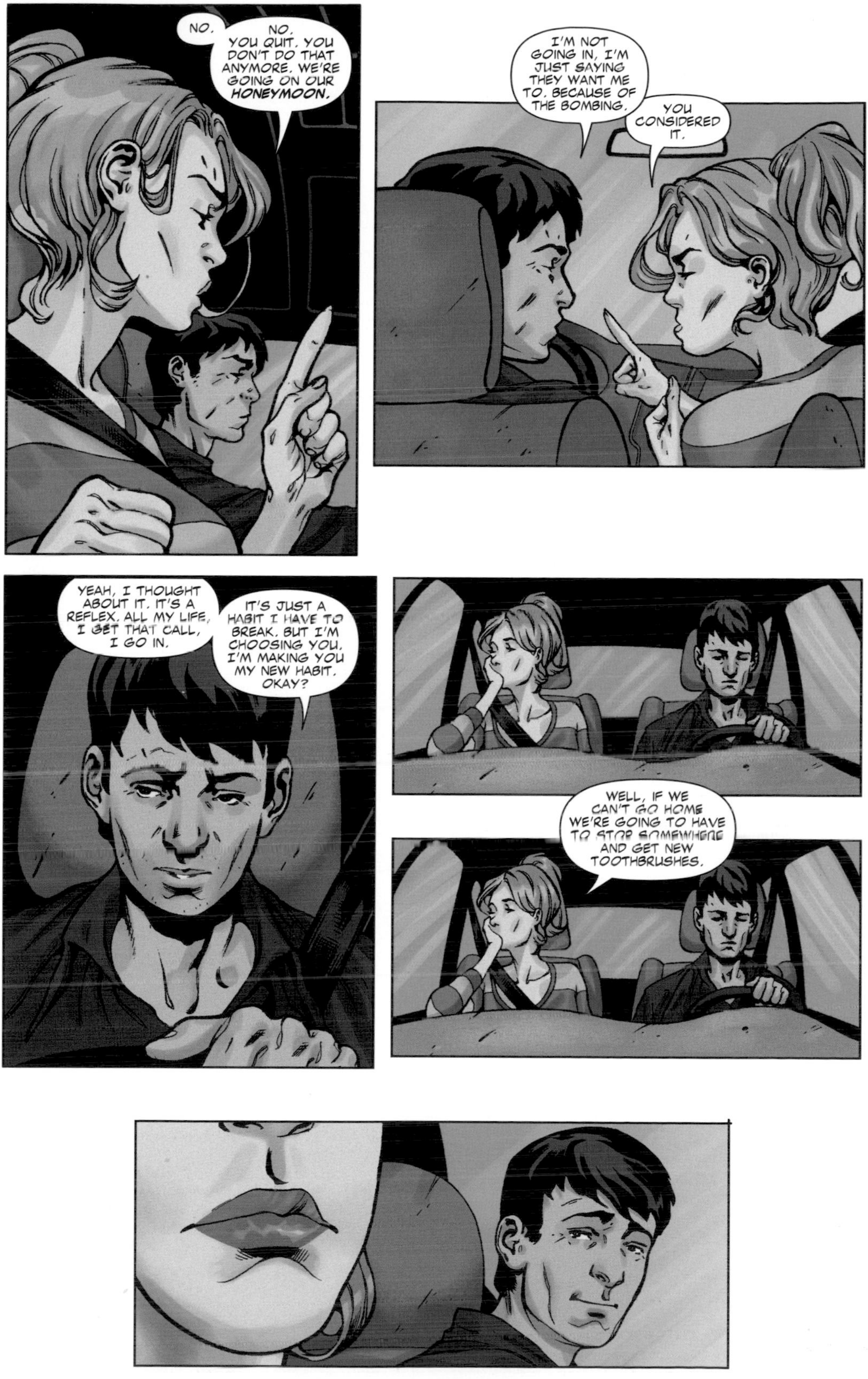
NO.
NO. YOU QUIT. YOU DON'T DO THAT ANYMORE. WE'RE GOING ON OUR HONEYMOON.
I'M NOT GOING IN, I'M JUST SAYING THEY WANT ME TO, BECAUSE OF THE BOMBING.
YOU CONSIDERED IT.
YEAH, I THOUGHT ABOUT IT. IT'S A REFLEX. ALL MY LIFE, I GET THAT CALL, I GO IN.
IT'S JUST A HABIT I HAVE TO BREAK. BUT I'M CHOOSING YOU. I'M MAKING YOU MY NEW HABIT. OKAY?
WELL, IF WE CAN'T GO HOME WE'RE GOING TO HAVE TO STOP SOMEWHERE AND GET NEW TOOTHBRUSHES.

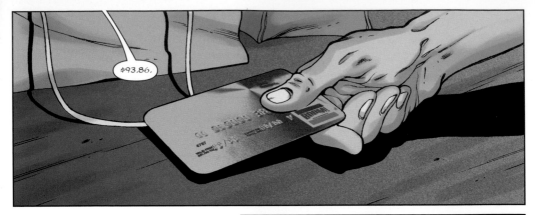

$93.86.

YOU KNOW WHAT? I FORGOT DEODORANT. TAKE THOSE TO THE CAR AND I'LL MEET YOU IN JUST A SEC.

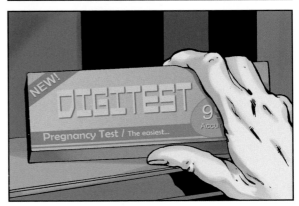

NEW!
DIGITEST
Pregnancy Test / The easiest...

ANDY?

OH, HEY. SORRY I MISSED YOUR CALL EARLIER. I WAS--

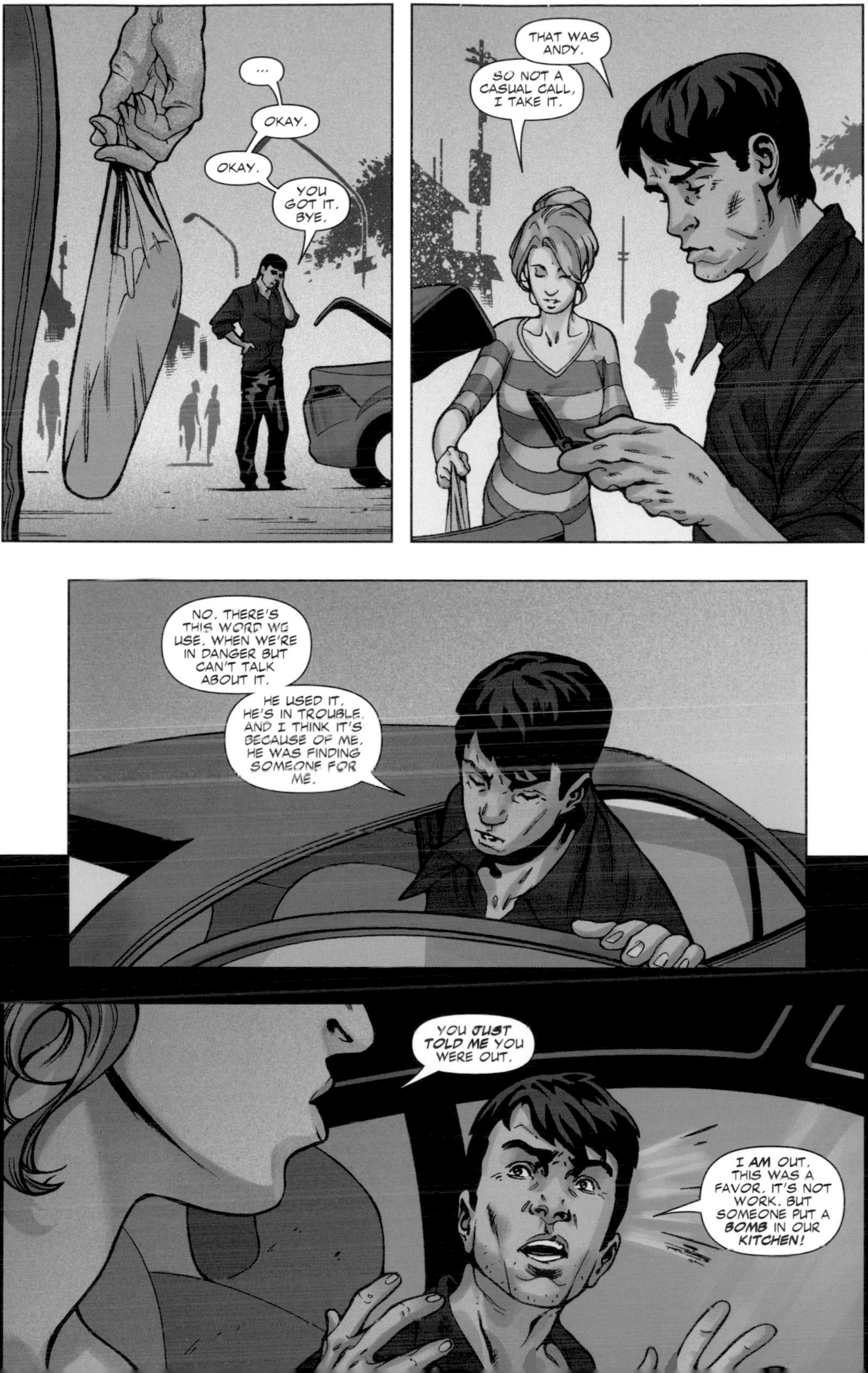
...
OKAY.
OKAY.
YOU GOT IT. BYE.
THAT WAS ANDY.
SO NOT A CASUAL CALL, I TAKE IT.
NO. THERE'S THIS WORD WE USE. WHEN WE'RE IN DANGER BUT CAN'T TALK ABOUT IT.
HE USED IT. HE'S IN TROUBLE. AND I THINK IT'S BECAUSE OF ME. HE WAS FINDING SOMEONE FOR ME.
YOU JUST TOLD ME YOU WERE OUT.
I AM OUT. THIS WAS A FAVOR. IT'S NOT WORK. BUT SOMEONE PUT A BOMB IN OUR KITCHEN!

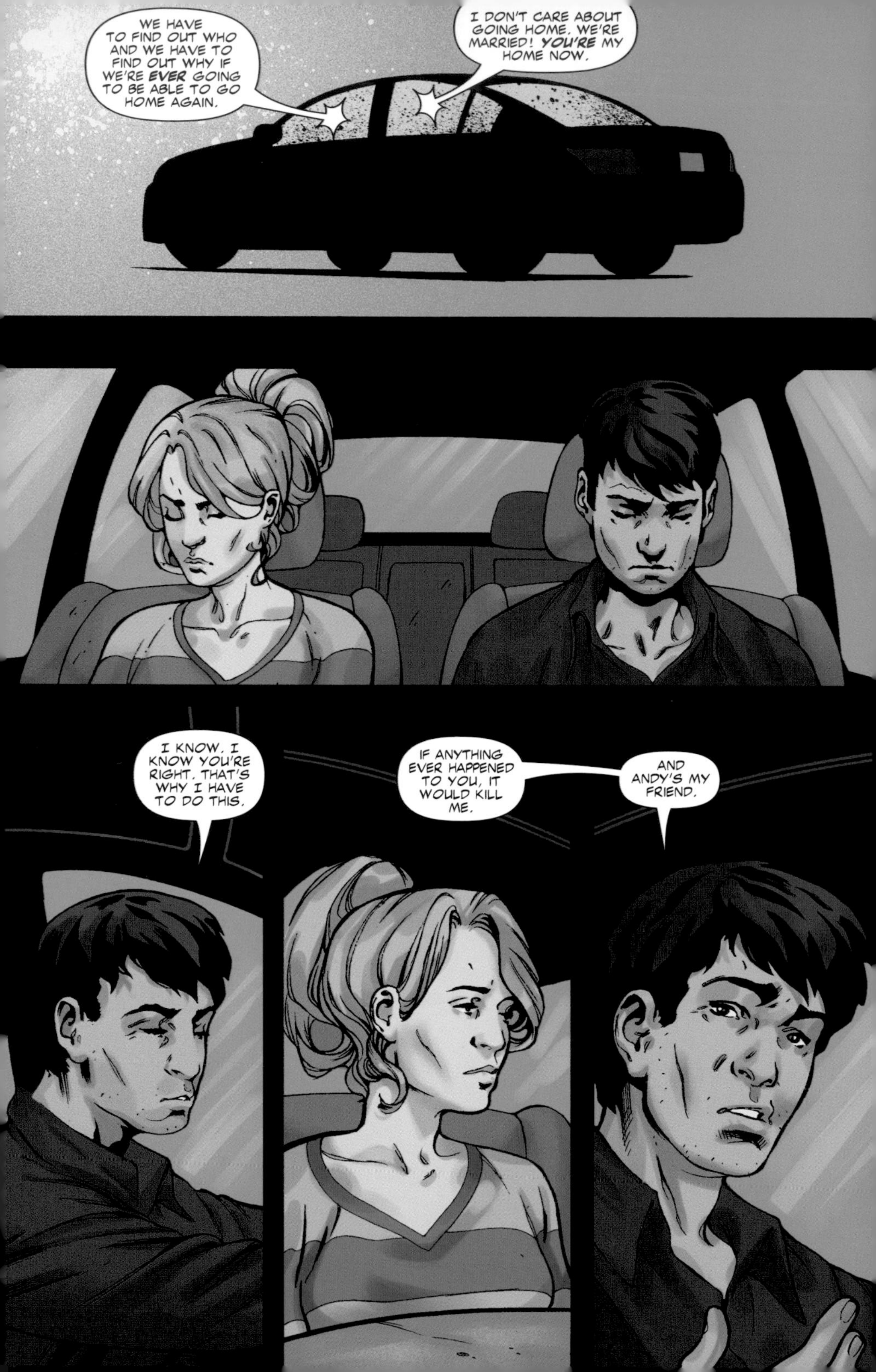
WE HAVE TO FIND OUT WHO AND WE HAVE TO FIND OUT WHY IF WE'RE **EVER** GOING TO BE ABLE TO GO HOME AGAIN.
I DON'T CARE ABOUT GOING HOME. WE'RE MARRIED! **YOU'RE** MY HOME NOW.
I KNOW. I KNOW YOU'RE RIGHT. THAT'S WHY I HAVE TO DO THIS.
IF ANYTHING EVER HAPPENED TO YOU, IT WOULD KILL ME.
AND ANDY'S MY FRIEND.

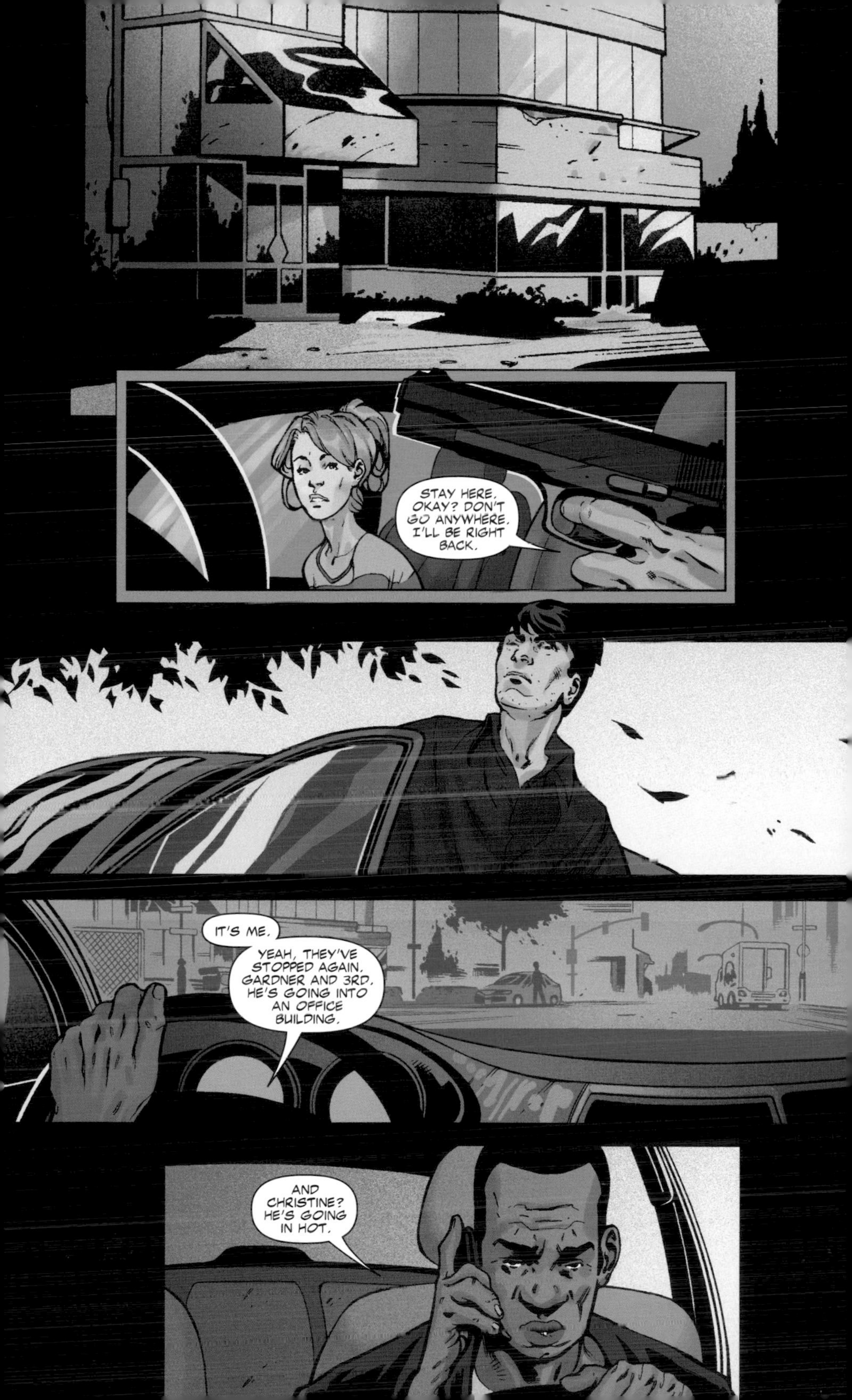
STAY HERE. OKAY? DON'T GO ANYWHERE. I'LL BE RIGHT BACK.
IT'S ME.
YEAH, THEY'VE STOPPED AGAIN. GARDNER AND 3RD. HE'S GOING INTO AN OFFICE BUILDING.
AND CHRISTINE? HE'S GOING IN HOT.

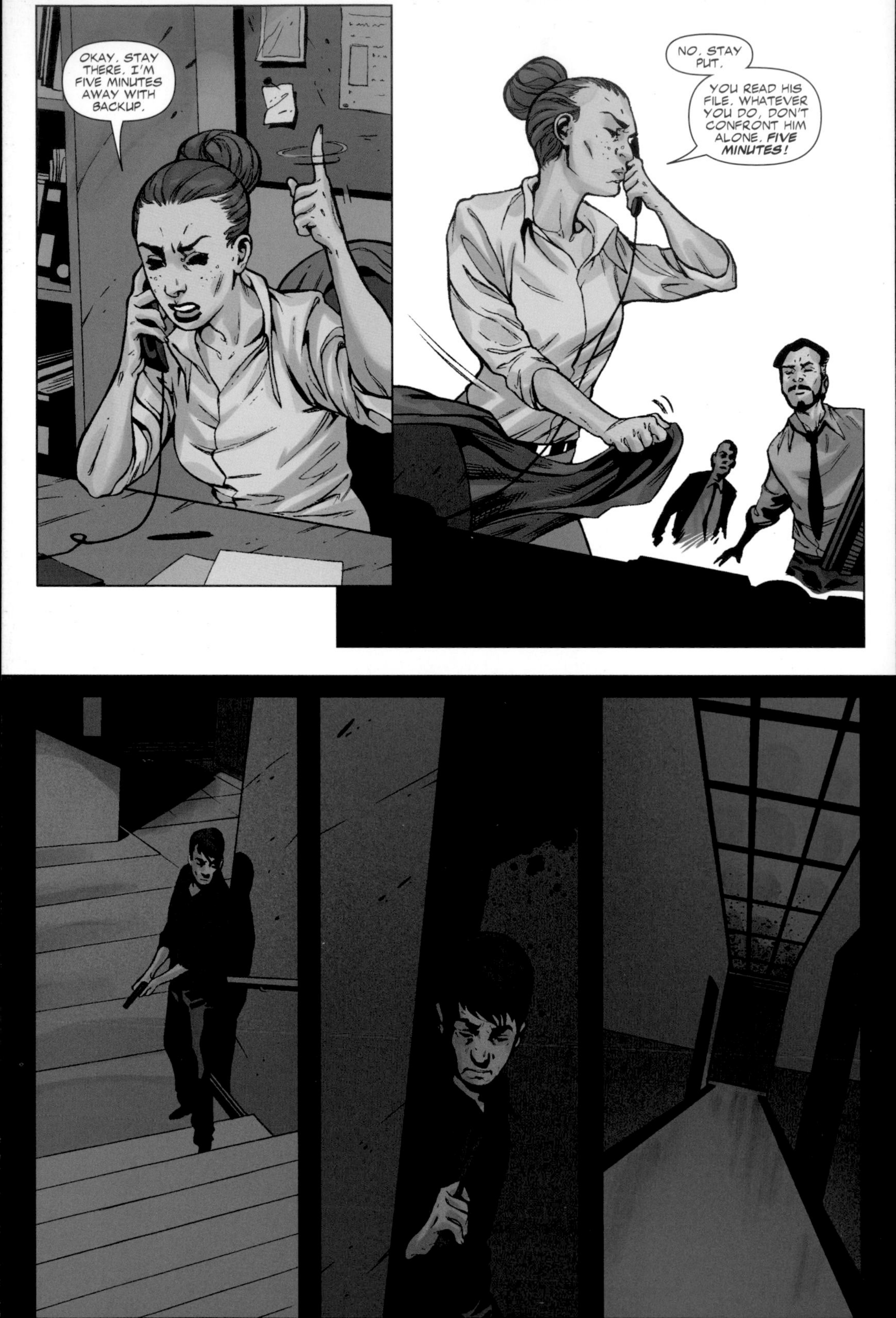
OKAY, STAY THERE. I'M FIVE MINUTES AWAY WITH BACKUP.
NO, STAY PUT.
YOU READ HIS FILE. WHATEVER YOU DO, DON'T CONFRONT HIM ALONE. FIVE MINUTES!

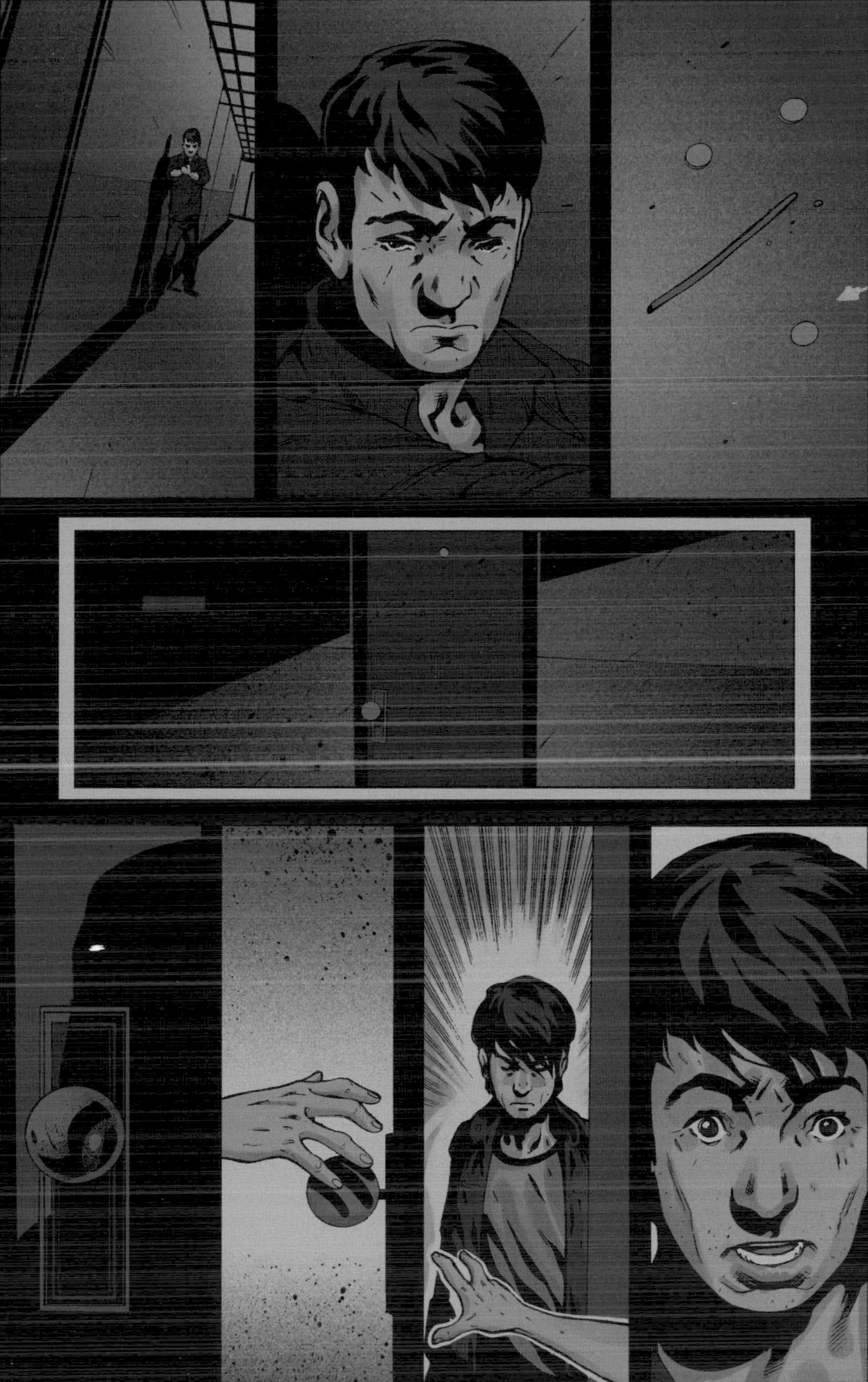

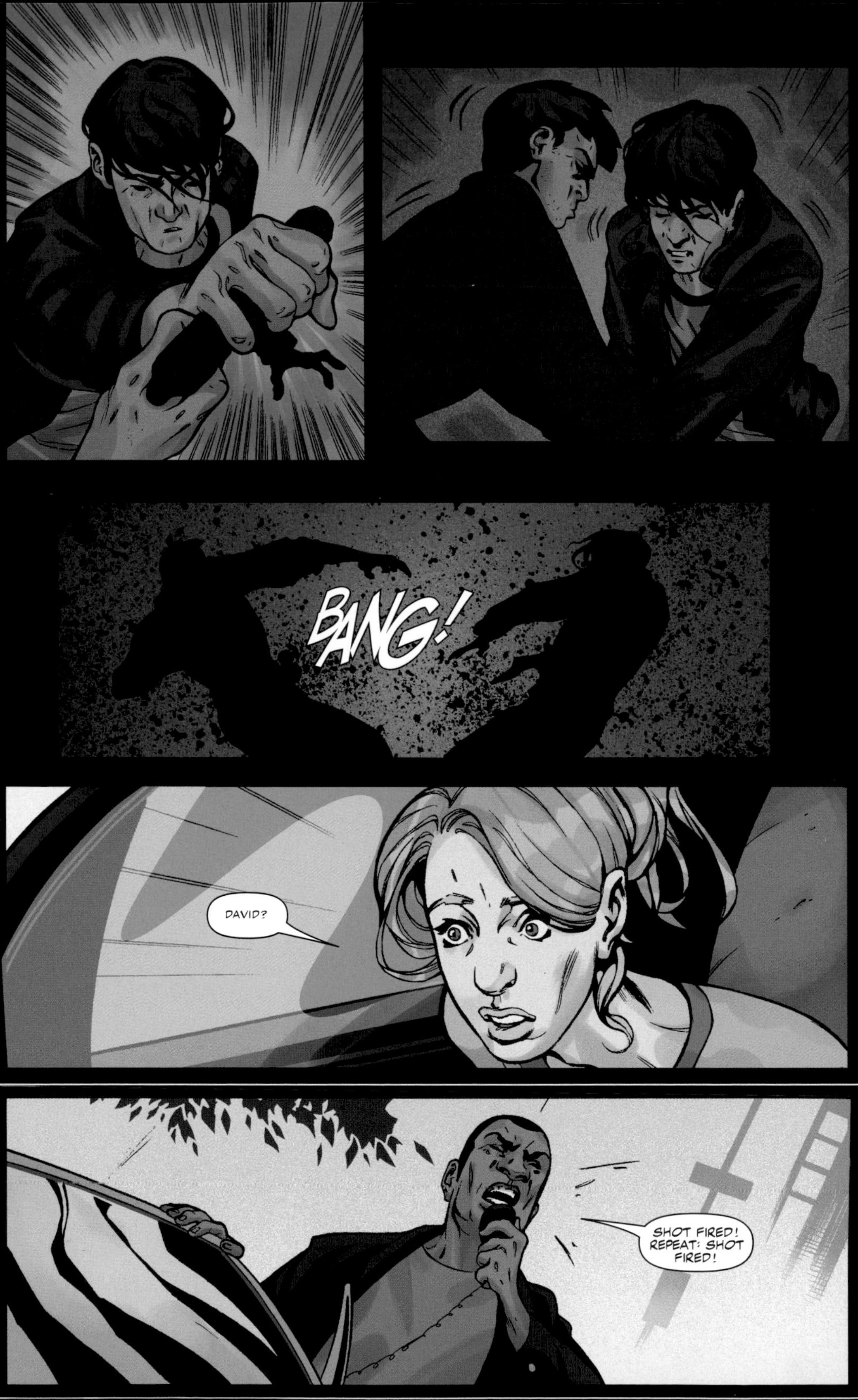
BANG!
DAVID?
SHOT FIRED! REPEAT: SHOT FIRED!

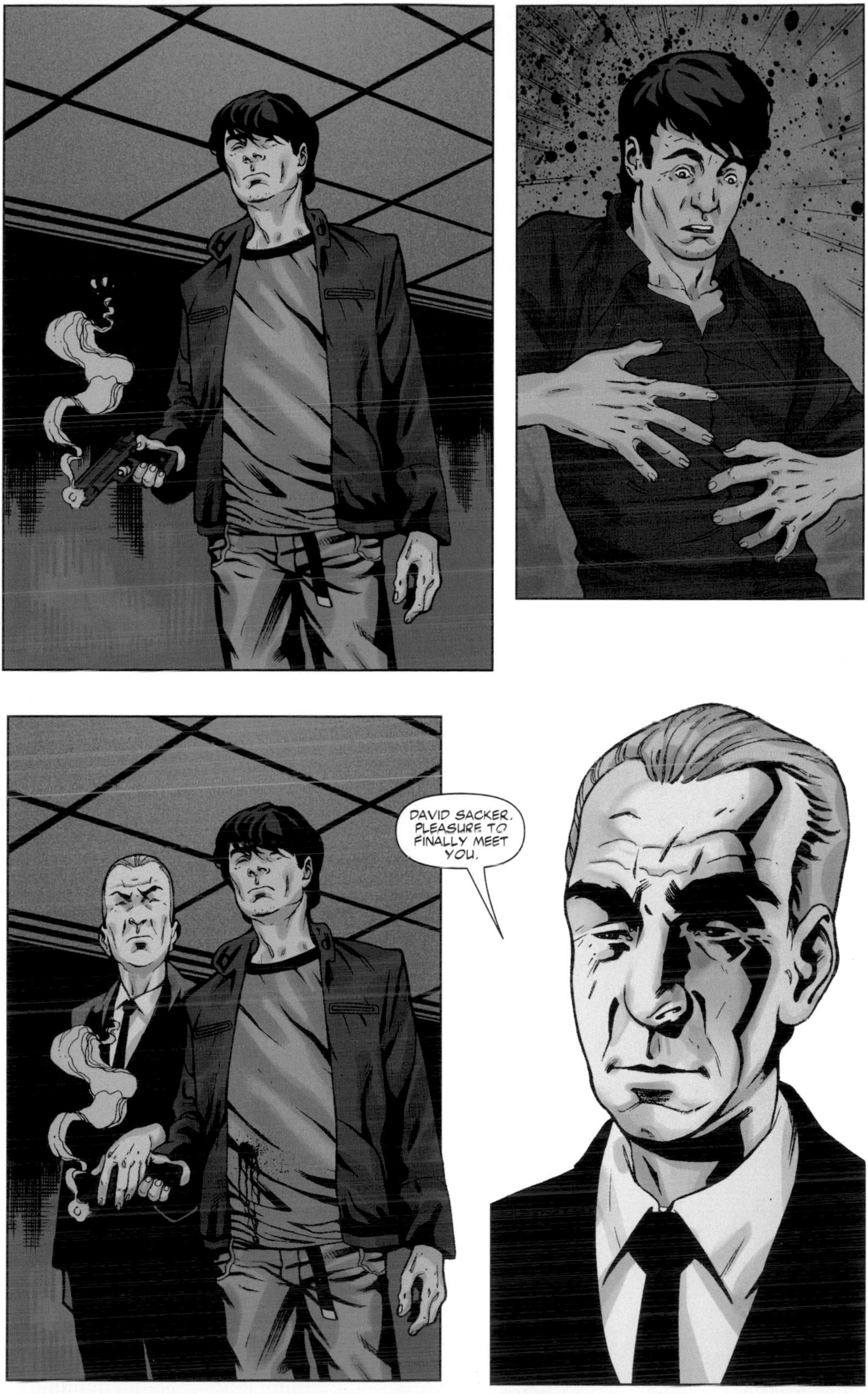
DAVID SACKER. PLEASURE TO FINALLY MEET YOU.

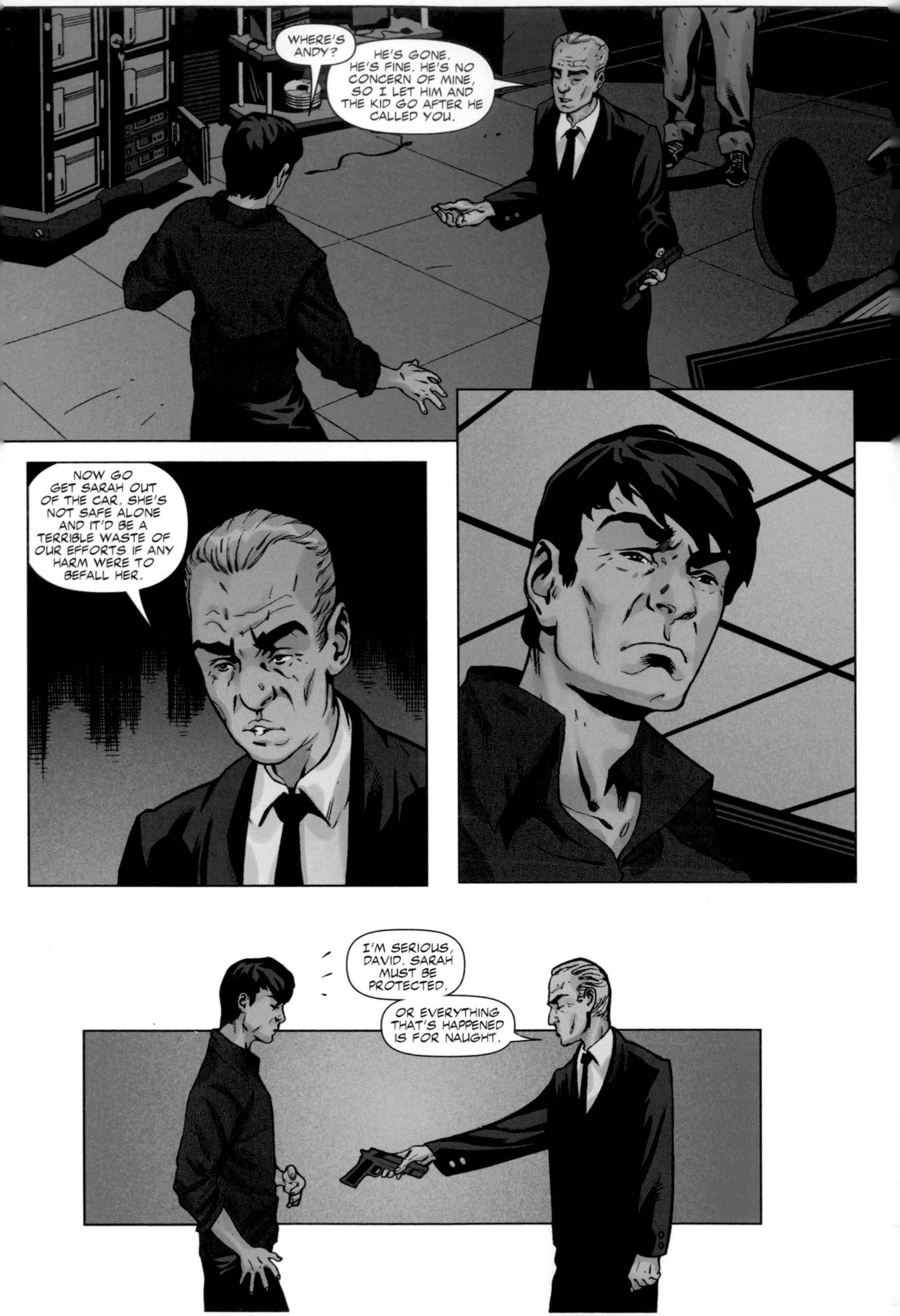
WHERE'S ANDY?
HE'S GONE. HE'S FINE. HE'S NO CONCERN OF MINE, SO I LET HIM AND THE KID GO AFTER HE CALLED YOU.
NOW GO GET SARAH OUT OF THE CAR. SHE'S NOT SAFE ALONE AND IT'D BE A TERRIBLE WASTE OF OUR EFFORTS IF ANY HARM WERE TO BEFALL HER.
I'M SERIOUS, DAVID. SARAH MUST BE PROTECTED.
OR EVERYTHING THAT'S HAPPENED IS FOR NAUGHT.

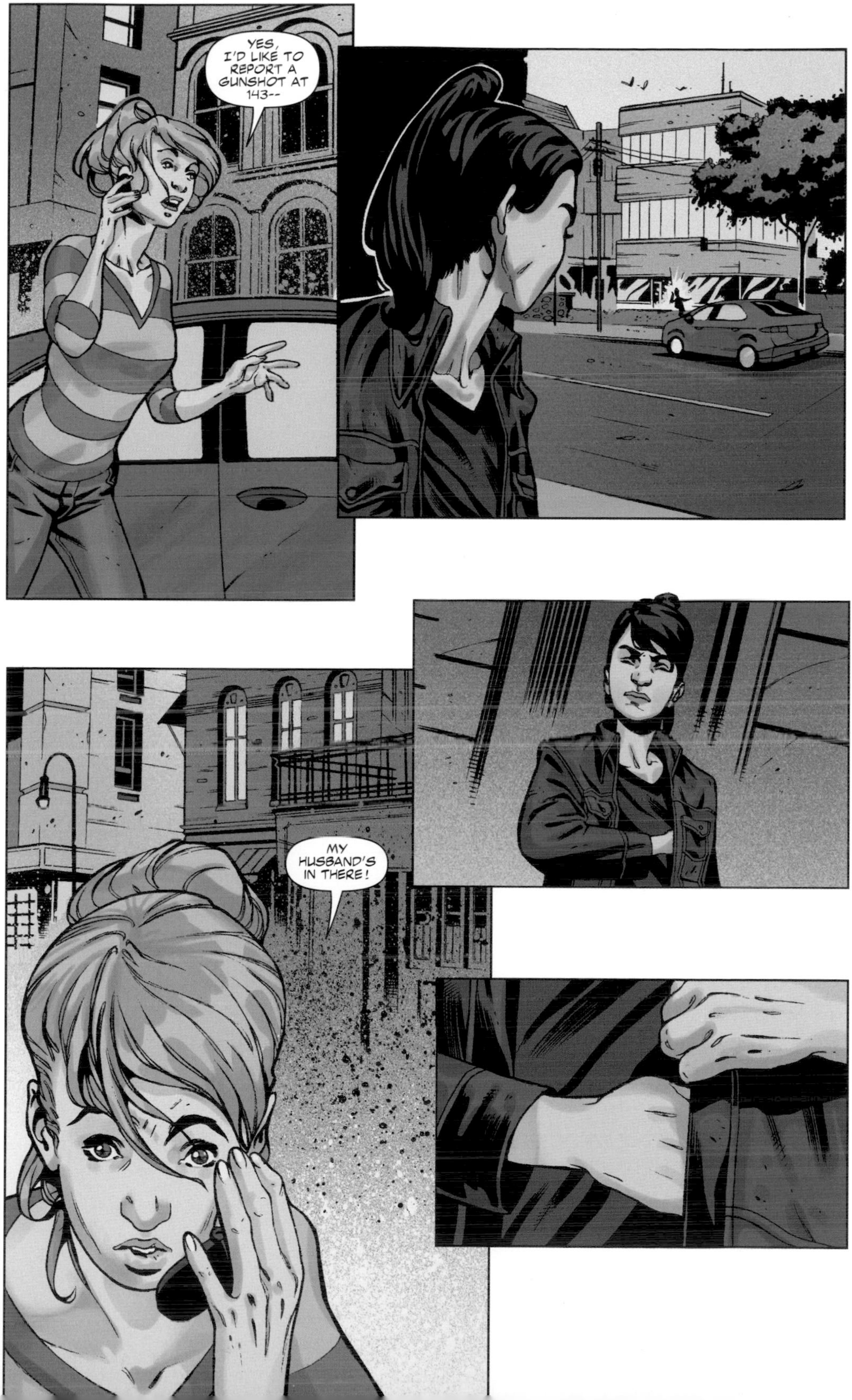
YES, I'D LIKE TO REPORT A GUNSHOT AT 143--
MY HUSBAND'S IN THERE!

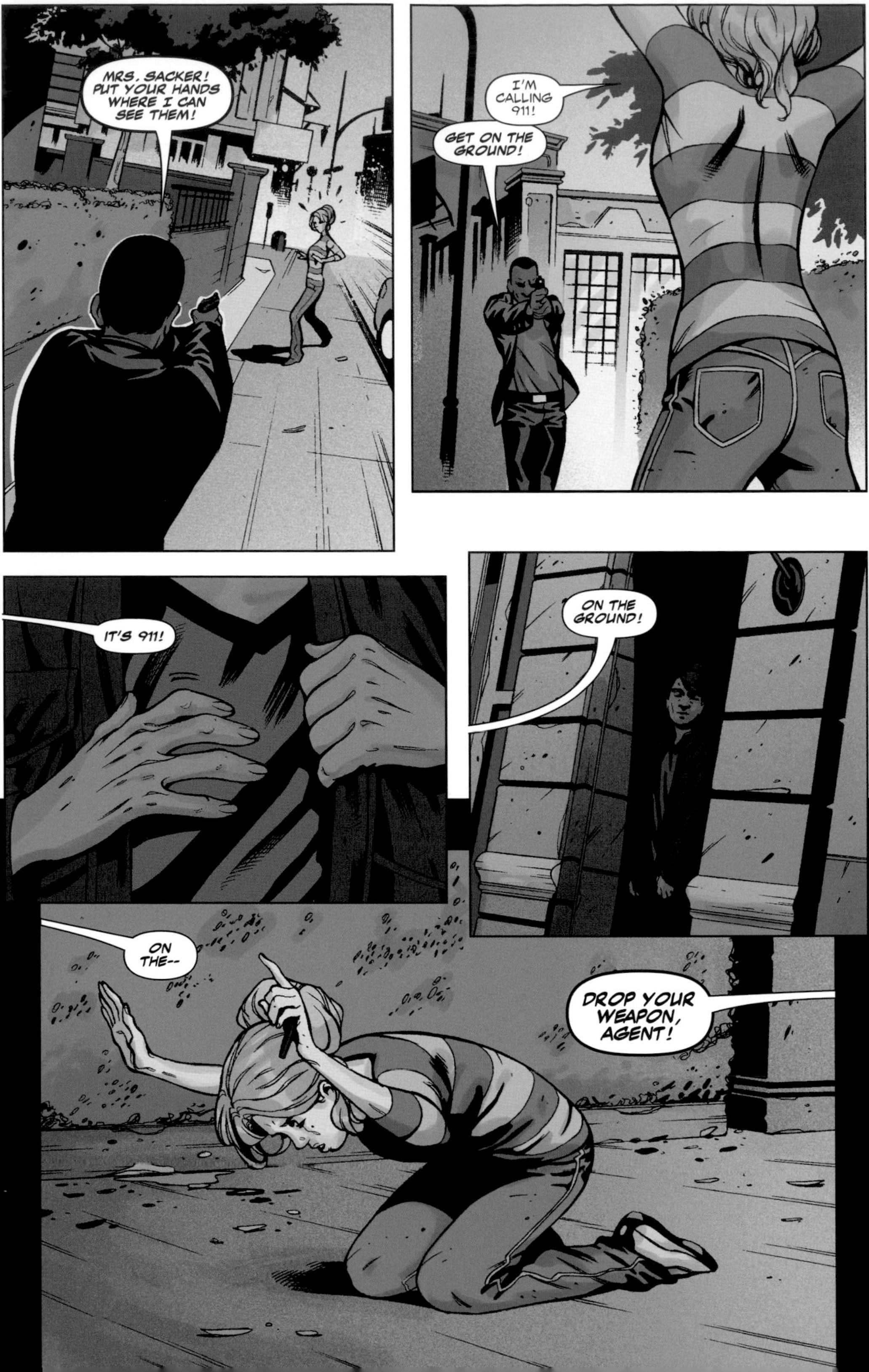
MRS. SACKER! PUT YOUR HANDS WHERE I CAN SEE THEM!
I'M CALLING 911!
GET ON THE GROUND!
IT'S 911!
ON THE GROUND!
ON THE--
DROP YOUR WEAPON, AGENT!

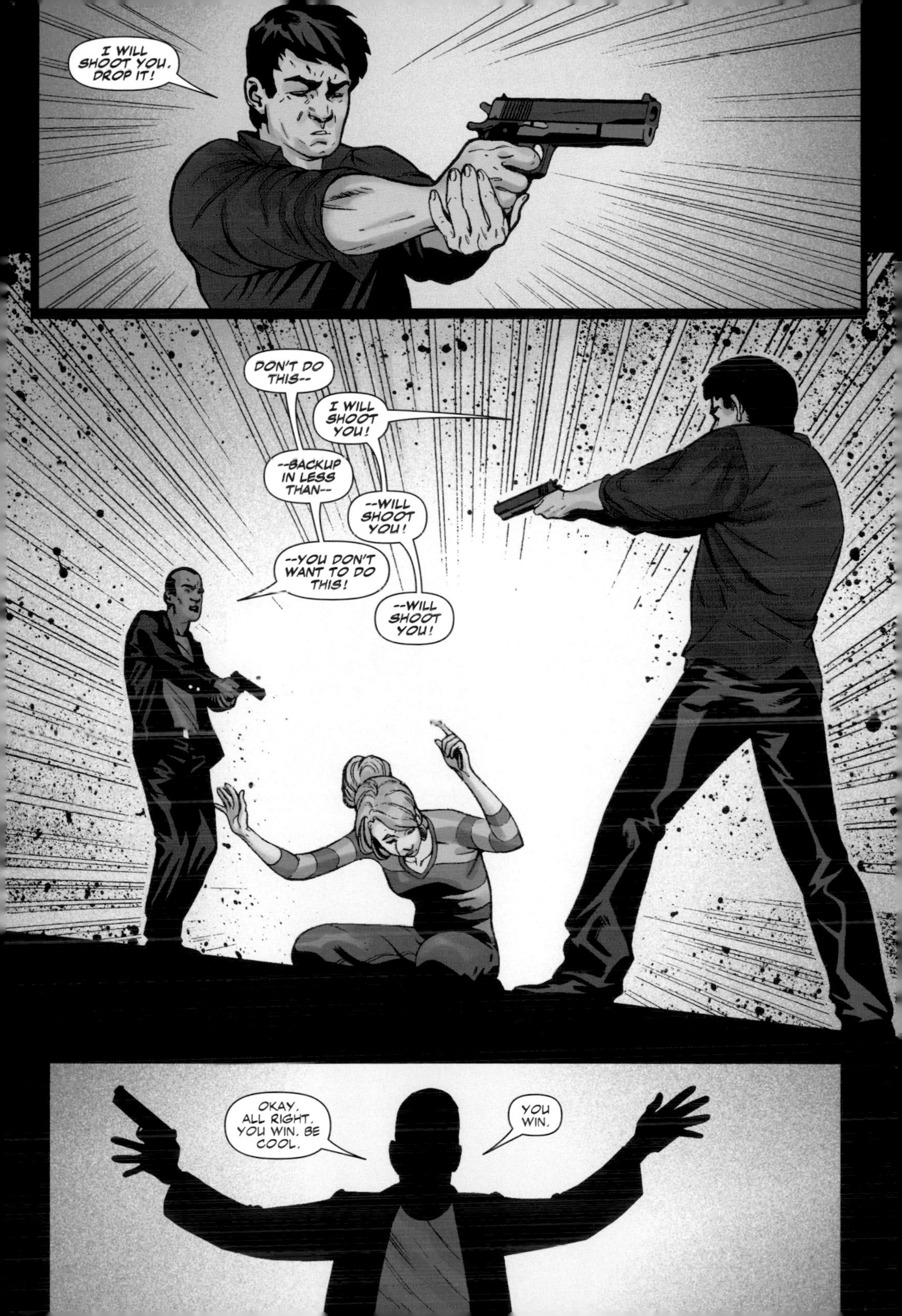
I WILL SHOOT YOU. DROP IT!
DON'T DO THIS--
I WILL SHOOT YOU!
--BACKUP IN LESS THAN--
--WILL SHOOT YOU!
--YOU DON'T WANT TO DO THIS!
--WILL SHOOT YOU!
OKAY. ALL RIGHT. YOU WIN. BE COOL.
YOU WIN.

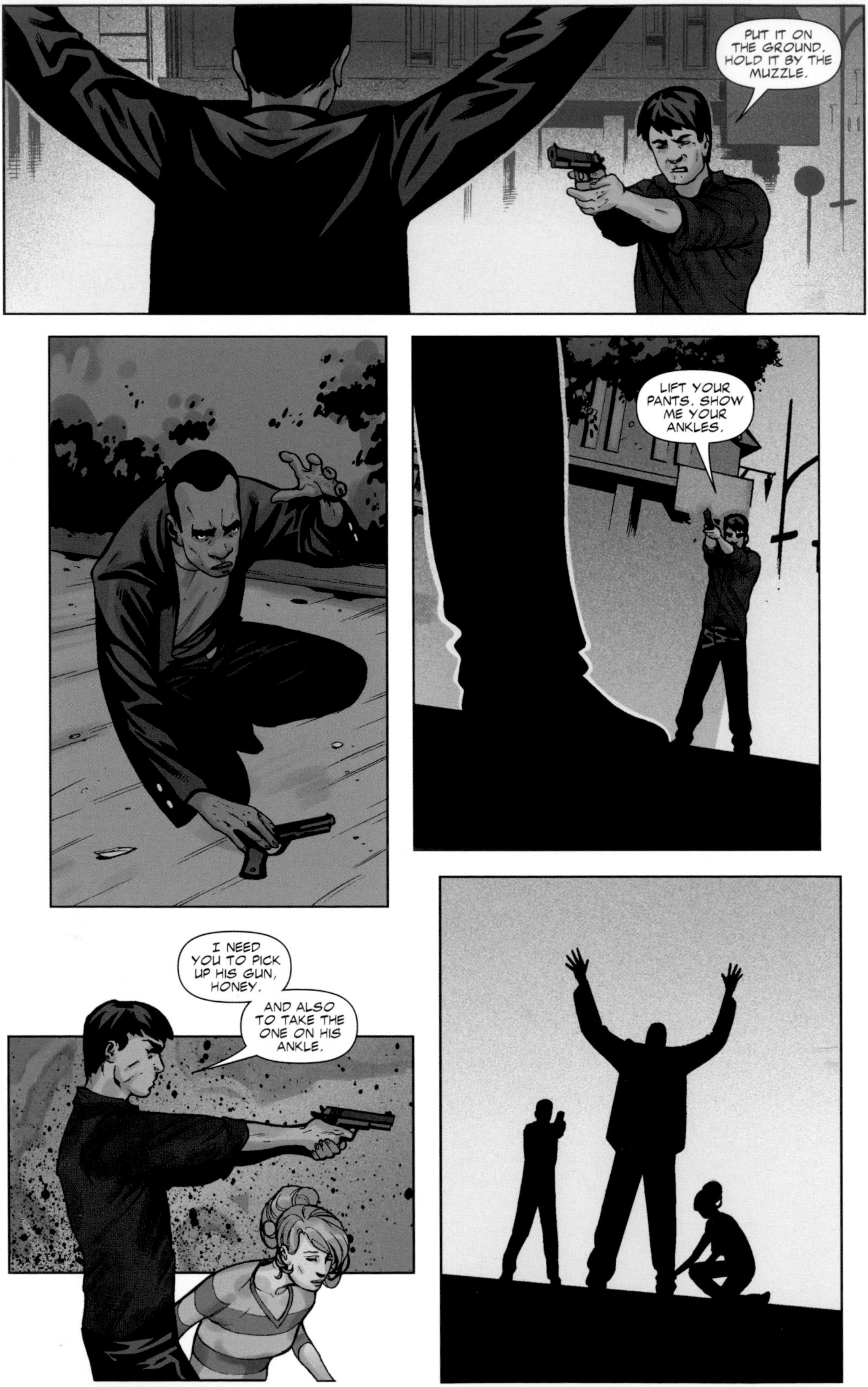
PUT IT ON THE GROUND. HOLD IT BY THE MUZZLE.
LIFT YOUR PANTS. SHOW ME YOUR ANKLES.
I NEED YOU TO PICK UP HIS GUN, HONEY.
AND ALSO TO TAKE THE ONE ON HIS ANKLE.

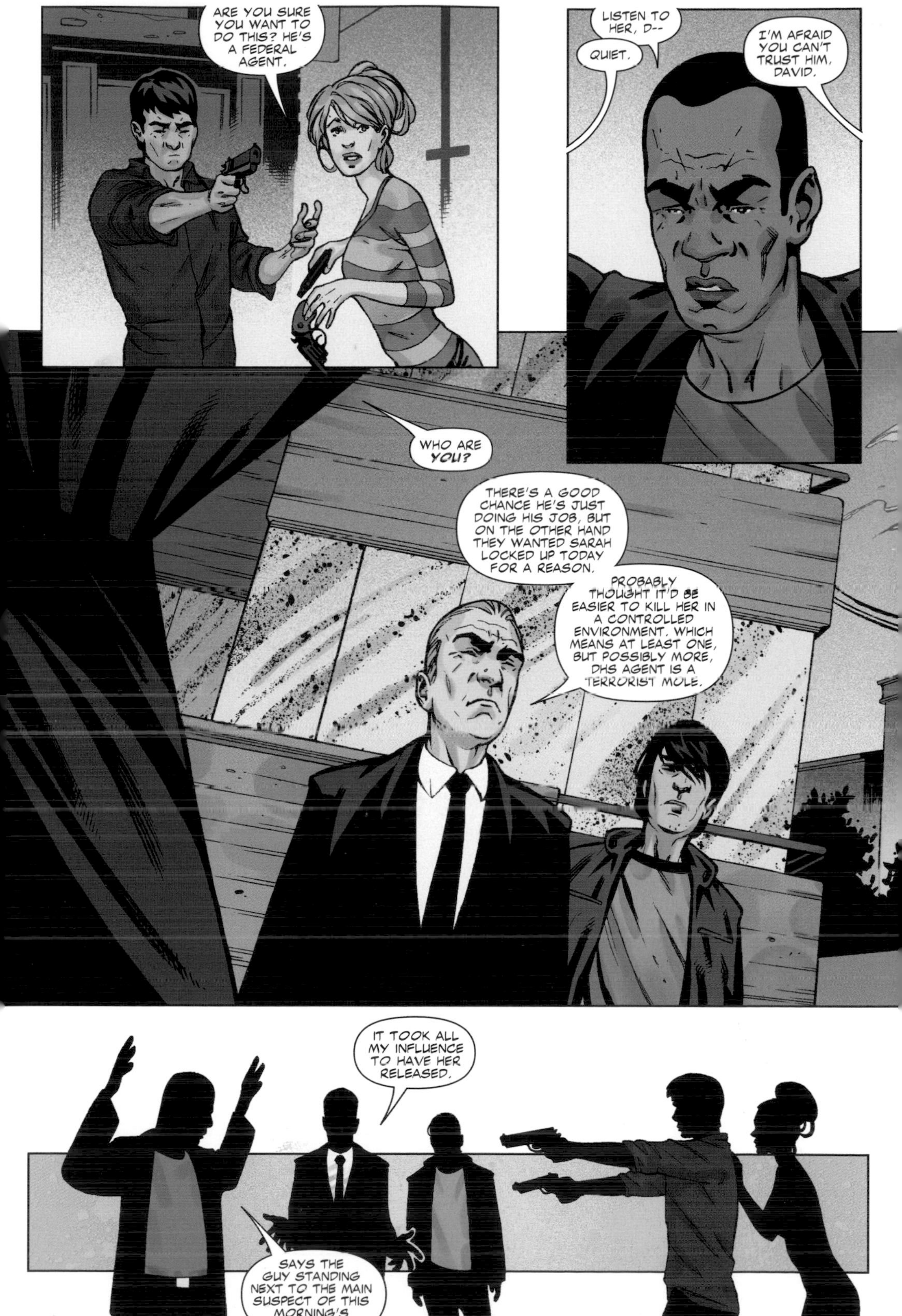
ARE YOU SURE YOU WANT TO DO THIS? HE'S A FEDERAL AGENT.
LISTEN TO HER, D--
QUIET.
I'M AFRAID YOU CAN'T TRUST HIM, DAVID.
WHO ARE YOU?
THERE'S A GOOD CHANCE HE'S JUST DOING HIS JOB, BUT ON THE OTHER HAND THEY WANTED SARAH LOCKED UP TODAY FOR A REASON.
PROBABLY THOUGHT IT'D BE EASIER TO KILL HER IN A CONTROLLED ENVIRONMENT. WHICH MEANS AT LEAST ONE, BUT POSSIBLY MORE, DHS AGENT IS A TERRORIST MOLE.
IT TOOK ALL MY INFLUENCE TO HAVE HER RELEASED.
SAYS THE GUY STANDING NEXT TO THE MAIN SUSPECT OF THIS MORNING'S ATTACK.

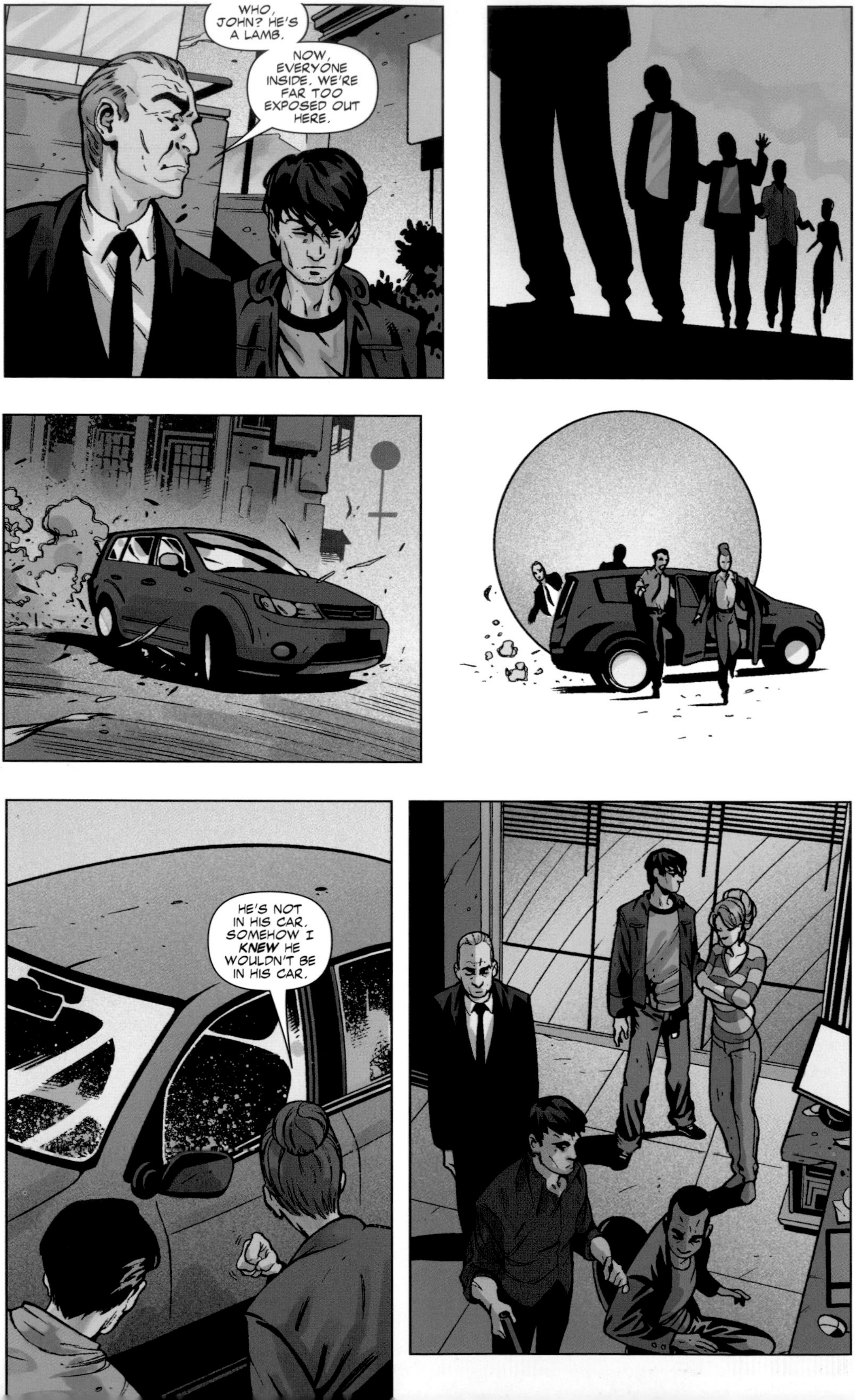
WHO, JOHN? HE'S A LAMB.
NOW, EVERYONE INSIDE. WE'RE FAR TOO EXPOSED OUT HERE.
HE'S NOT IN HIS CAR. SOMEHOW I KNEW HE WOULDN'T BE IN HIS CAR.

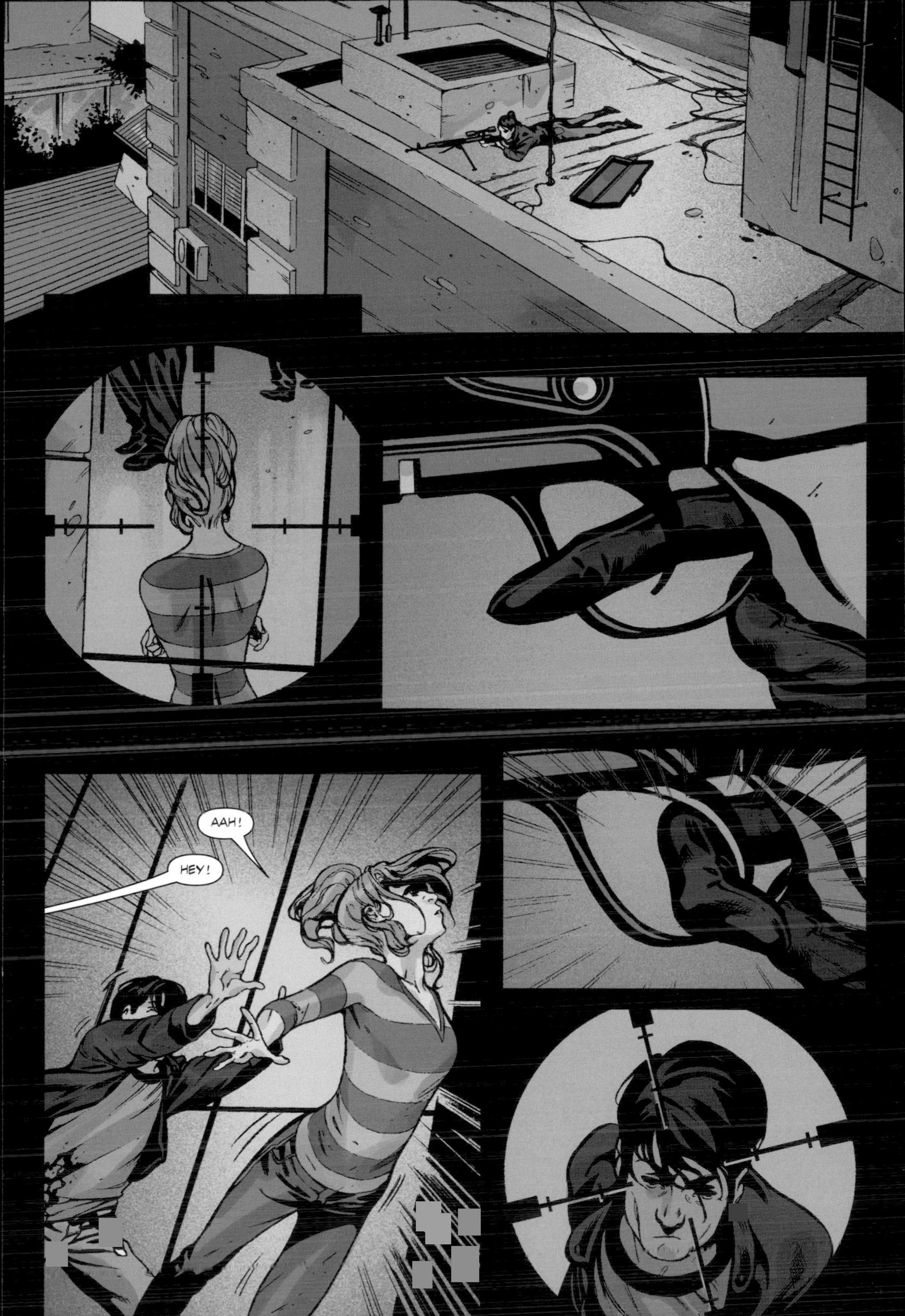
AAH!
HEY!

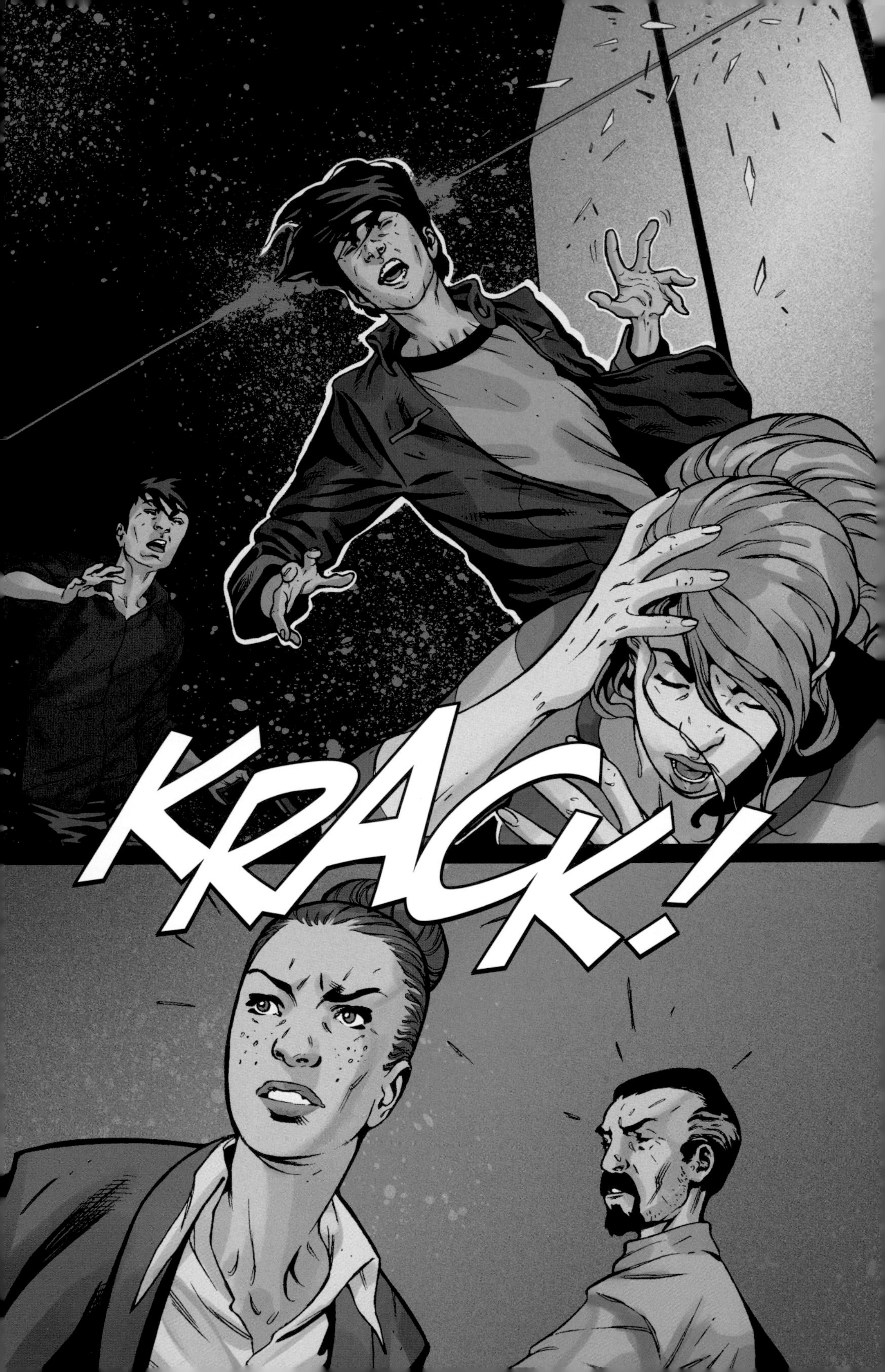
KRACK!

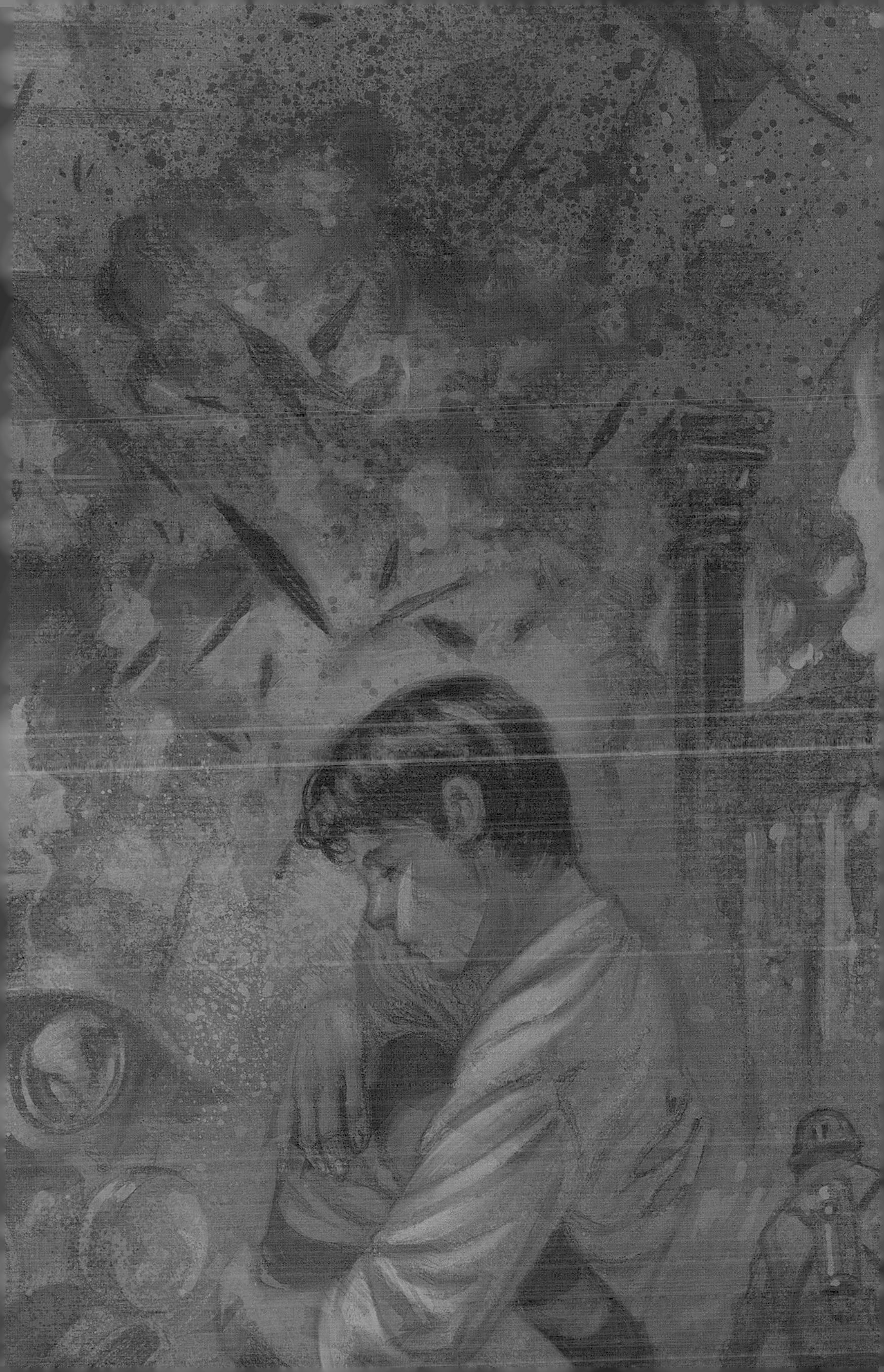

CHAPTER FOUR

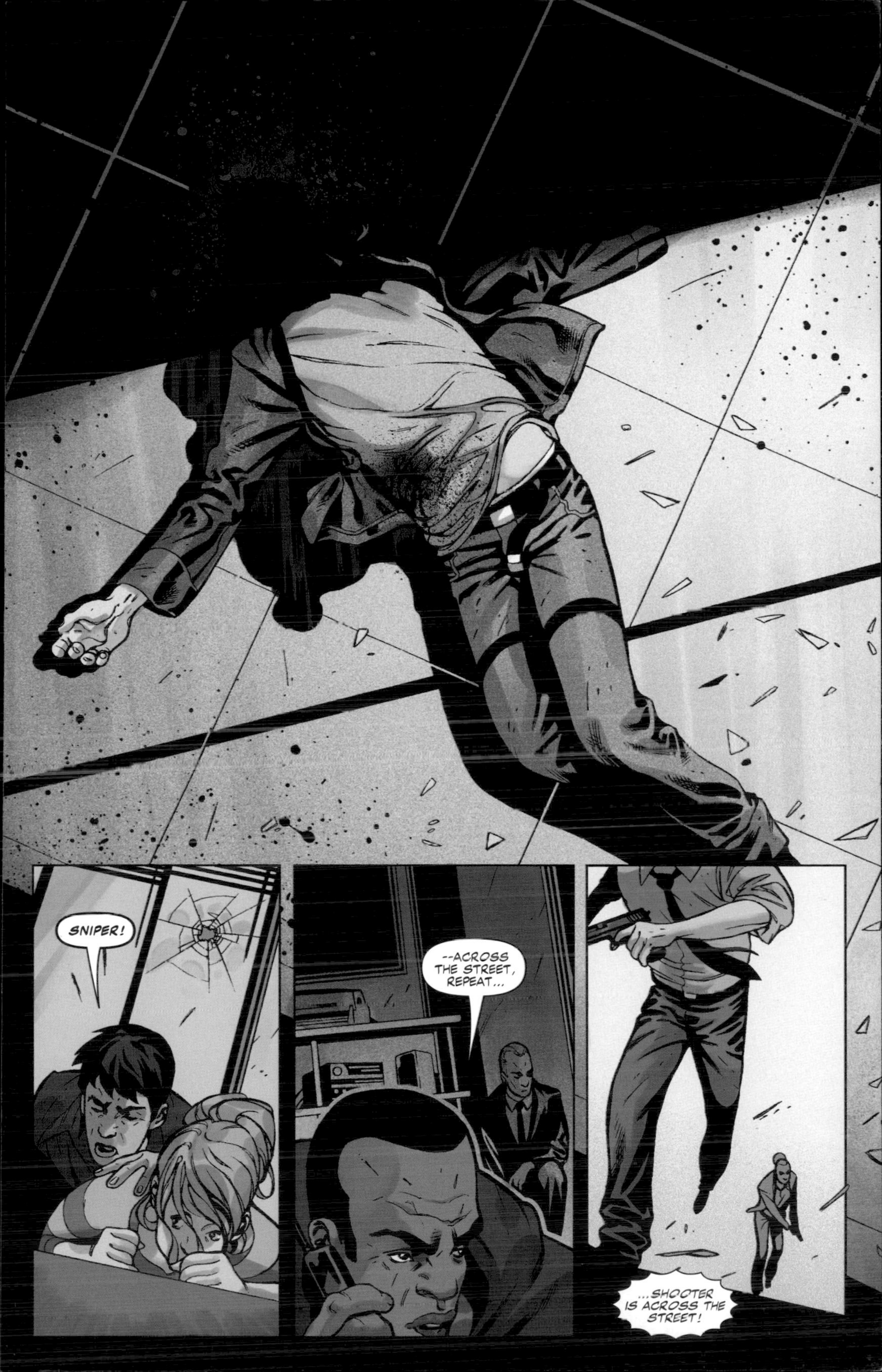
SNIPER!
--ACROSS THE STREET, REPEAT...
...SHOOTER IS ACROSS THE STREET!

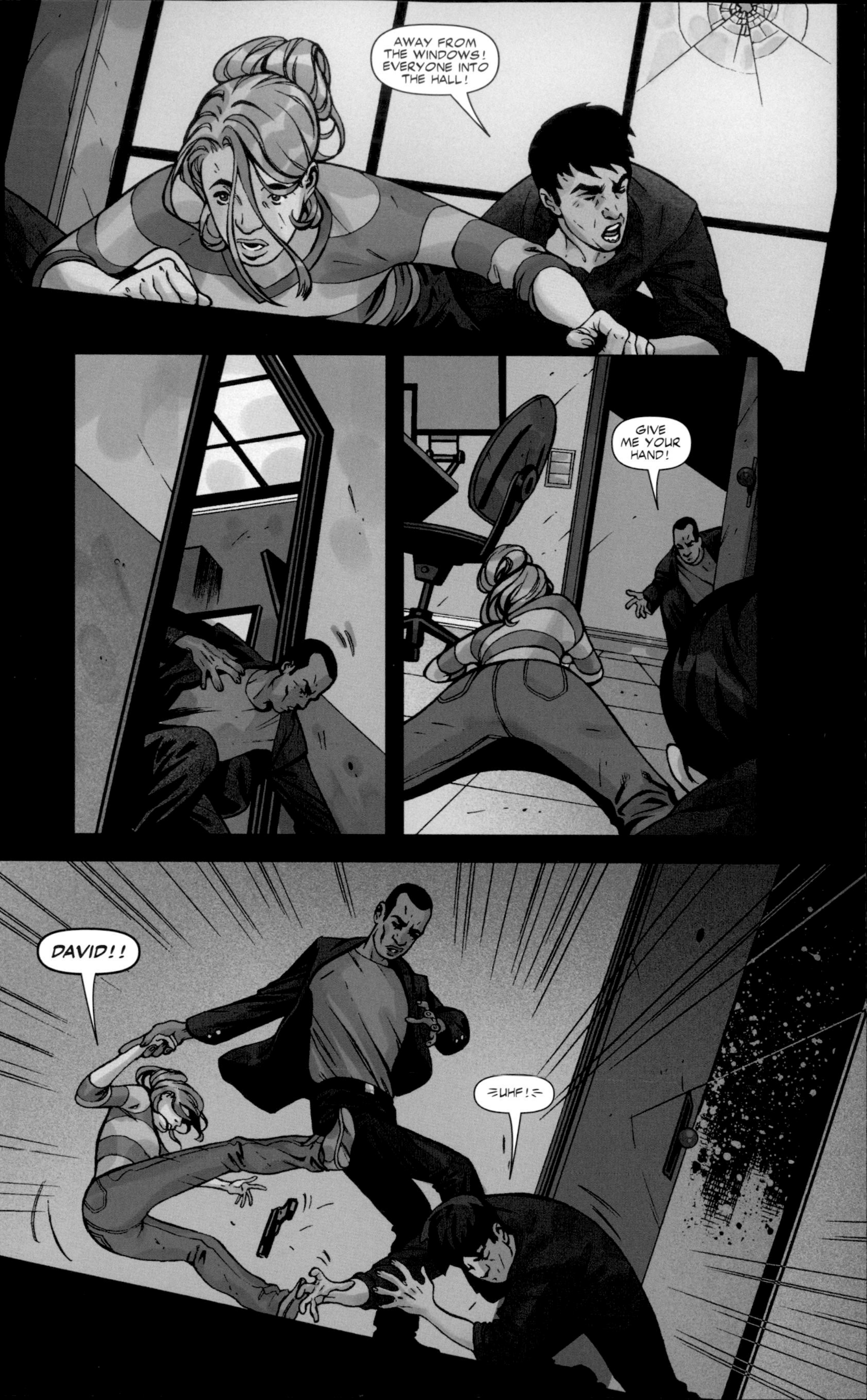
AWAY FROM THE WINDOWS! EVERYONE INTO THE HALL!
GIVE ME YOUR HAND!
DAVID!!
UHF!

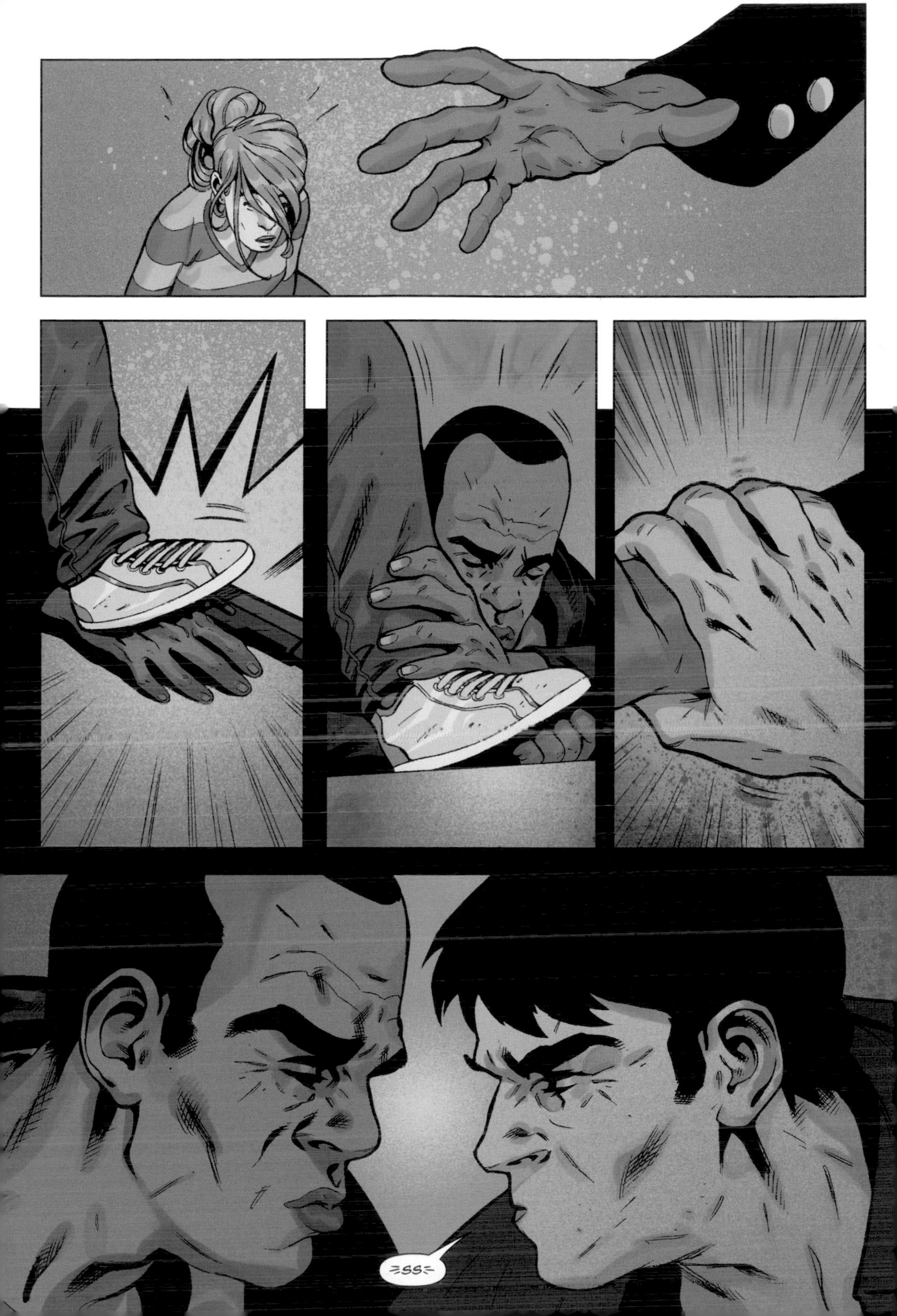
SS

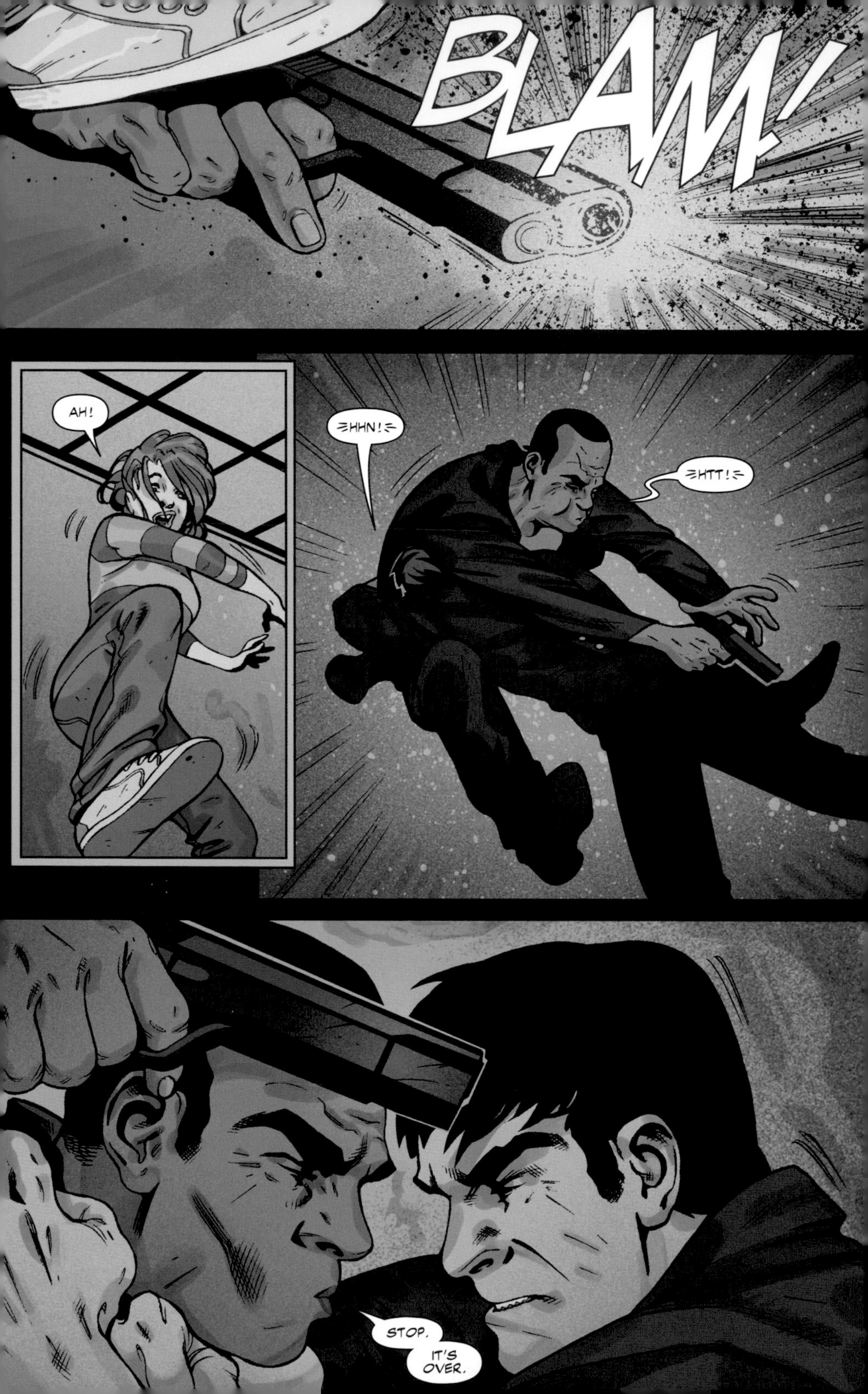
BLAM!
AH!
HHN!
HTT!
STOP.
IT'S OVER.

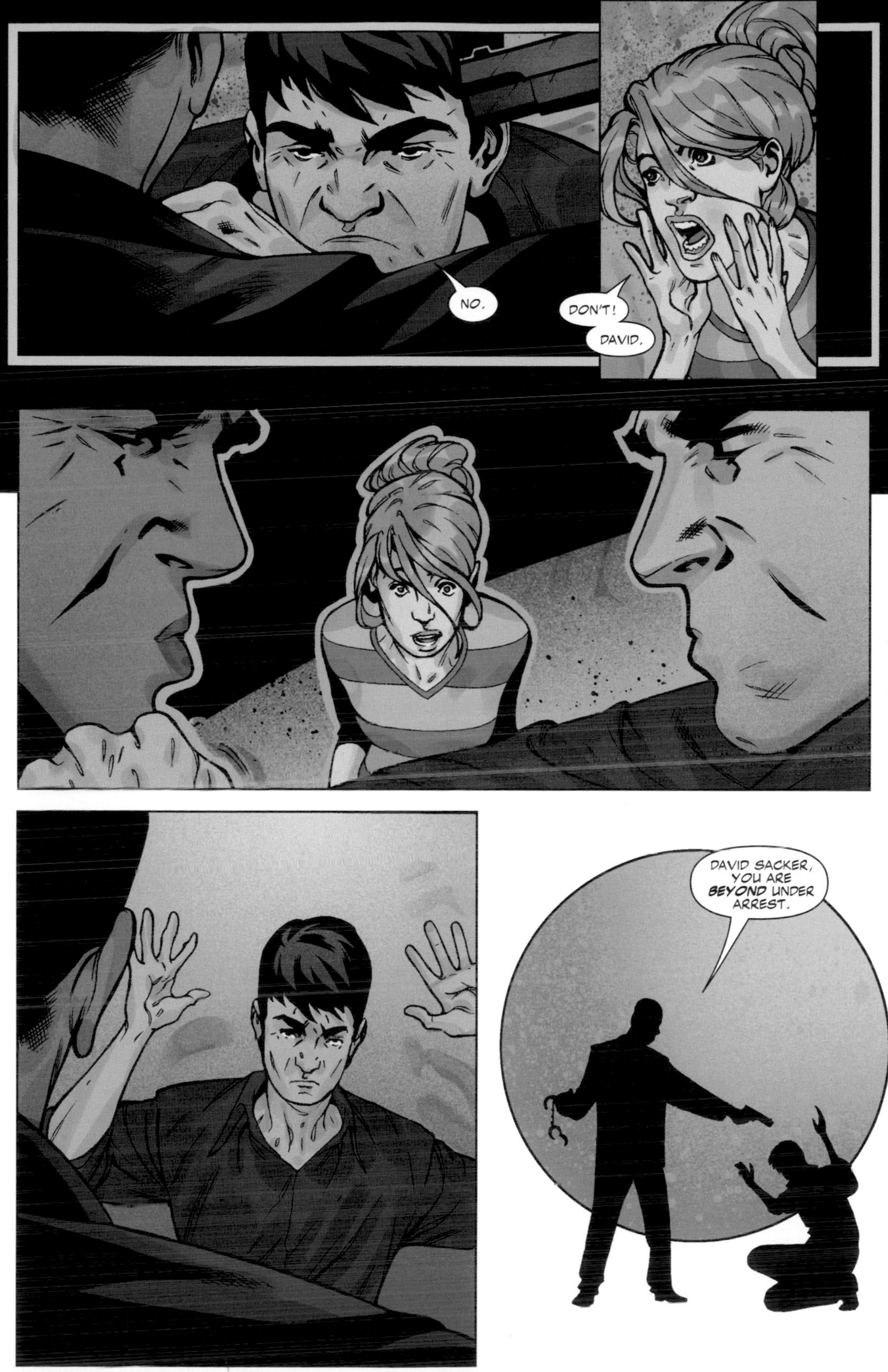
NO.
DON'T!
DAVID.
DAVID SACKER, YOU ARE BEYOND UNDER ARREST.

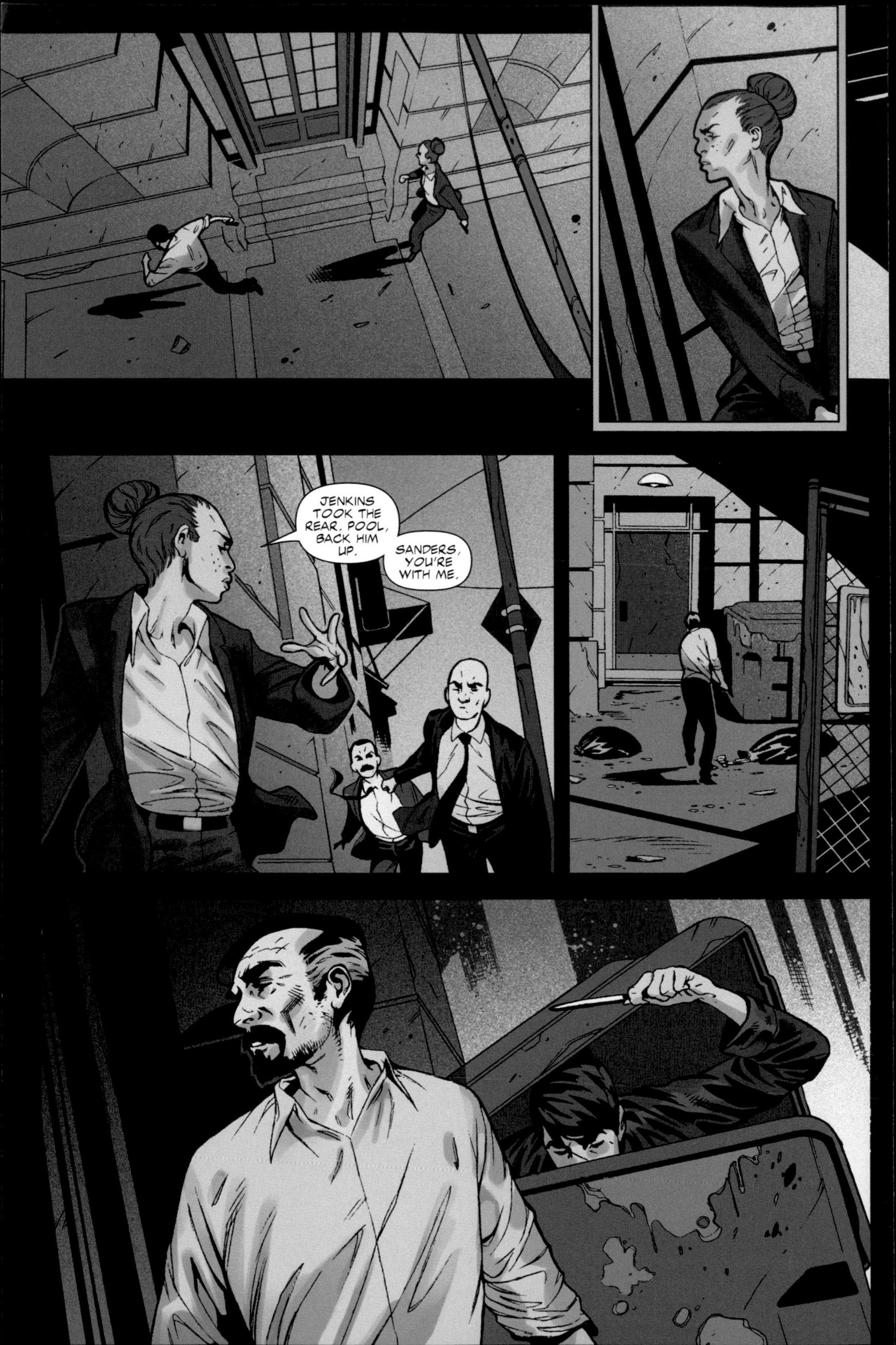
JENKINS TOOK THE REAR. POOL, BACK HIM UP.
SANDERS, YOU'RE WITH ME.

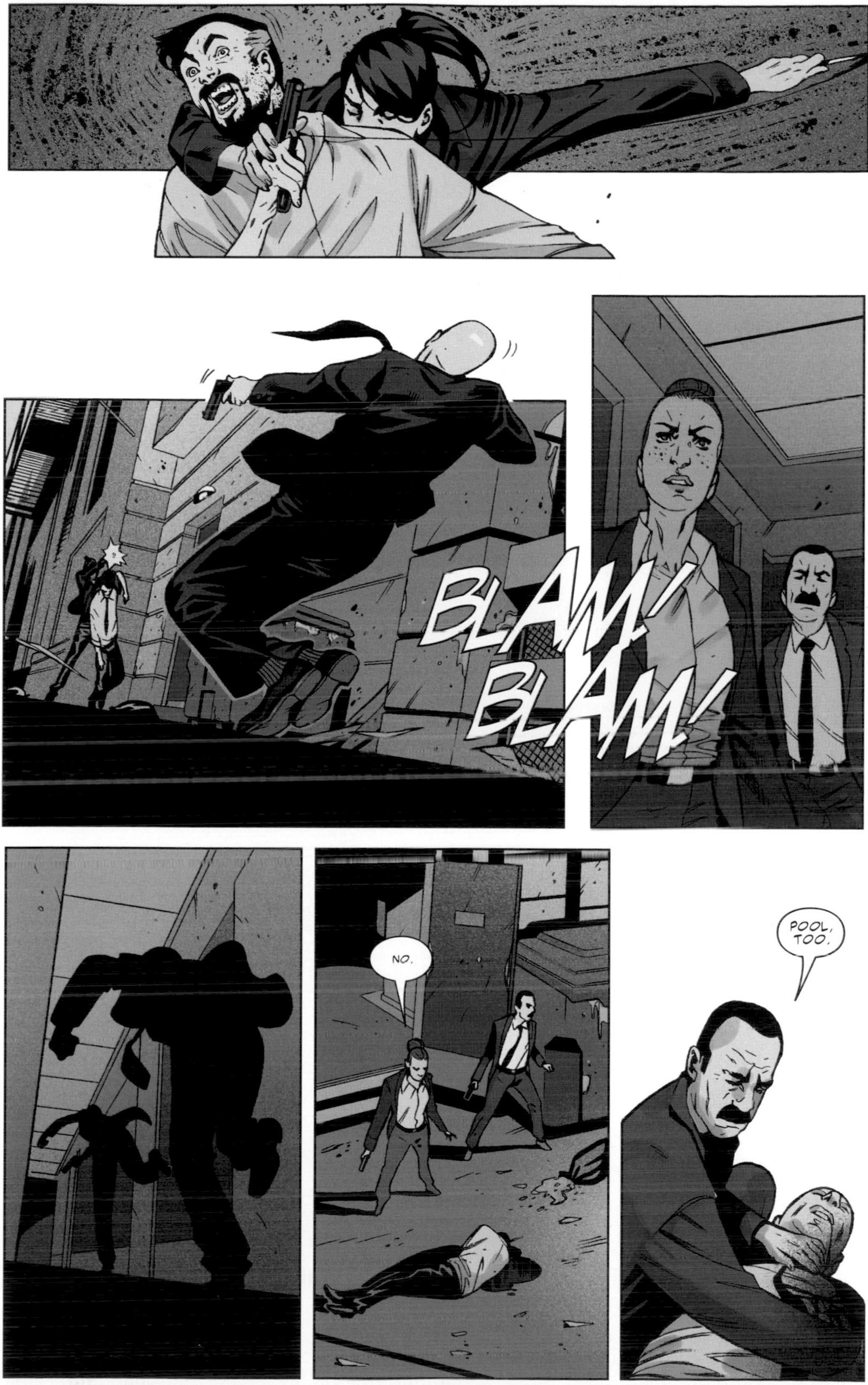
BLAM!
BLAM!
NO.
POOL, TOO.

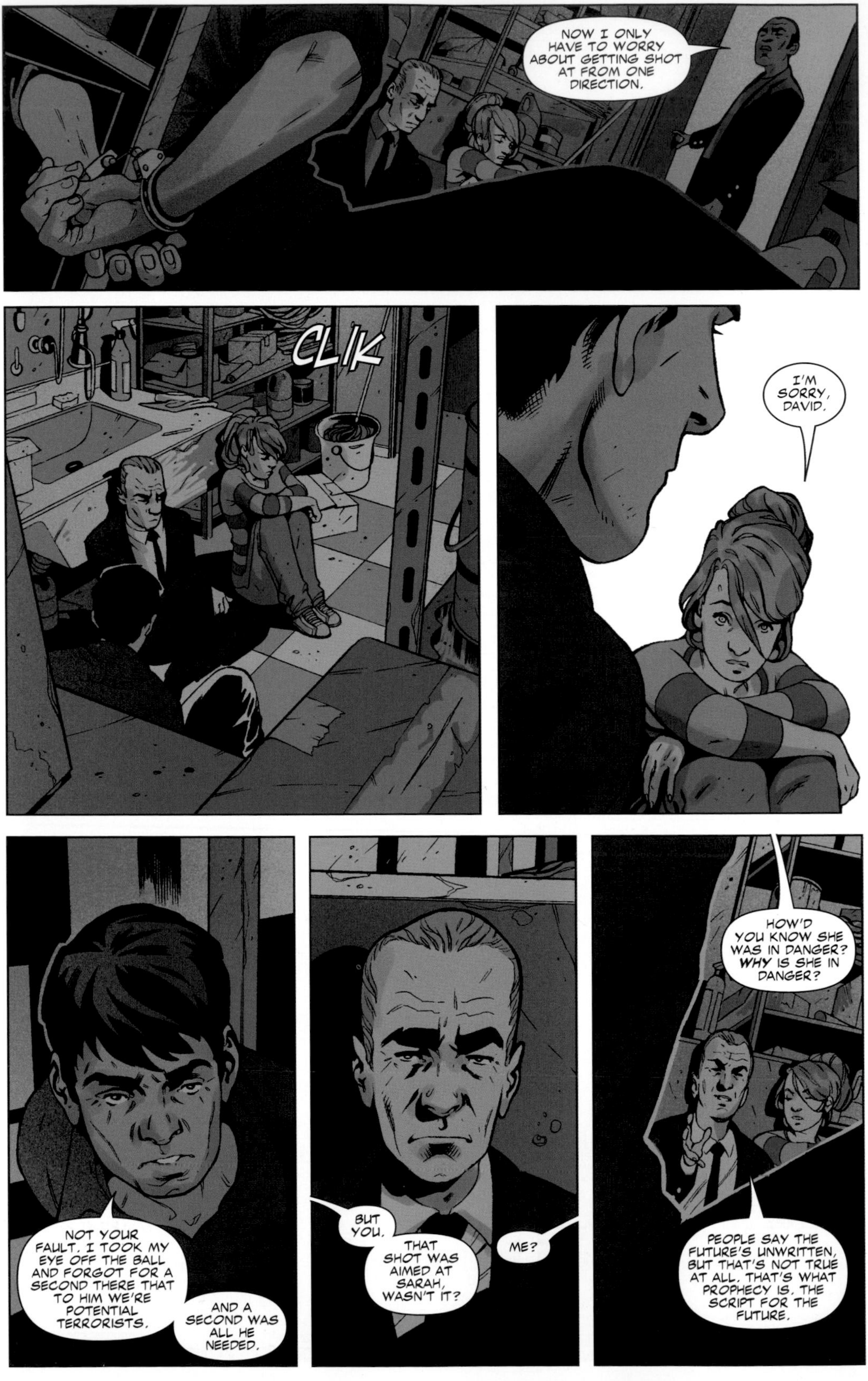
NOW I ONLY HAVE TO WORRY ABOUT GETTING SHOT AT FROM ONE DIRECTION.
CLIK
I'M SORRY, DAVID.
NOT YOUR FAULT. I TOOK MY EYE OFF THE BALL AND FORGOT FOR A SECOND THERE THAT TO HIM WE'RE POTENTIAL TERRORISTS.
AND A SECOND WAS ALL HE NEEDED.
BUT YOU.
THAT SHOT WAS AIMED AT SARAH, WASN'T IT?
ME?
HOW'D YOU KNOW SHE WAS IN DANGER? WHY IS SHE IN DANGER?
PEOPLE SAY THE FUTURE'S UNWRITTEN, BUT THAT'S NOT TRUE AT ALL. THAT'S WHAT PROPHECY IS. THE SCRIPT FOR THE FUTURE.

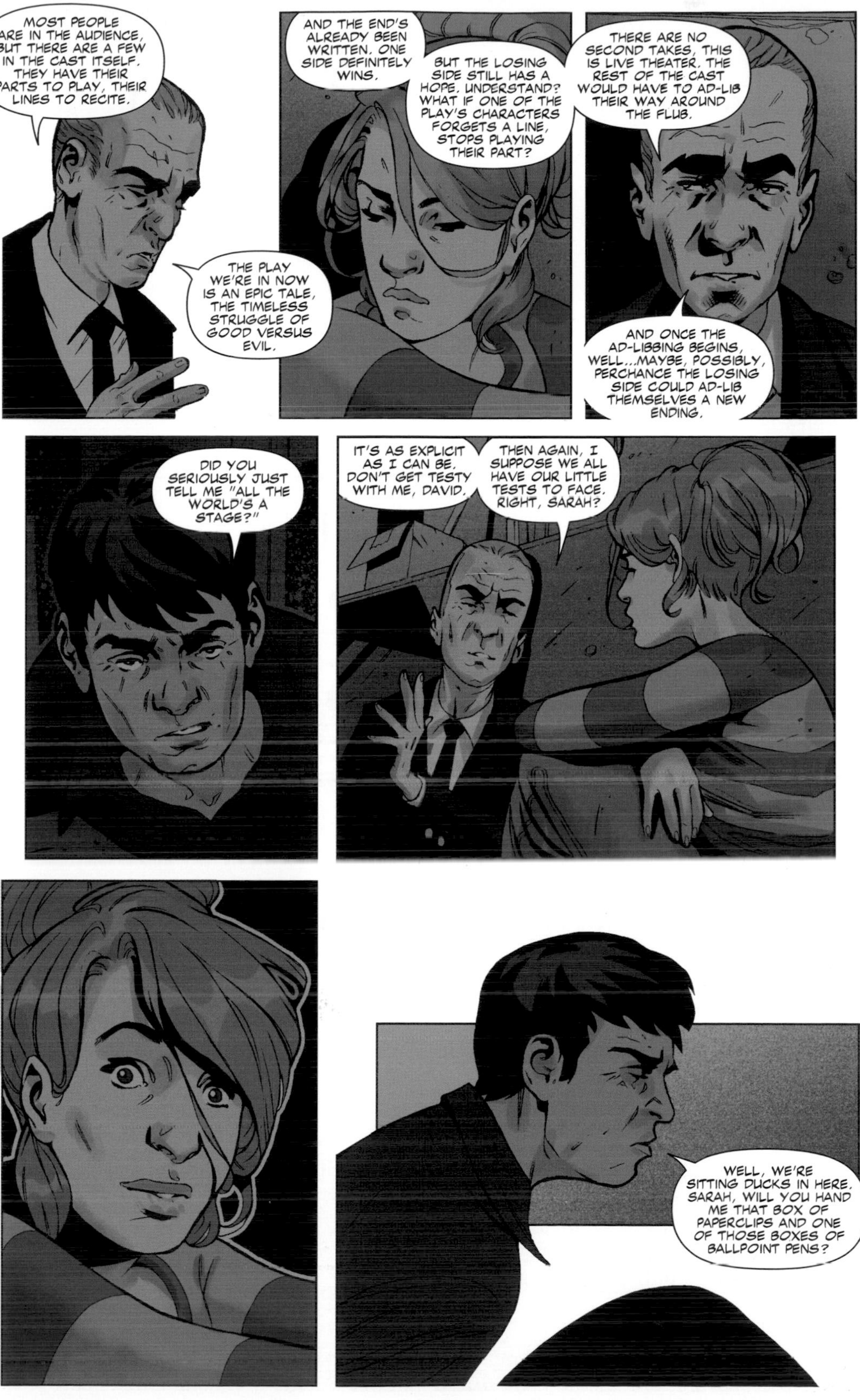
MOST PEOPLE ARE IN THE AUDIENCE, BUT THERE ARE A FEW IN THE CAST ITSELF. THEY HAVE THEIR PARTS TO PLAY, THEIR LINES TO RECITE.
THE PLAY WE'RE IN NOW IS AN EPIC TALE, THE TIMELESS STRUGGLE OF GOOD VERSUS EVIL.
AND THE END'S ALREADY BEEN WRITTEN. ONE SIDE DEFINITELY WINS.
BUT THE LOSING SIDE STILL HAS A HOPE, UNDERSTAND? WHAT IF ONE OF THE PLAY'S CHARACTERS FORGETS A LINE, STOPS PLAYING THEIR PART?
THERE ARE NO SECOND TAKES, THIS IS LIVE THEATER. THE REST OF THE CAST WOULD HAVE TO AD-LIB THEIR WAY AROUND THE FLUB.
AND ONCE THE AD-LIBBING BEGINS, WELL...MAYBE, POSSIBLY, PERCHANCE THE LOSING SIDE COULD AD-LIB THEMSELVES A NEW ENDING.
DID YOU SERIOUSLY JUST TELL ME "ALL THE WORLD'S A STAGE?"
IT'S AS EXPLICIT AS I CAN BE. DON'T GET TESTY WITH ME, DAVID.
THEN AGAIN, I SUPPOSE WE ALL HAVE OUR LITTLE TESTS TO FACE. RIGHT, SARAH?
WELL, WE'RE SITTING DUCKS IN HERE. SARAH, WILL YOU HAND ME THAT BOX OF PAPERCLIPS AND ONE OF THOSE BOXES OF BALLPOINT PENS?

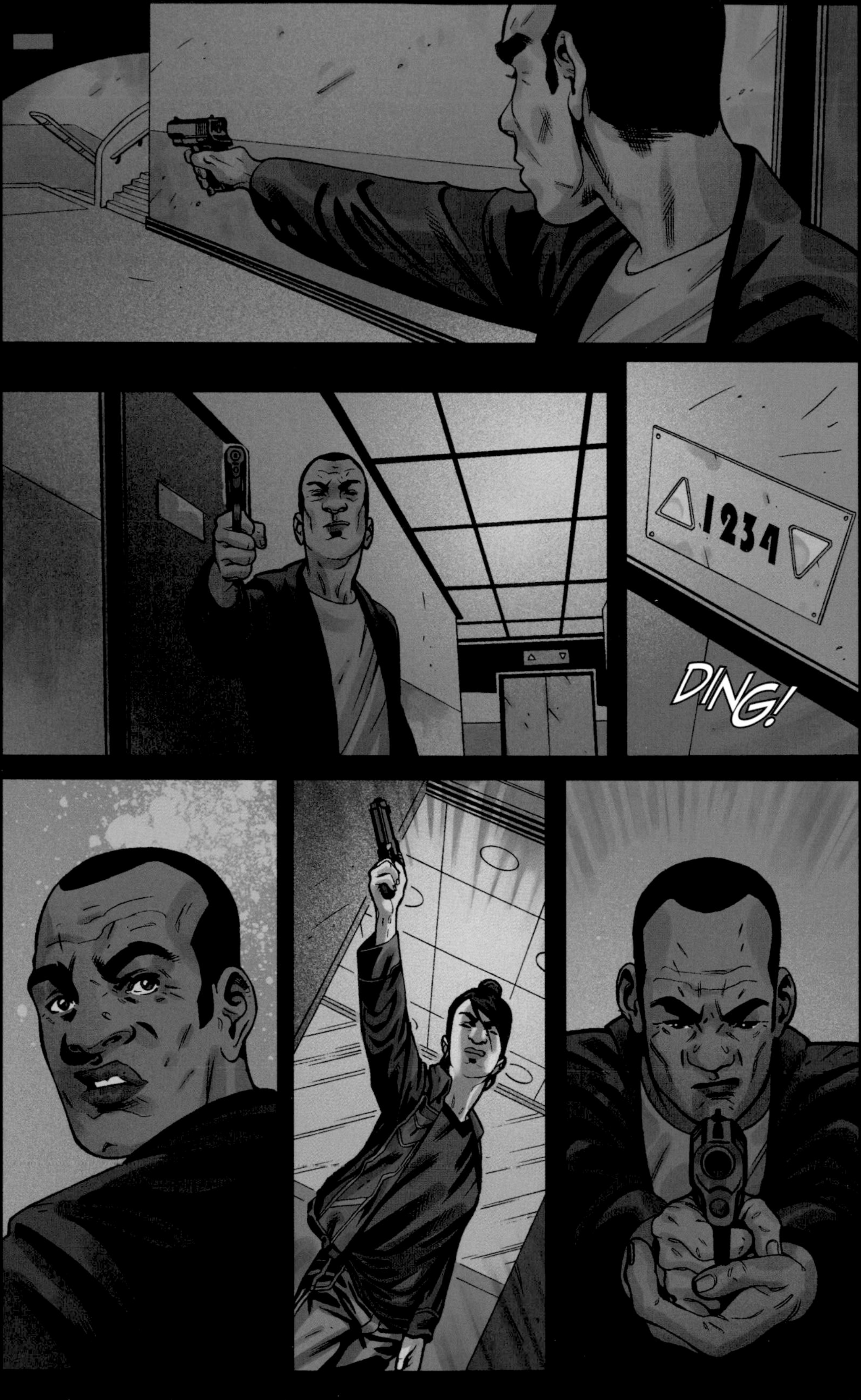
1234
DING!

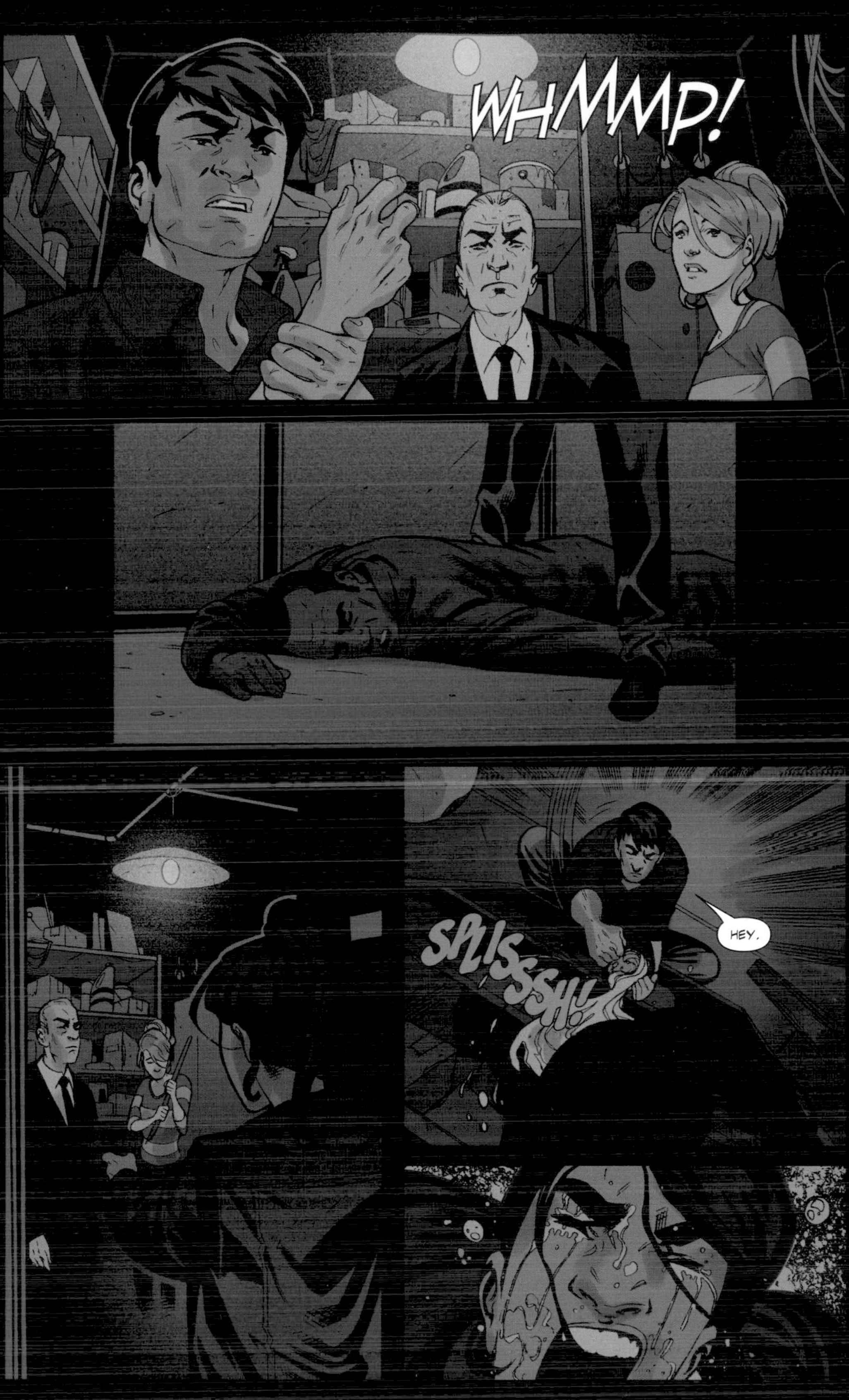
WHMMP!
SPLISSSH!
HEY.

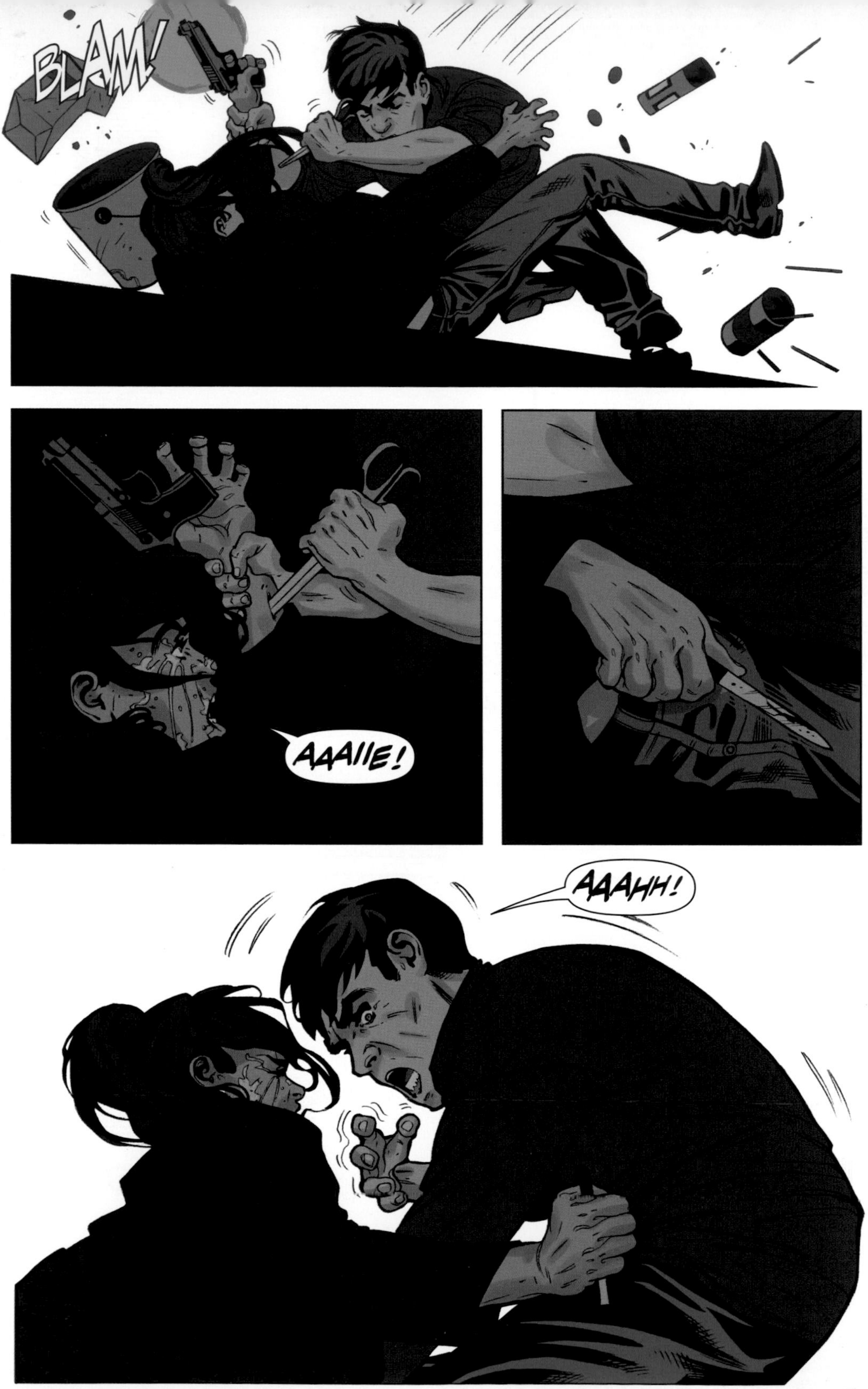
BLAM!
AAAIIE!
AAAHH!

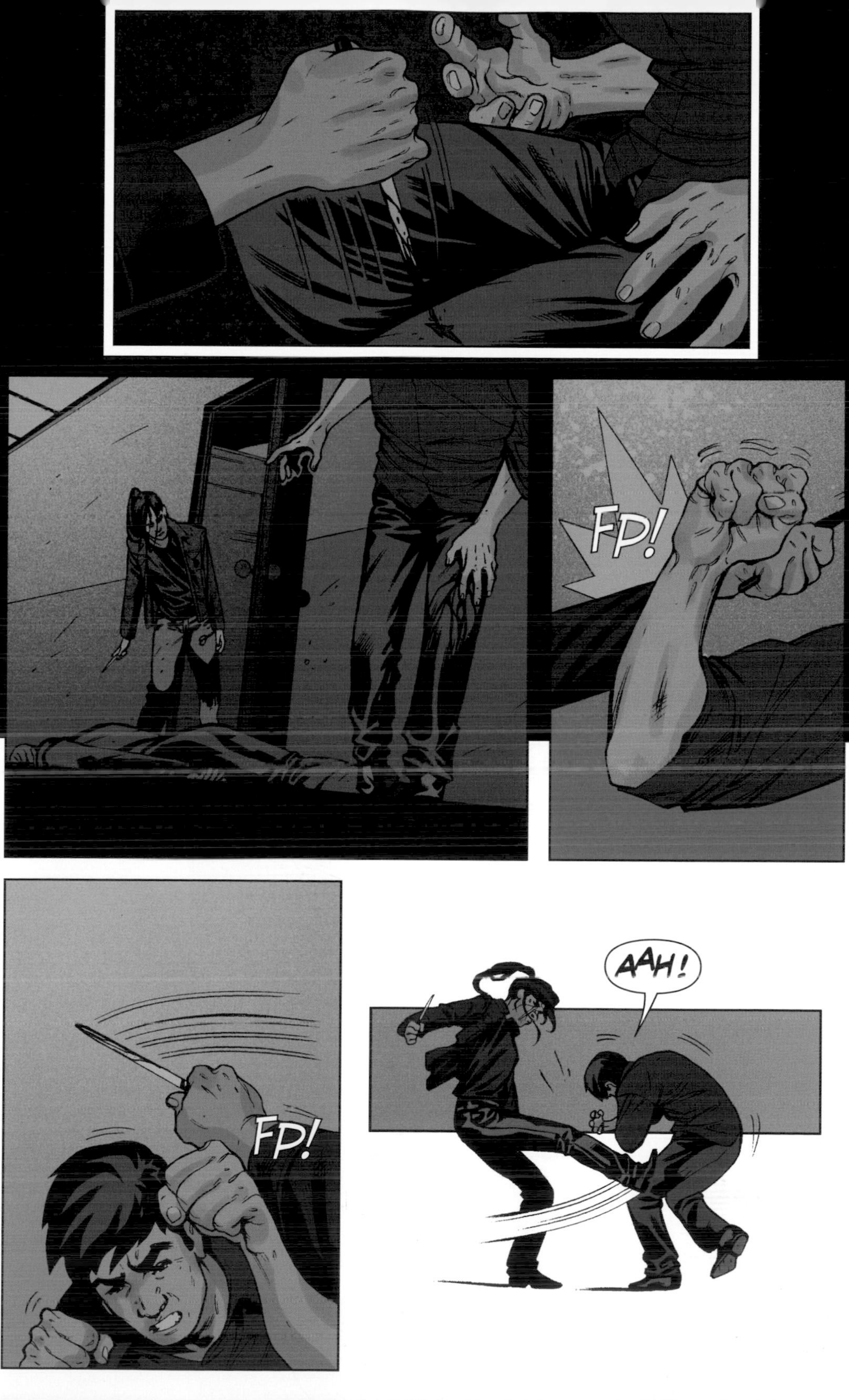
FP!
FP!
AAH!

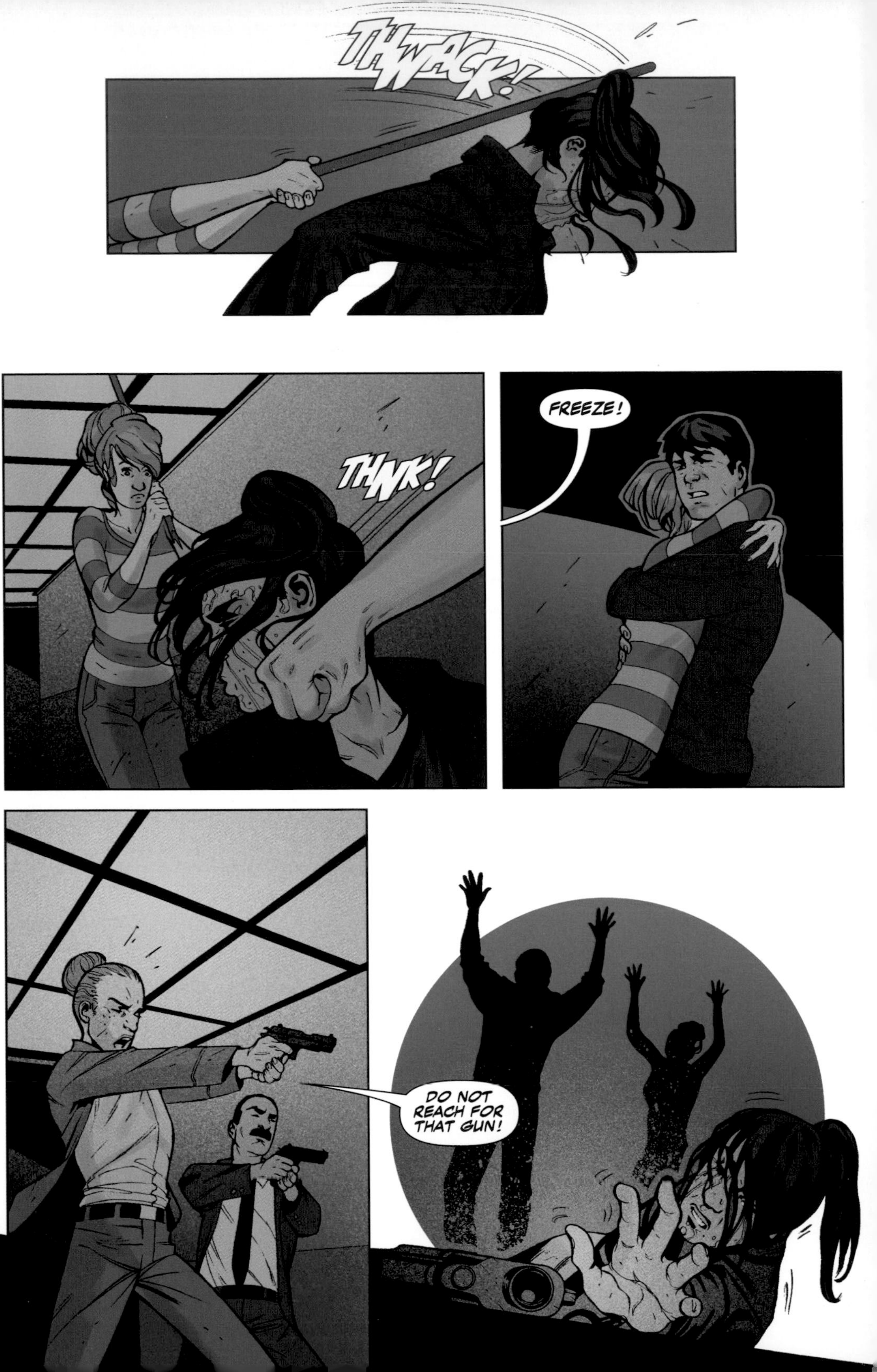
THWACK!
THNK!
FREEZE!
DO NOT REACH FOR THAT GUN!

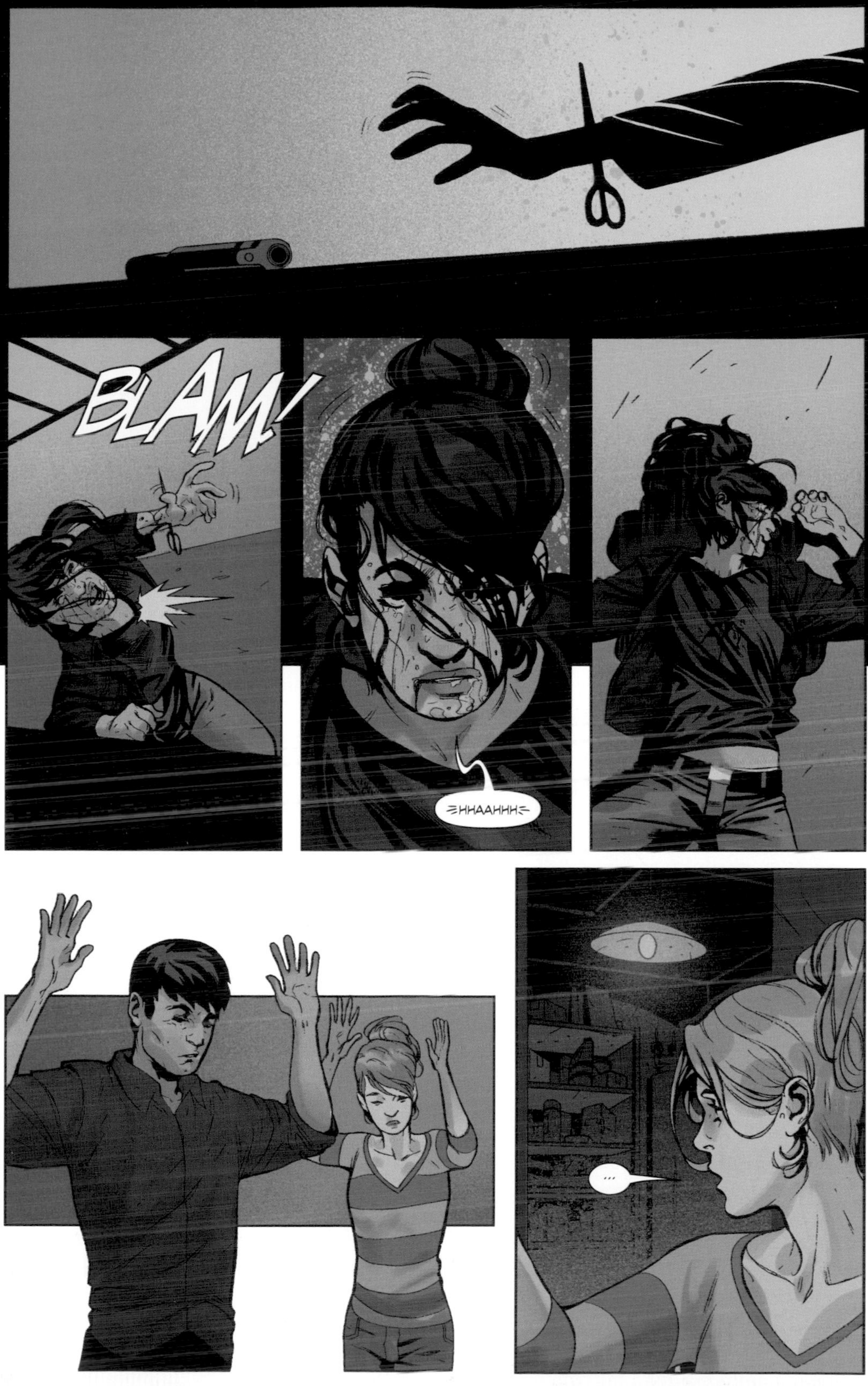
BLAM!
HHAAHHH
...

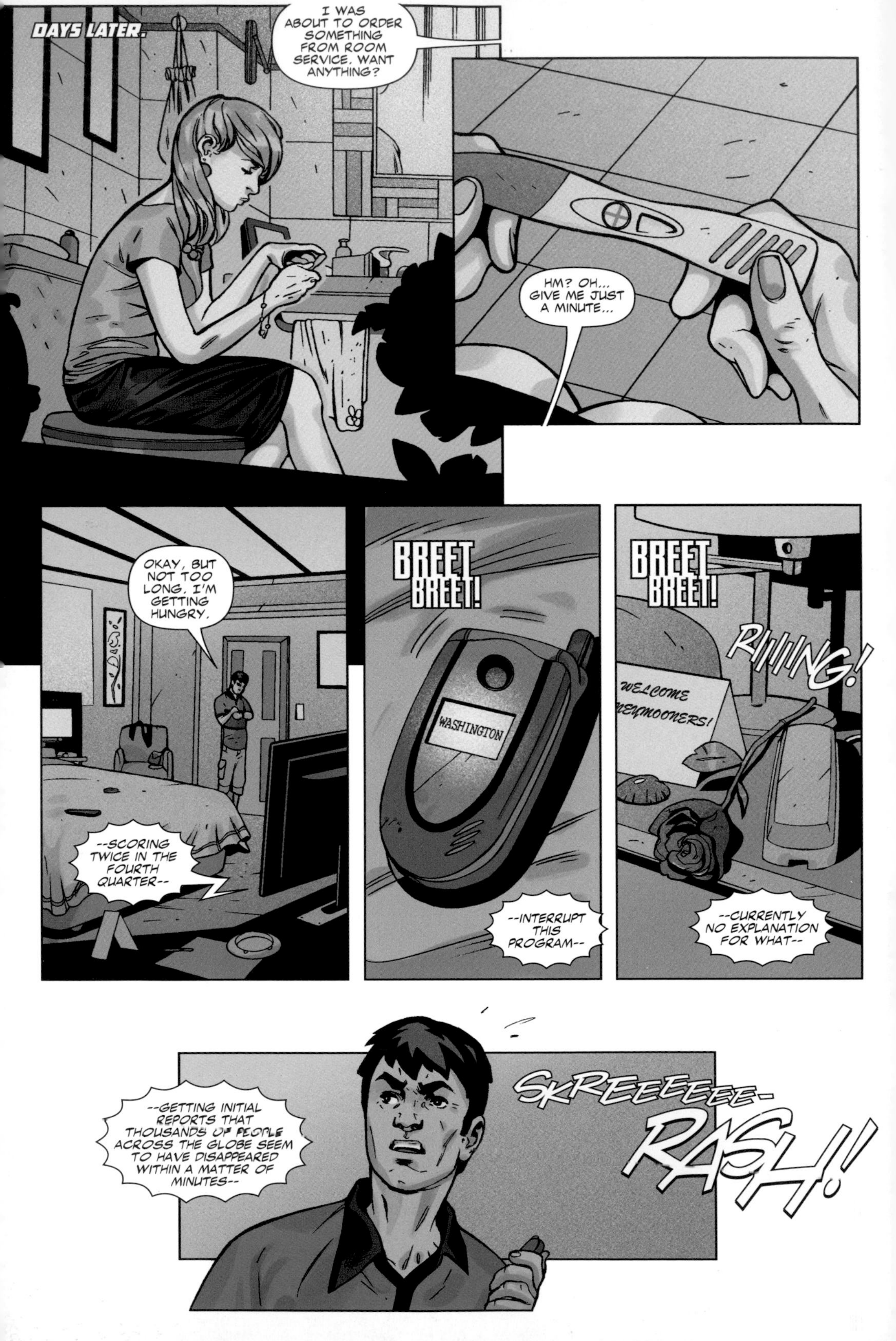
DAYS LATER.
I WAS ABOUT TO ORDER SOMETHING FROM ROOM SERVICE. WANT ANYTHING?
HM? OH... GIVE ME JUST A MINUTE...
OKAY, BUT NOT TOO LONG. I'M GETTING HUNGRY.
--SCORING TWICE IN THE FOURTH QUARTER--
BREET BREET!
WASHINGTON
--INTERRUPT THIS PROGRAM--
BREET BREET!
RIIIING!
WELCOME
NEYMOONERS!
--CURRENTLY NO EXPLANATION FOR WHAT--
--GETTING INITIAL REPORTS THAT THOUSANDS OF PEOPLE ACROSS THE GLOBE SEEM TO HAVE DISAPPEARED WITHIN A MATTER OF MINUTES--
SKREEEEEEE-RASH!

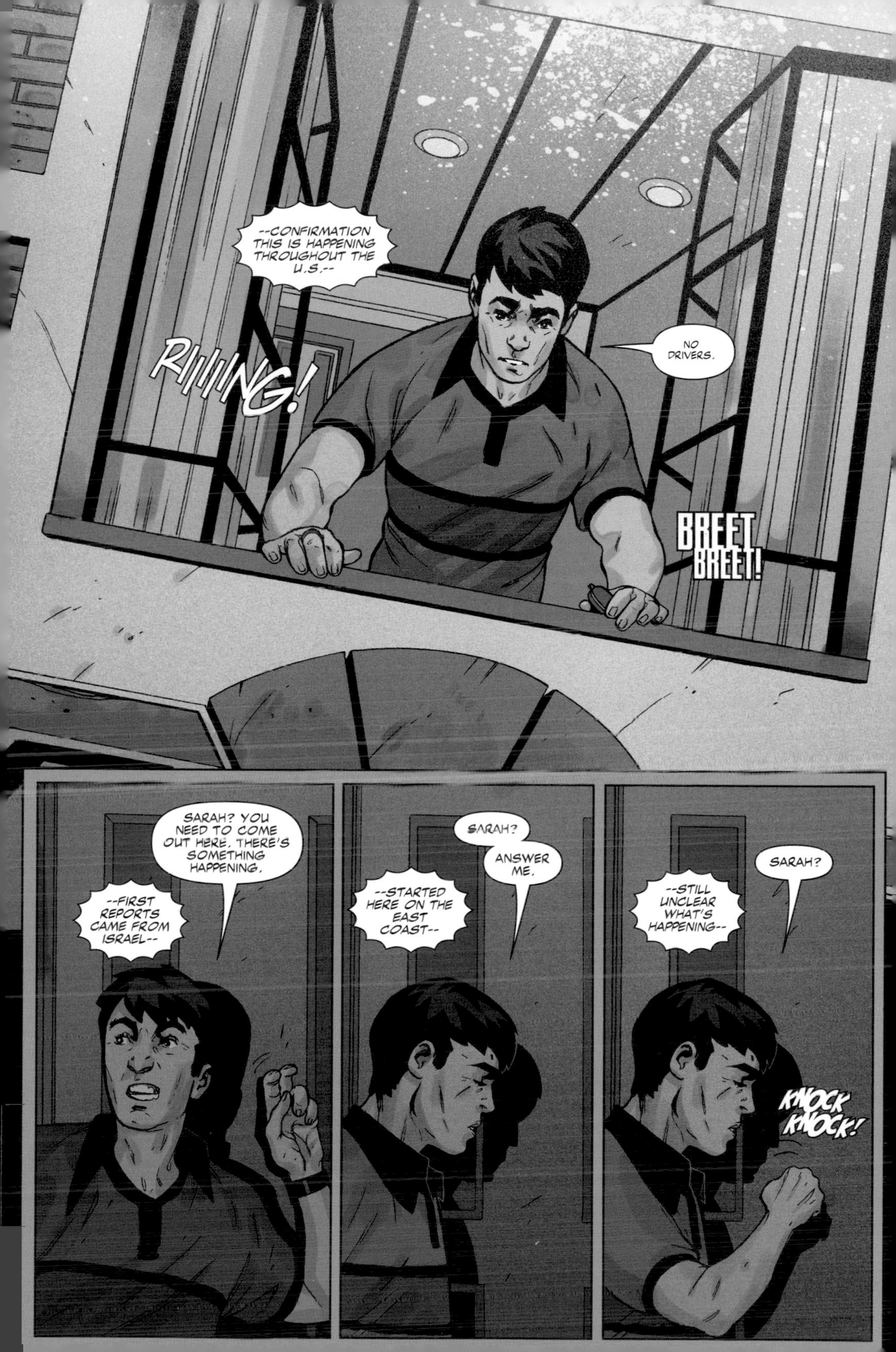
--CONFIRMATION THIS IS HAPPENING THROUGHOUT THE U.S.--
NO DRIVERS.
RIIIING!
BREET BREET!
SARAH? YOU NEED TO COME OUT HERE. THERE'S SOMETHING HAPPENING.
--FIRST REPORTS CAME FROM ISRAEL--
SARAH?
ANSWER ME.
--STARTED HERE ON THE EAST COAST--
SARAH?
--STILL UNCLEAR WHAT'S HAPPENING--
KNOCK KNOCK!

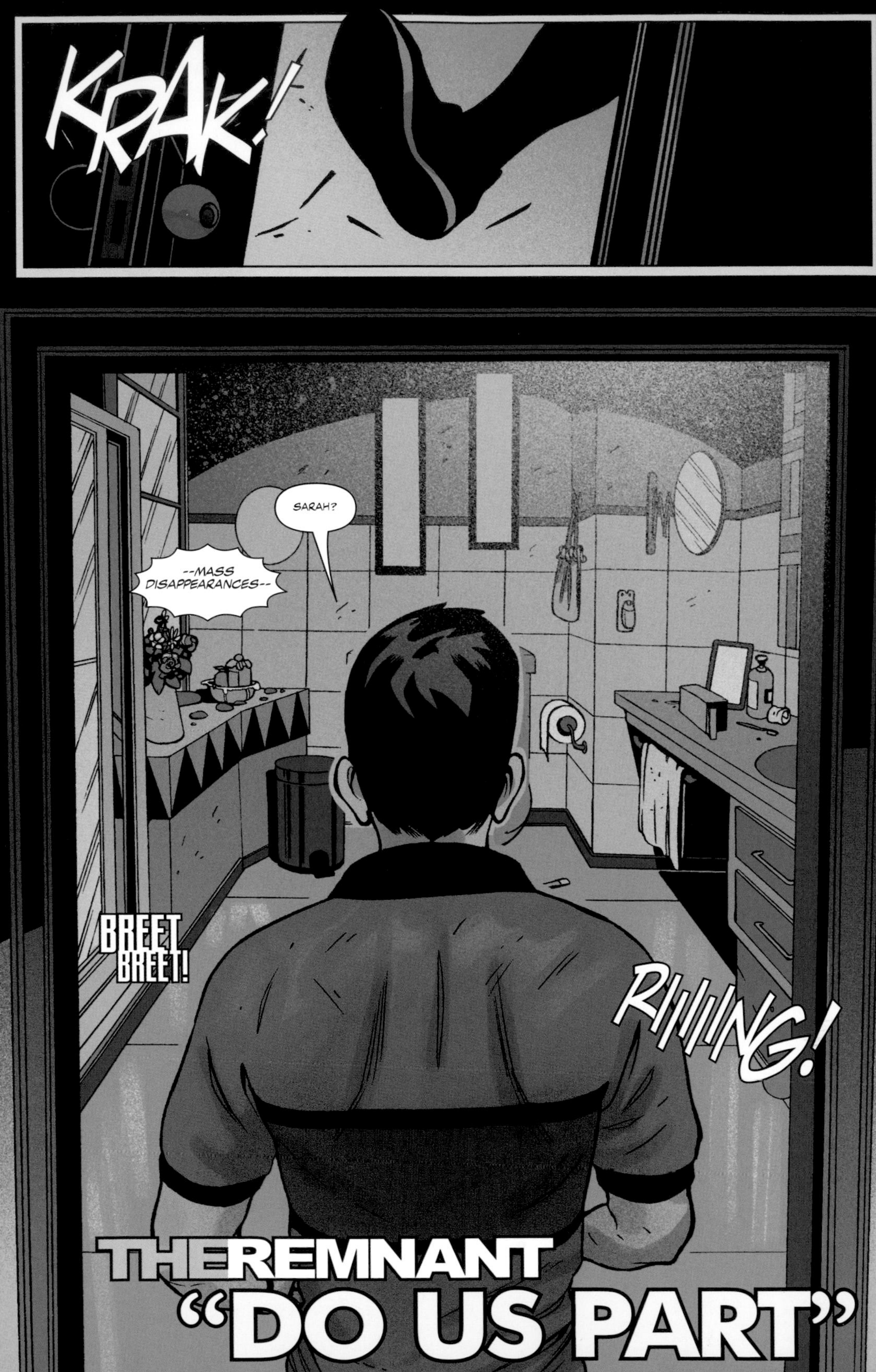
KRAK!
SARAH?
--MASS DISAPPEARANCES--
BREET BREET!
RIIIING!
THE REMNANT
"DO US PART"

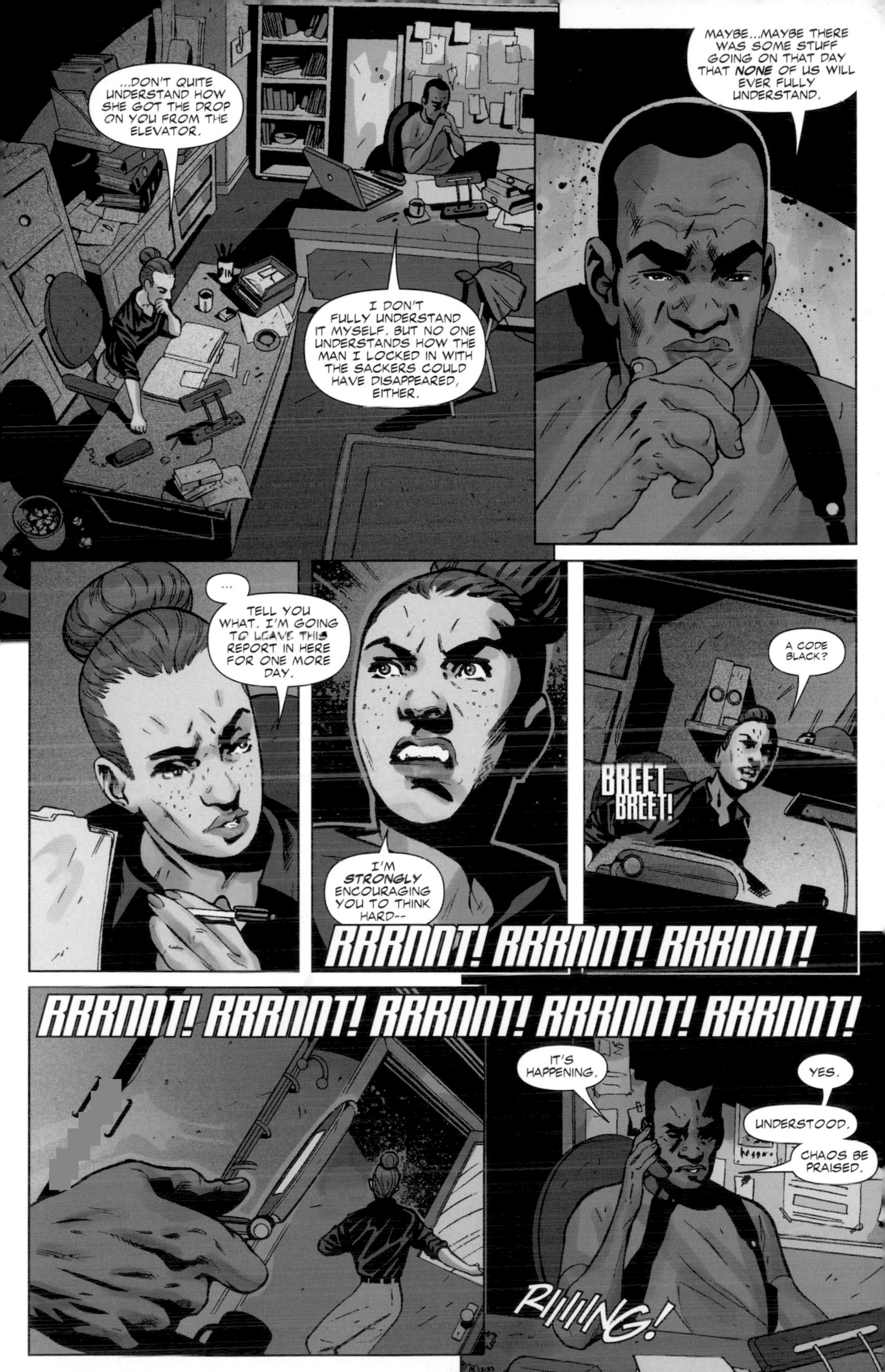
...DON'T QUITE UNDERSTAND HOW SHE GOT THE DROP ON YOU FROM THE ELEVATOR.
I DON'T FULLY UNDERSTAND IT MYSELF. BUT NO ONE UNDERSTANDS HOW THE MAN I LOCKED IN WITH THE SACKERS COULD HAVE DISAPPEARED, EITHER.
MAYBE...MAYBE THERE WAS SOME STUFF GOING ON THAT DAY THAT NONE OF US WILL EVER FULLY UNDERSTAND.
...
TELL YOU WHAT. I'M GOING TO LEAVE THIS REPORT IN HERE FOR ONE MORE DAY.
I'M STRONGLY ENCOURAGING YOU TO THINK HARD--
BREET BREET!
A CODE BLACK?
RRRNNT! RRRNNT! RRRNNT!
RRRNNT! RRRNNT! RRRNNT! RRRNNT! RRRNNT!
IT'S HAPPENING.
YES.
UNDERSTOOD.
CHAOS BE PRAISED.
RIIIING!

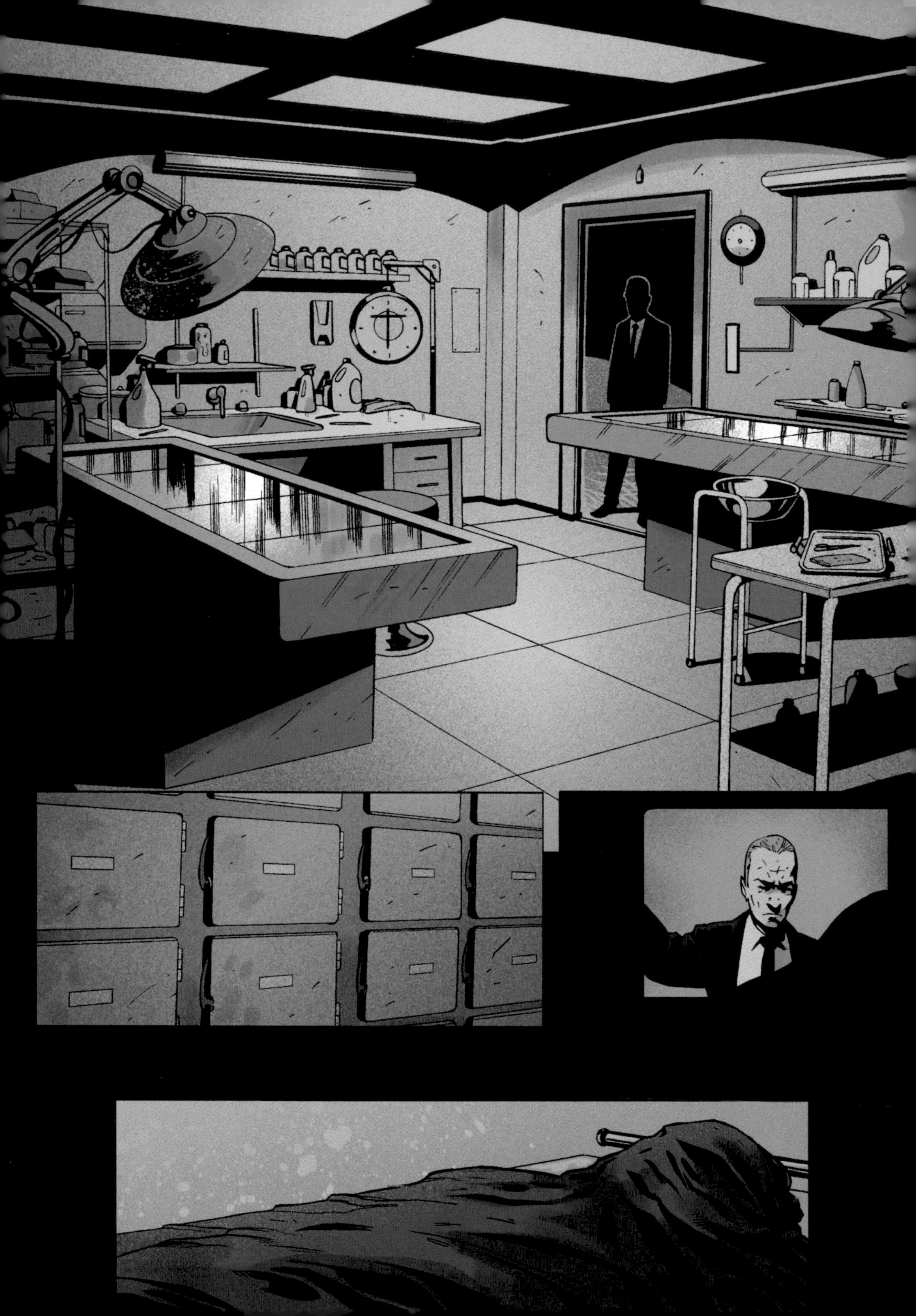

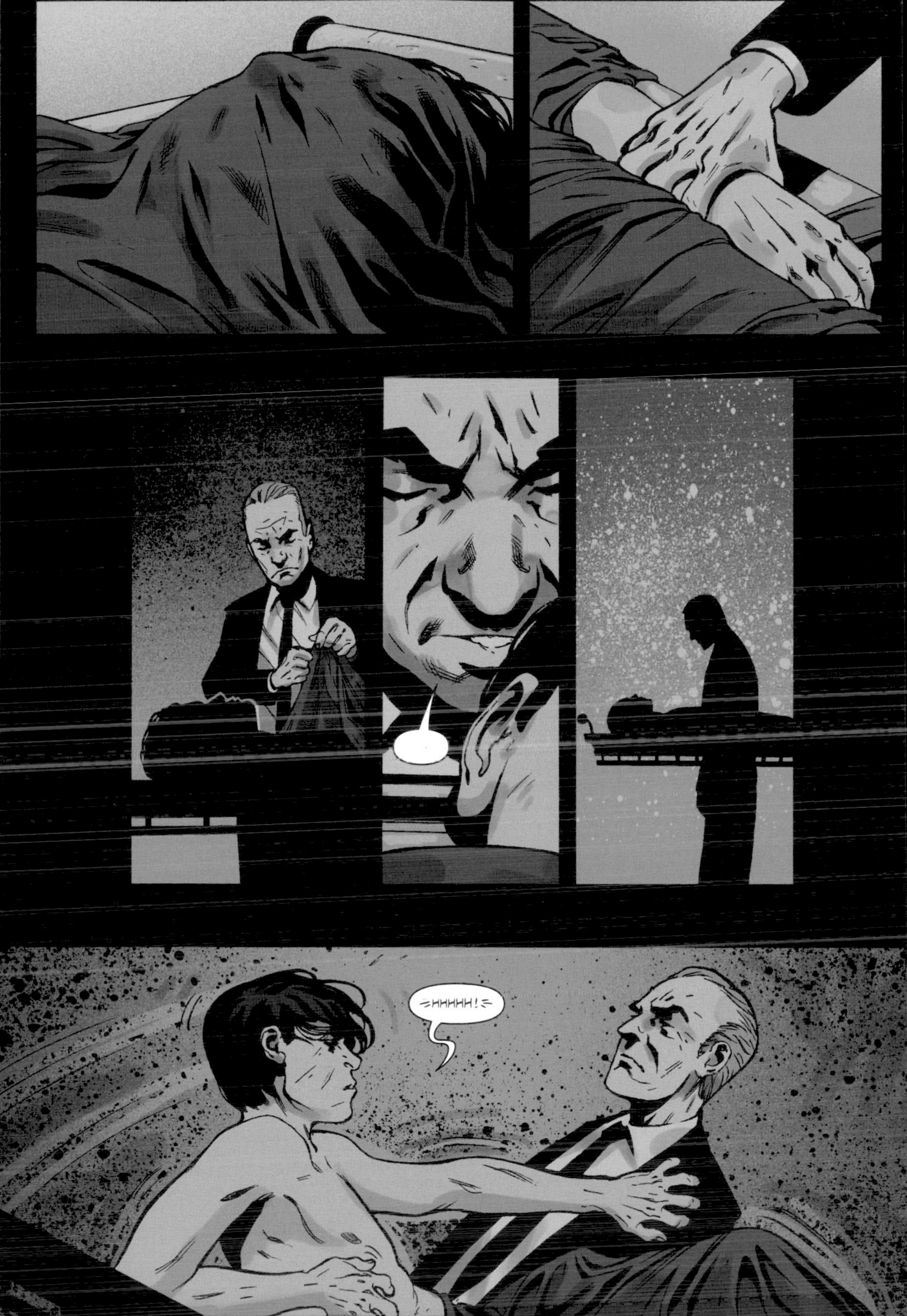
HHHHH!

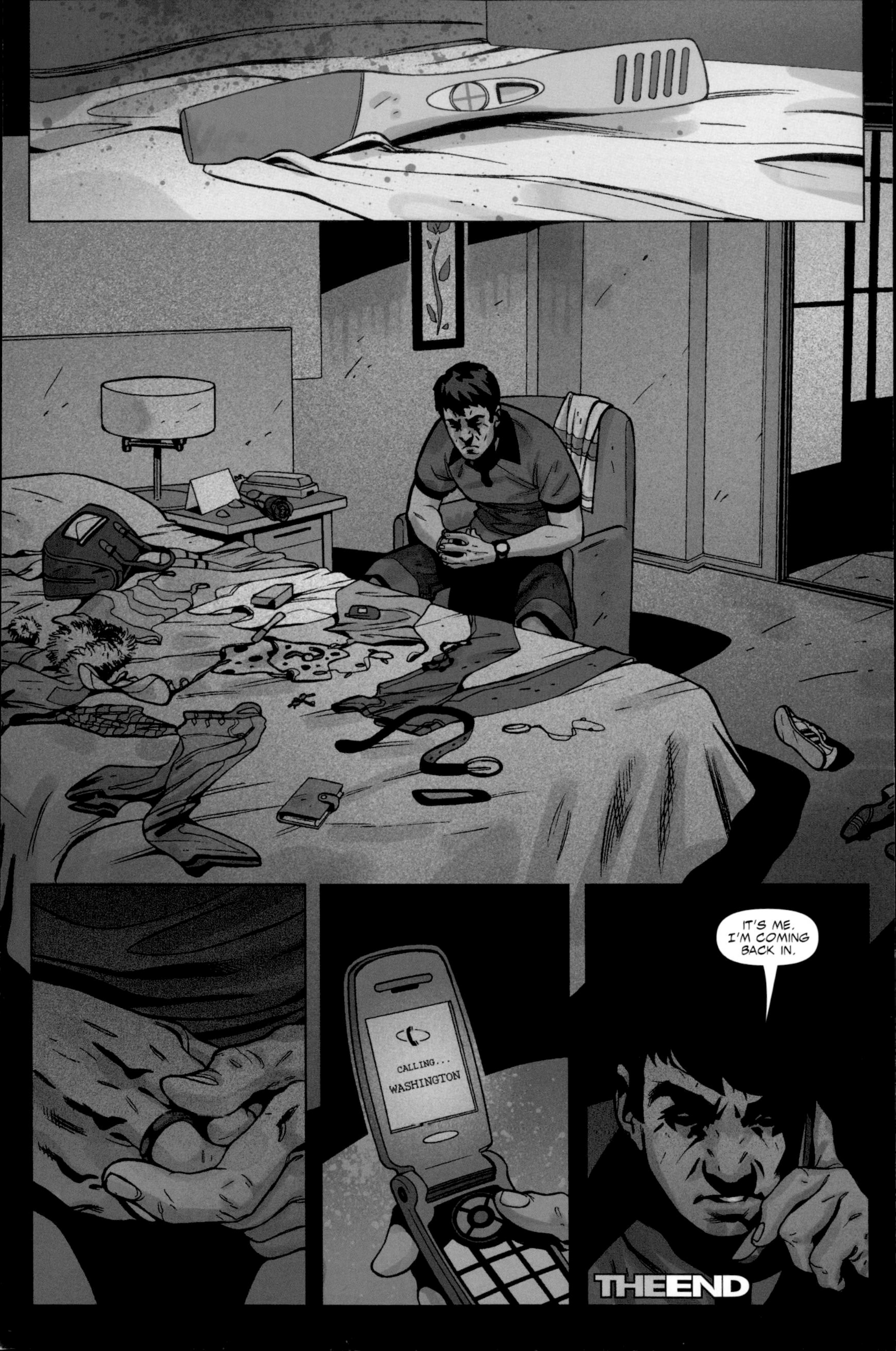
CALLING...
WASHINGTON
IT'S ME. I'M COMING BACK IN.
THE END

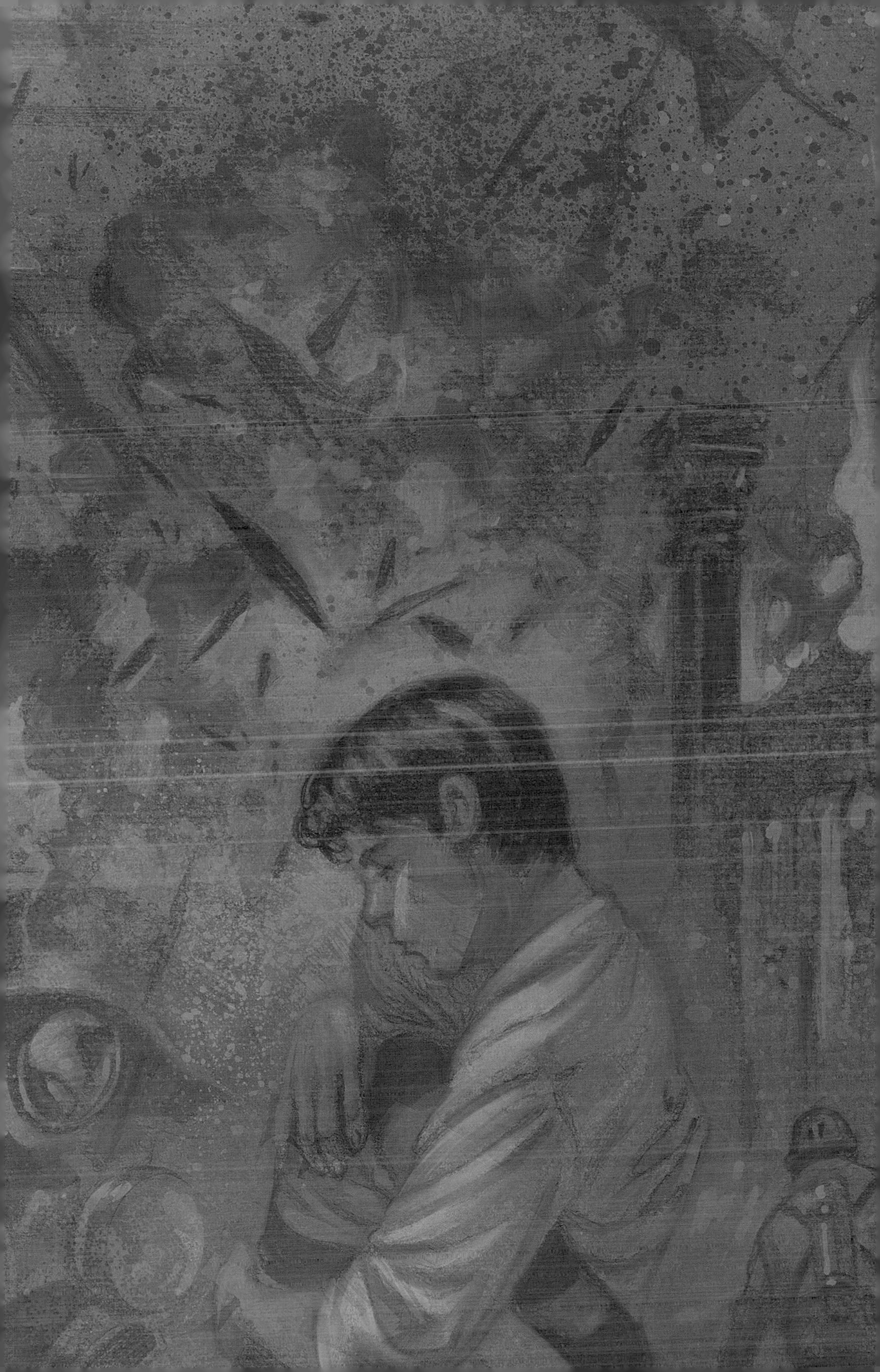

COVER
GALLERY

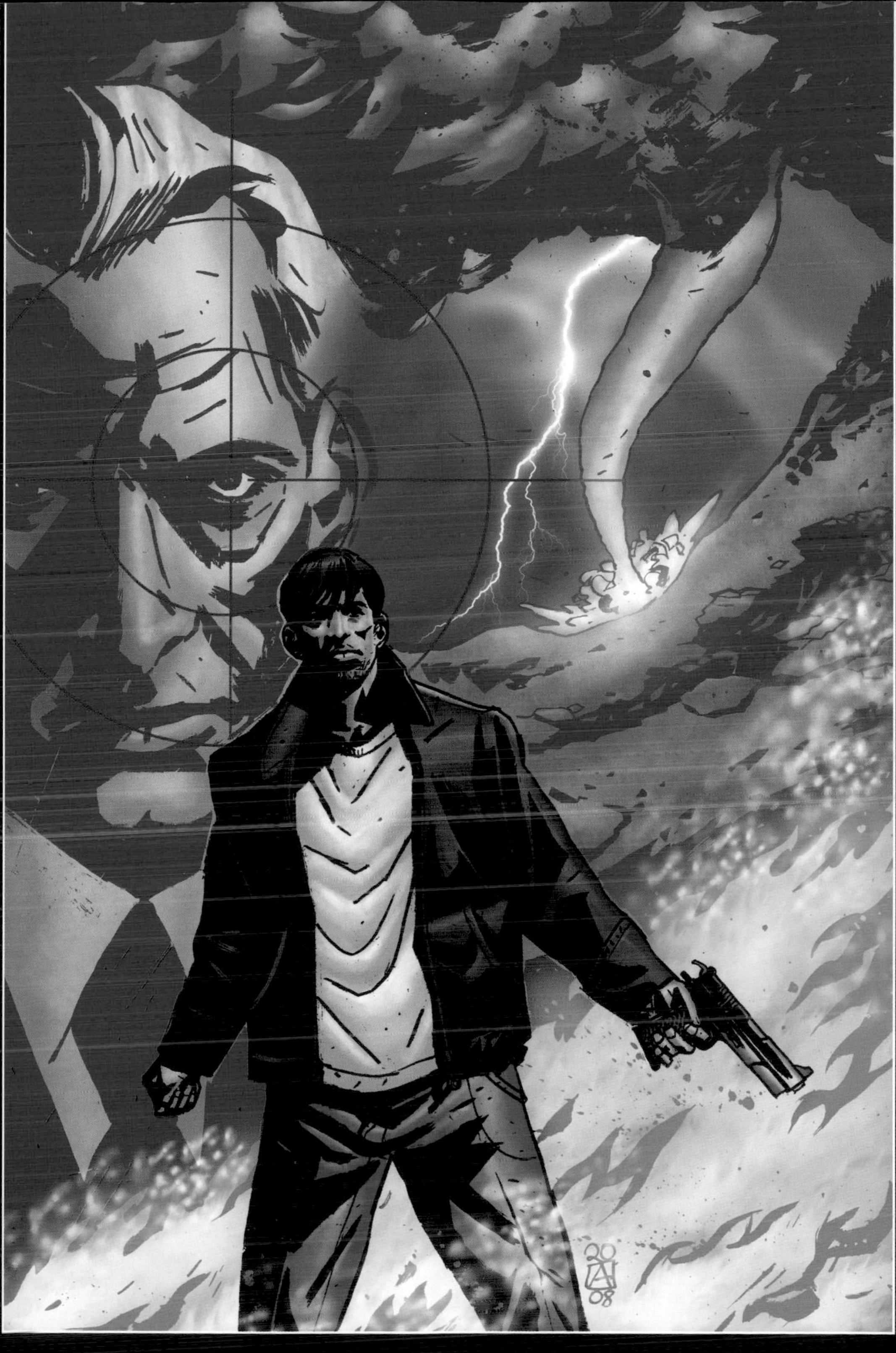
20
08

COVER 1A
PAUL AZACETA / COLORS BY ANDREW DALHOUSE

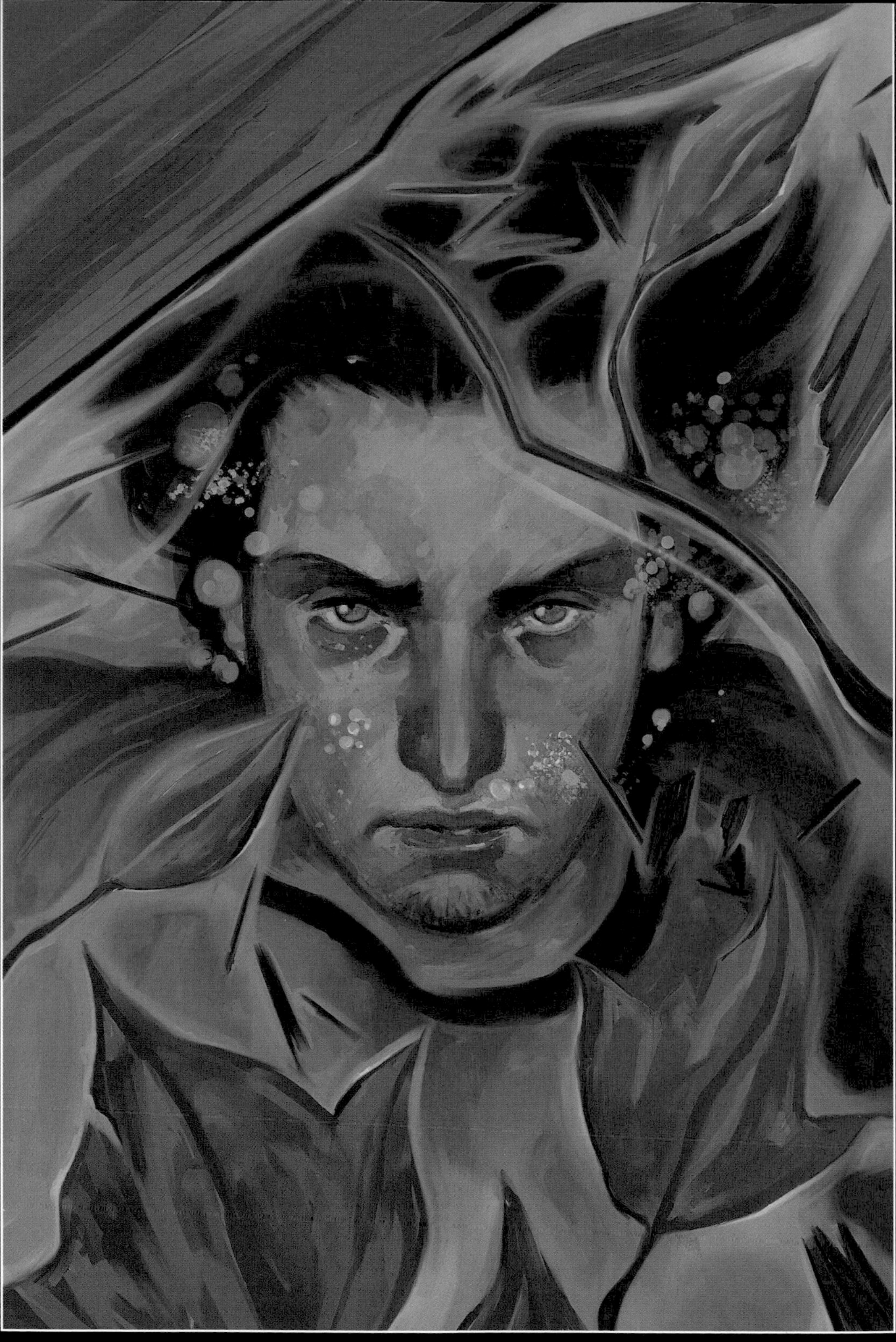

COVER 1B
JULIAN TOTINO TEDESCO

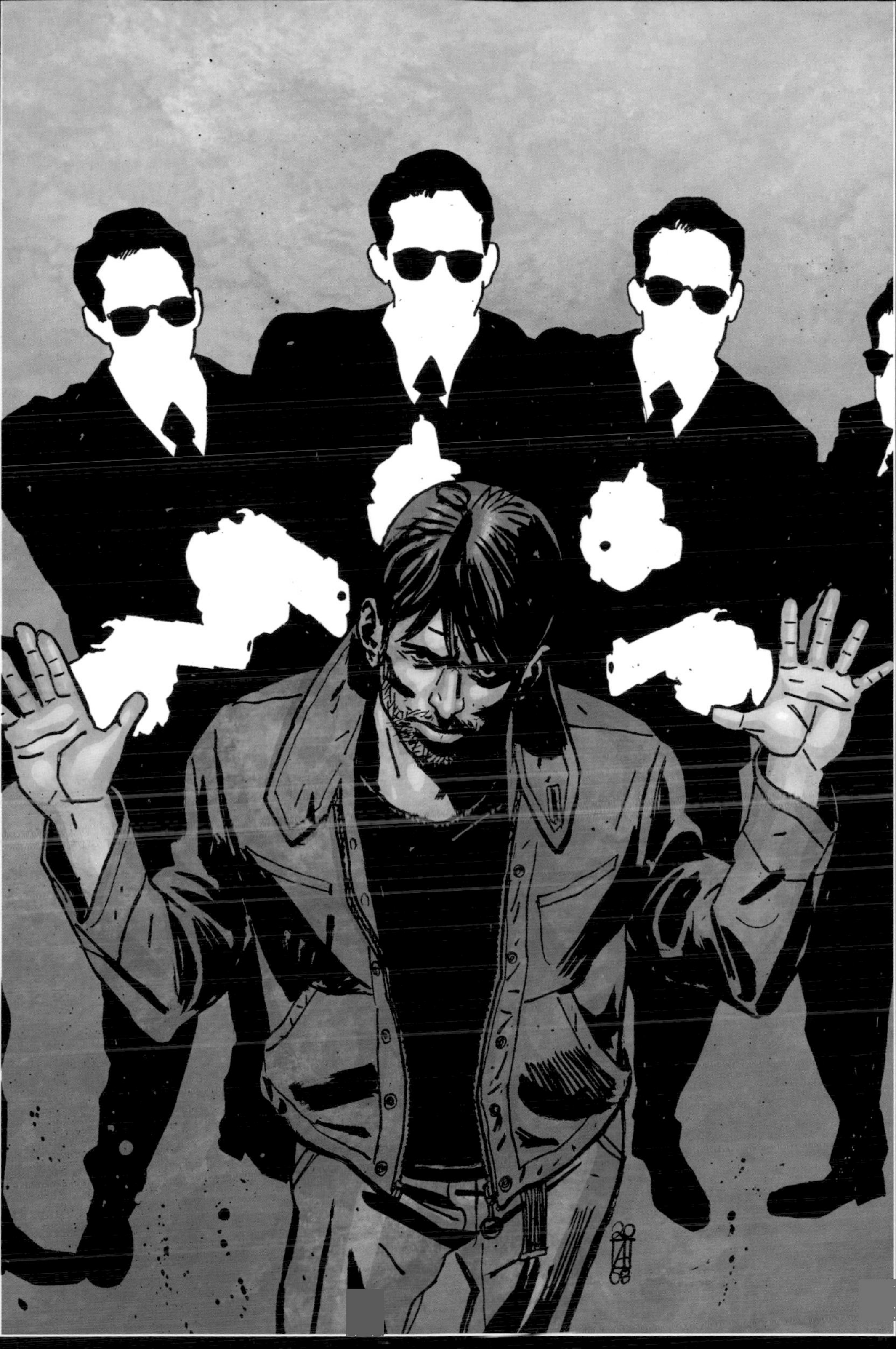

COVER 2A
PAUL AZACETA / COLORS BY ANDREW DALHOUSE

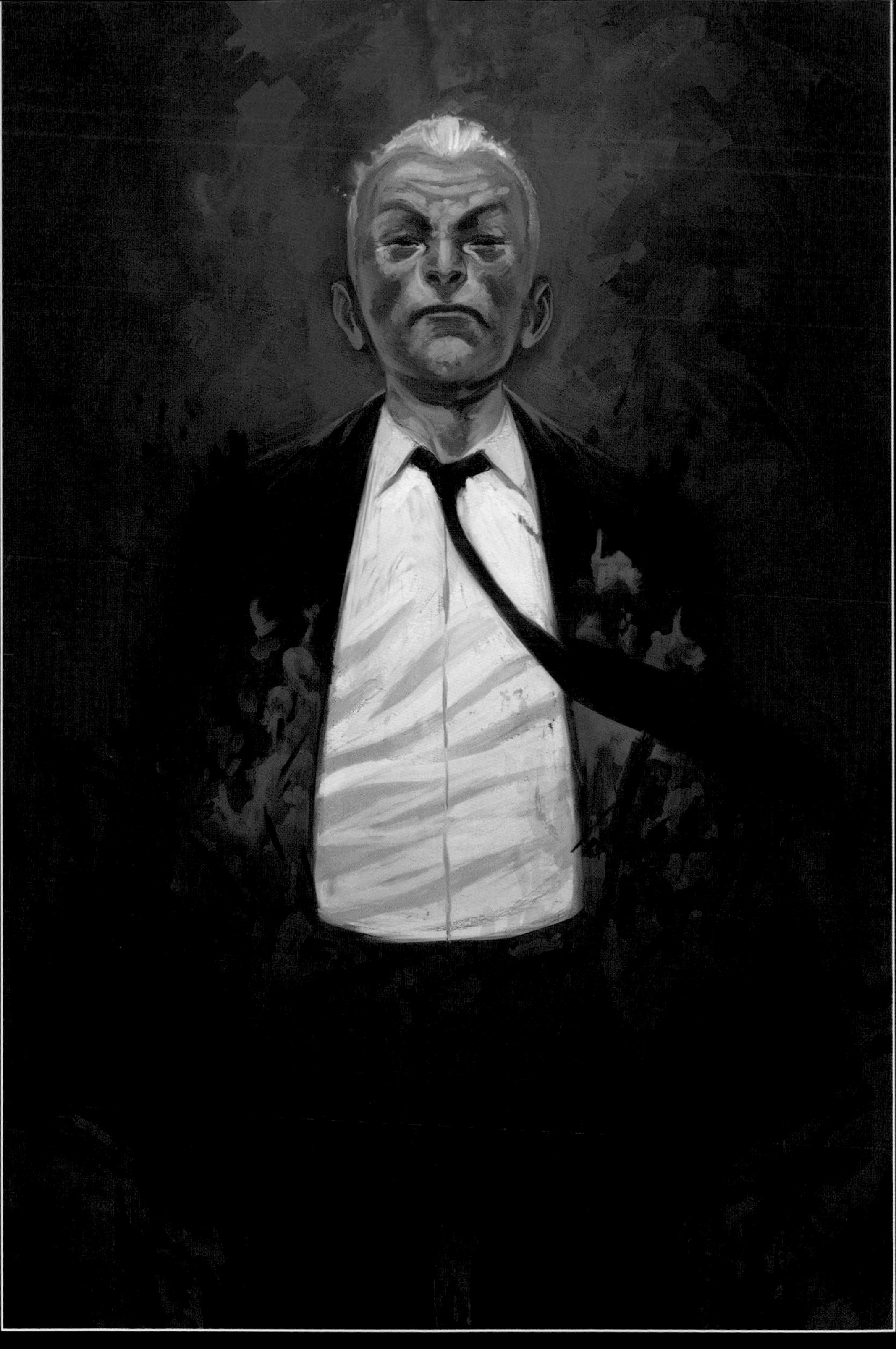

COVER 2B
JULIAN TOTINO TEDESCO

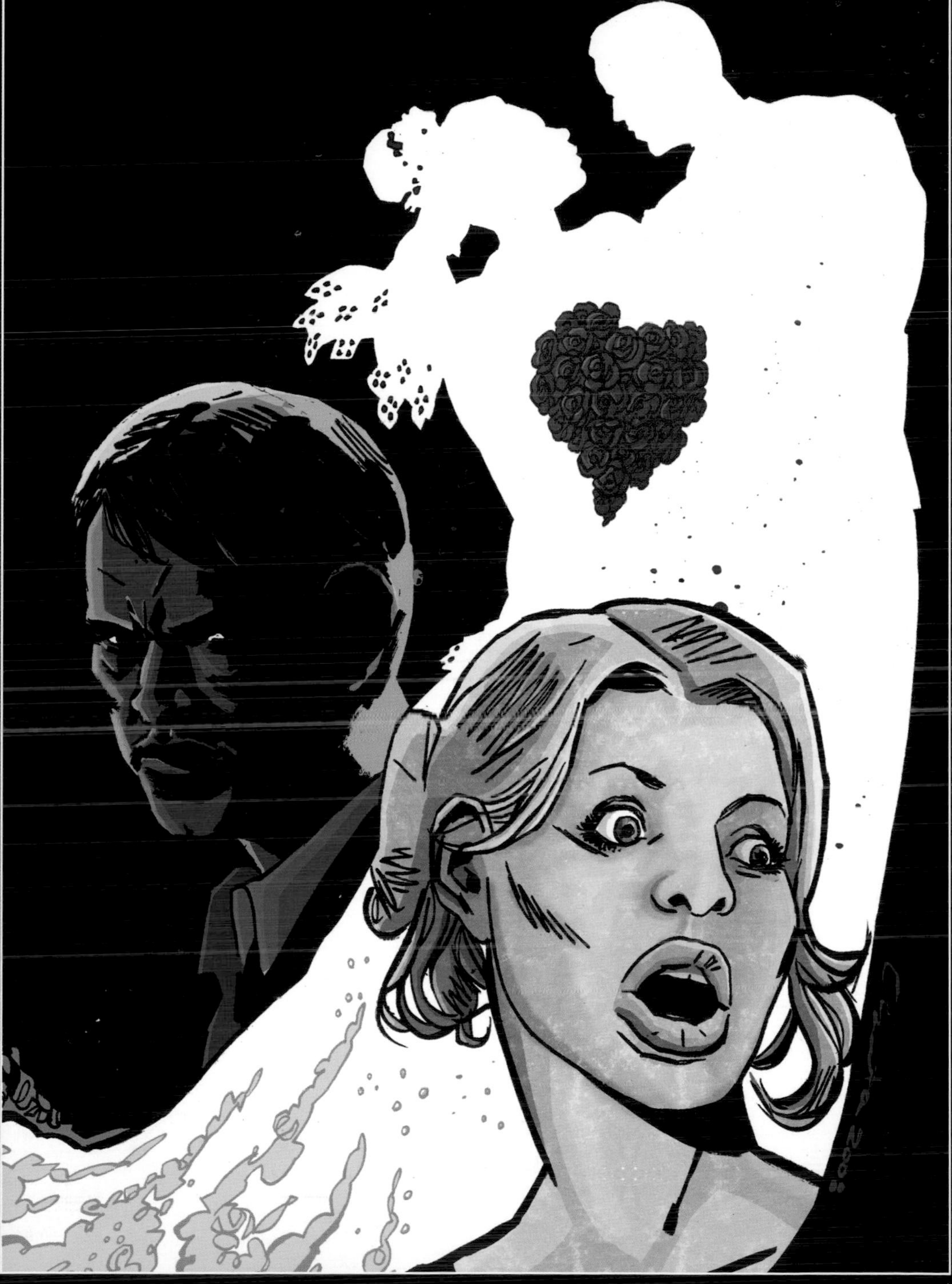

COVER 3A
PAUL AZACETA / COLORS BY NICK FILARDI

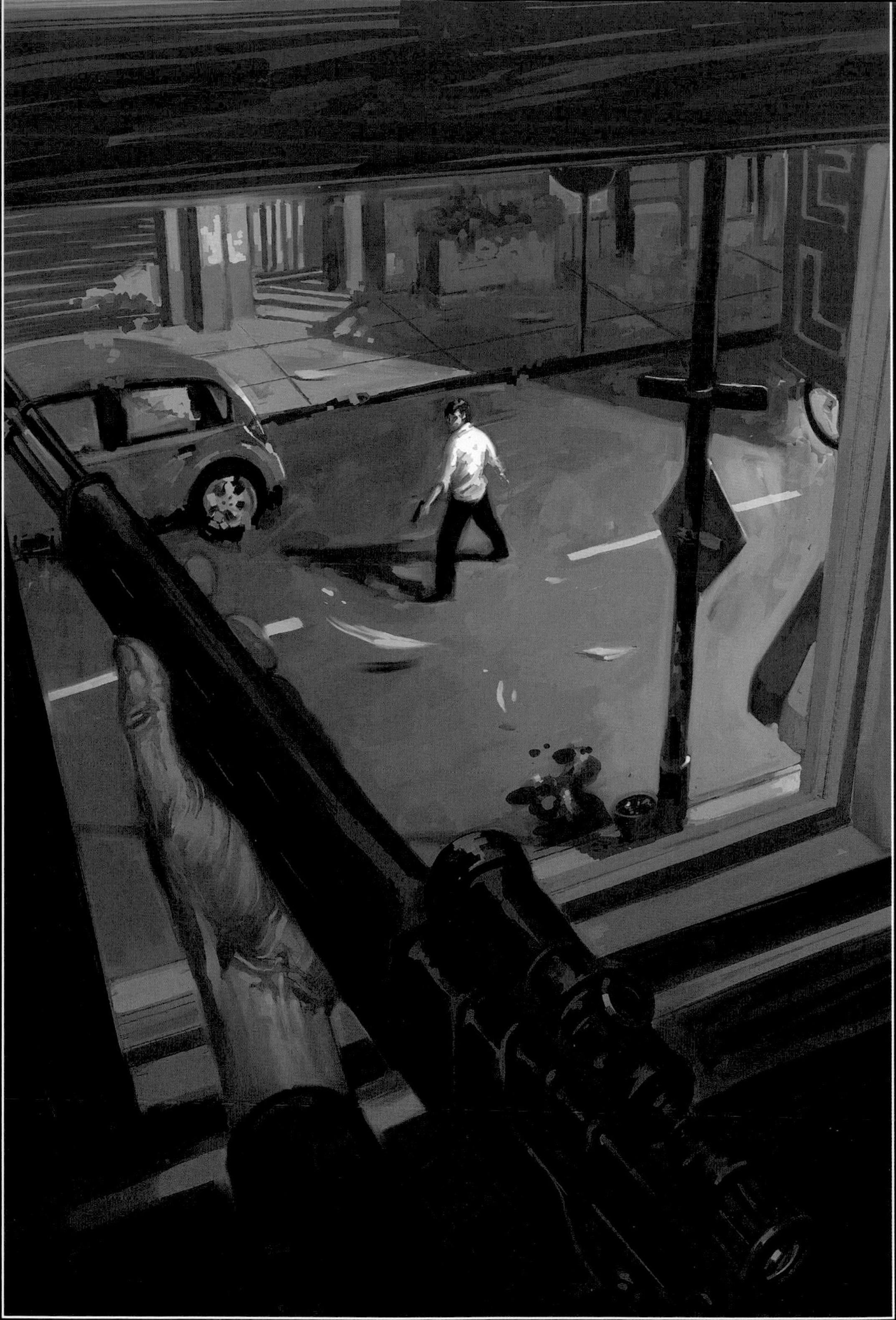

COVER 3B
JULIAN TOTINO TEDESCO

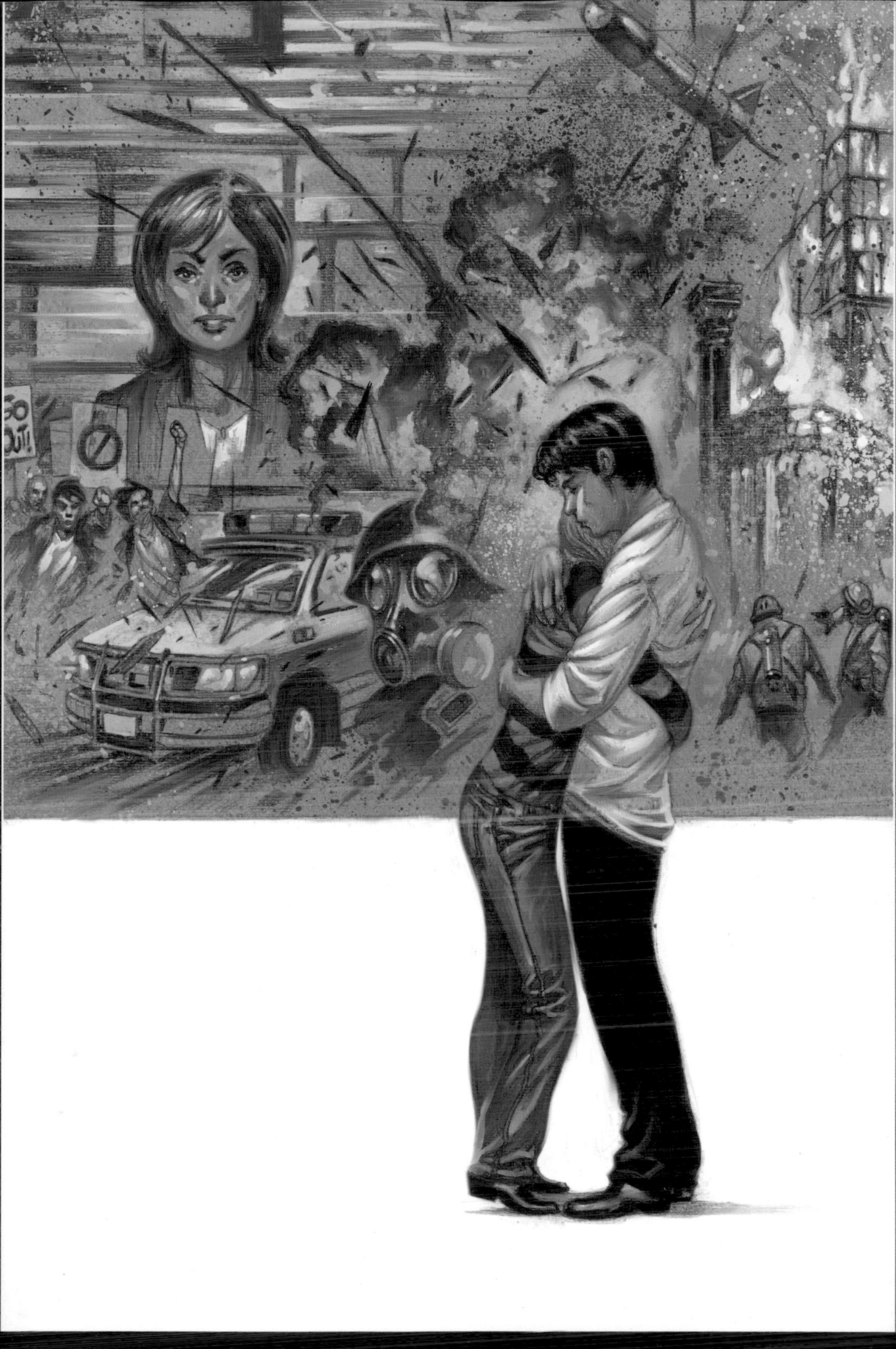
GO OUT!

COVER 4A
JULIAN TOTINO TEDESCO

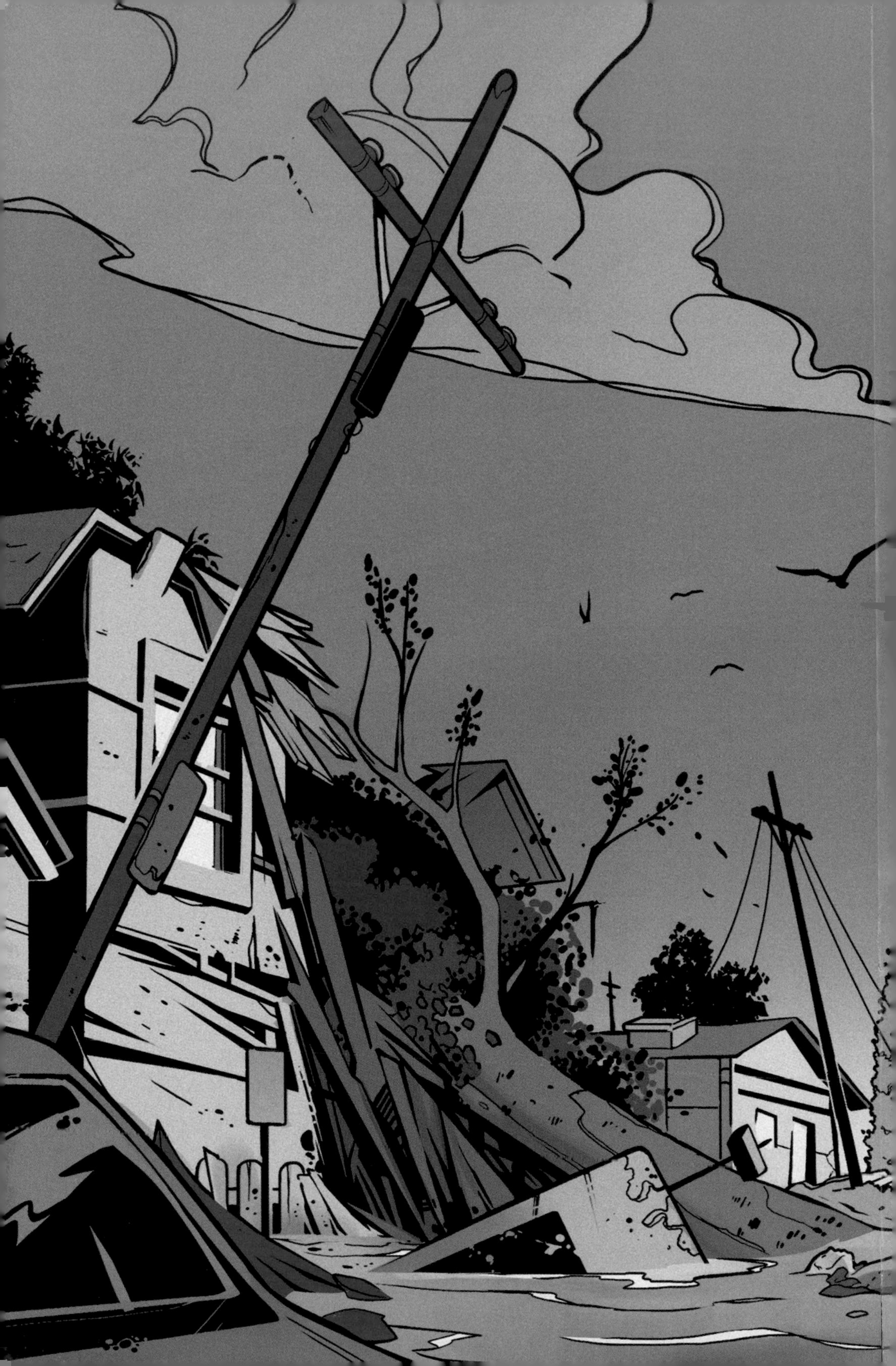

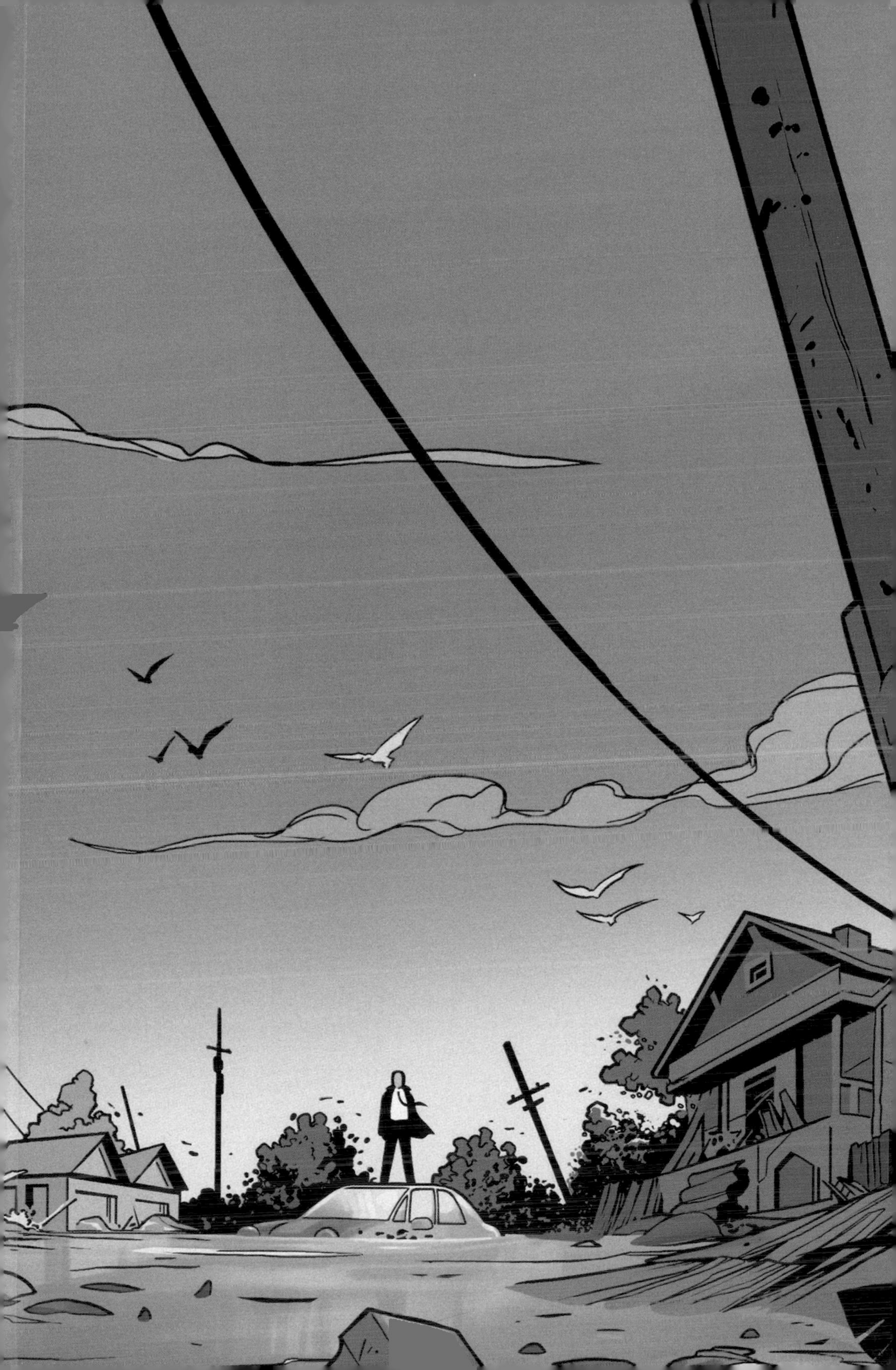

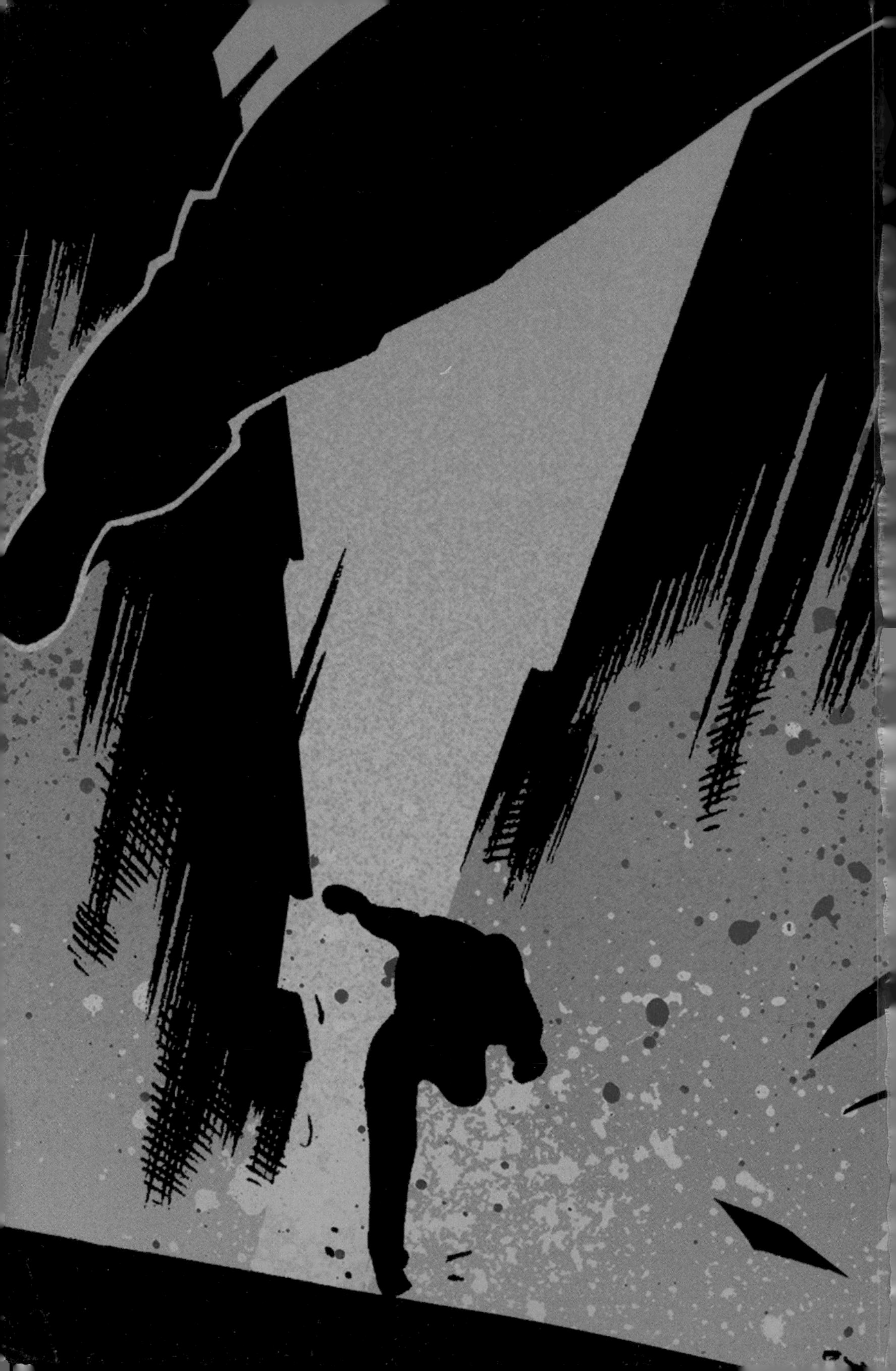